# The Critical Shaw

## on

# Theater

*Edited by*
D.A. Hadfield

RosettaBooks°

Published 2016 by RosettaBooks
ISBN (paperback): 978-0-7953-4897-6
Cover design by David Ter-Avanesyan / Ter33Design
Cover illustration by Shutterstock / LHF Graphics
ISBN (EPUB): 978-0-7953-4688-0
ISBN (Kindle): 978-0-7953-4770-2

www.RosettaBooks.com

RosettaBooks®

# Contents

# Acknowledgments

I owe a double gratitude to Leonard Conolly, general editor of this Critical Shaw series, first for offering me the opportunity to immerse myself in the vast range of Shaw's writing about theatre, and then also for his wisdom and guidance through the difficult process of paring the voluminous riches down to a manageable sampling. His patience and encouragement are much appreciated.

I am also grateful to my fellow editors in this series—Michel Pharand, Gustavo Rodriguez Martin, Christopher Innes, and Brigitte Bogar—for their enthusiasm and collaborative professionalism in negotiating a coordinated framework for the volumes, and to Jay McNair and the editorial team at Rosetta for bringing the series together.

And finally, I want to thank the members of the International Shaw Society, who provide such enriching opportunities for keeping the critical conversation about Shaw alive.

# General Editor's Preface

Bernard Shaw is not the household name he once was, but in the 1920s and 1930s he was certainly the world's most famous English-language playwright, and arguably one of the most famous people in the world. His plays were internationally performed and acclaimed, his views on matters great and small were relentlessly solicited by the media, he was pursued by paparazzi long before the word was even invented, the biggest names in politics, the arts, entertainment, even sports—Gandhi, Nehru, Churchill, Rodin, Twain, Wells, Lawrence of Arabia, Elgar, Einstein, Garbo, Chaplin, Stalin, Tunney and many more—welcomed his company, and his correspondents in the tens of thousands of letters he wrote during his long lifetime constitute a veritable who's who of world culture and politics. And Shaw remains the only person ever to have been awarded both a Nobel Prize and an Oscar.

Shaw's reputation rests securely not just on his plays, a dozen or so of which have come to be recognized as classics—*Man and Superman, Major Barbara, Pygmalion*, and *Saint Joan* perhaps now the most familiar of them—but also on his early work as a music, art, literary, and theater critic, and on his lifelong political activism. After he moved to London from his native Dublin in 1876, and after completing five novels, he established himself as one of London's most controversial, feared, and admired critics, and while he eventually retired from earning his living as a critic in order to focus on playwriting, he continued to lecture and write about cultural

and other issues—religion, for example—with scorching intelligence. As for politics, his early commitment to Socialism,
and his later expressed admiration for Communism and contempt for Capitalism, meant that while his views were relentlessly refuted by the establishment press they could rarely be
ignored—hardly surprising given the logic and passion that
underpinned them.

Winston Churchill once declared Shaw to be "the greatest
living master of letters in the English-speaking world," and
the selections from Shaw's reviews, essays, speeches, and correspondence contained in the five volumes of this Critcal
Shaw series provide abundant evidence to validate
Churchill's high regard. Shaw wrote—and spoke—volumi-
nously, and his complete works on the topics covered by this
series—Literature, Music, Religion, Theater, and Politics—would fill many more than five volumes. The topics
reflect Shaw's deepest interests and they inspired some of his
most brilliant nondramatic writing. The selections in each
volume give a comprehensive and representative survey of
his thinking, and show him to be not just the great rhetori-
cian that Churchill and others acknowledged, but also one of
the great public intellectuals of the twentieth century.

Leonard Conolly
Robinson College, Cambridge
December 2015

# Introduction

On 2 November 1950, the lights on Broadway and in Times Square went dark for a moment to acknowledge the passing of George Bernard Shaw, one of the most important dramatic figures of the twentieth century. Several weeks earlier, the 94-year-old Shaw had fallen while pruning branches in his garden, and the world had kept vigil, via regular posts from the aggressive mob of journalists who maintained a round-the-clock presence, while Shaw's extraordinary store of abundant vitality finally, inexorably, faded.

The man whose death occasioned such a public display of mourning was actually a relatively late bloomer as a public figure. Bernard Shaw (he hated the "George," and rarely used it), or G.B.S. as he was also known, was born into shabby-genteel poverty in Dublin on 26 July 1856, the youngest child and only son of an alcoholic father and the disillusioned wife who eventually left for London with her music teacher. Shaw was almost 20 when he joined his mother in London, determined to become a literary success. But that success didn't come easily, and for the next decade Shaw was forced to live off his mother's earnings as a music teacher while one publisher after another rejected his novels and articles. As he later famously explained, "I did not throw myself into the struggle for life: I threw my mother into it."

It was through his mother, in fact, that he got his first start in the world of paid journalism, ghost-writing a music criticism column for Vandeleur Lee, the music teacher who had convinced Bessie Shaw to leave Dublin. But when that commission ended without any better prospects, the under-employed Shaw took himself to the British Museum Reading Room, where he essentially gave himself a world-class education for the price of a reader's ticket. It was here that he got his first real literary break in 1883, through a chance meeting with a well-known and respected journalist, William Archer. Archer's attention was arrested both by Shaw's unusual appearance—tall, skinny, red hair and beard, clad in a beige woolen Jaeger suit that matched his pale complexion—and his reading material: Shaw was simultaneously reading a French translation of Marx's *Das Kapital* and the full orchestral score of Wagner's opera *Tristan und Isolde*. The two hit it off immediately, and Archer helped Shaw to various journalistic opportunities in music, art, and literary criticism, eventually getting him the position of full-time music critic for *The World*, where Archer was theatre critic. Archer also indirectly enabled Shaw's second real literary break, by suggesting that they collaborate on a play. The attempt ended disastrously with Shaw using up the entire plot of Archer's "well-made play" in the first two acts, and Archer highly critical of Shaw's expanded plot that turned a romantic comedy into an indictment of slum landlords and the wealthy property owners who profit from them. Instead of launching Shaw's dramatic career at that moment, the experience was enough to turn Shaw off any further attempts at playwriting for the next seven years.

But Shaw eventually returned to that aborted play, completing it in his way for a première at J.T. Grein's Independent Theatre in 1892. The notoriety of *Widowers' Houses* gave 36-year-old Shaw his first taste of dramatic celebrity. Or, as he described it, "I had not achieved a success; but I had provoked an uproar; and the sensation was so agreeable that I resolved to try again." The uproar was provoked by precisely the kinds of changes through which Shaw had turned

Archer's "well-made play" into a trenchant social critique. Shaw had discovered his dramatic idiom.

From the outset of his career as a dramatist, Shaw's insistence that the stage was an appropriate venue to debate urgent social problems and their solutions set him apart from the popular playwrights of the day, whose formulaic plots, morally empty farces, and idealized characters filled him mostly with boredom and dismay. Instead, Shaw took his cue from Norwegian playwright Henrik Ibsen, who showed his characters in the process of stripping away idealistic illusions and grappling with the existential crises and very real social injustices that they exposed. Ibsen's plays, too, had provoked an uproar when they first appeared on the London stage, a sure sign, Shaw felt, that they were indeed forcing audiences to recognize and confront important social realities rather than allowing them to escape into mindless entertainments.

Shaw had first encountered Ibsen when he took the part of Krogstadt in a private reading of *A Doll's House* organized by Eleanor Marx (Karl's daughter), but it was the notorious first production of that play in 1889, managed and acted by Janet Achurch (1864–1916) and Charles Charrington (1854–1926), that confirmed Shaw's sense of his dramatic kinship with Ibsen. Watching the characters act out Ibsen's idea that women should insist on their right to an independent existence in the world resonated strongly in a society that was grappling with early feminist consciousness-raising in the form of "the Woman Question" in the homes and streets outside the theatre. The agitation for women's personal and political emancipation was becoming increasingly organized through legislative amendments to marriage and property laws, and through the efforts of suffrage activists such as Millicent Fawcett (1847–1929) and Emmeline Pankhurst (1858–1928). For Shaw, the Achurch-Charrington production of *A Doll's House* represented a breakthrough in the way it used theatre as a medium for audiences to examine and understand contemporary social issues. Ironically, that production was based on a translation of Ibsen's play by none other than William Archer, who had earlier discouraged Shaw from turning his own well-made play idea into a similar type of social problem play.

After the agreeable uproar of *Widower's Houses*, however, Shaw's own attempts to dramatize the Woman Question proved so disagreeable to theatre managers that he had trouble interesting any of them in producing these "unpleasant" plays. Still, one of them, *Mrs Warren's Profession*, did manage to provoke an uproar even though — or more accurately precisely because — it wasn't produced.

Managers unanimously declined Shaw's second play, *The Philanderer*, a partially autobiographical drama about Ibsen, theatrical idealism, and ideologies of women's emancipation, but Grein expressed interest in commercially producing Shaw's third play, *Mrs Warren's Profession*, about a wealthy, successful brothel owner and the daughter she has raised to be a lady, who has no idea that her Cambridge education has been financed by the proceeds of prostitution. Mrs Warren initially earns her daughter's admiration and respect when she explains that prostitution was a lucrative and strategic career choice in a society that excluded women from most professions and forced them to trade sex for financial security one way or another. *Mrs Warren's Profession* provoked the first major battle in Shaw's lifelong war with theatre censorship when the Lord Chamberlain refused to license the play, making it illegal to stage any public performance of it. Shaw had predicted the Lord Chamberlain's decision, and had hoped that Grein would offer to stage it privately, which would exempt it from the licensing requirement. (In this workaround, audiences didn't buy tickets for a performance, they bought a membership to a theatre society, and plays were performed at what was technically the society's meetings.) When Grein declined the private option, Shaw used every print and public forum he could access to denounce the Lord Chamberlain's power of censorship. Shaw's vocal and visible anti-censorship campaign arguably helped to establish his reputation as a major theatrical figure and modern playwright as effectively as any play production could have. (See Part 4 for selections from Shaw's more than 50-year battle against government censorship of the theatre.) It also, ironically, helped him attract the attention of book publishers in a way that his earlier novels never did. Publishing plays in reading editions was virtually unheard-of, but like private performances, it was an ingenious way to get around the Lord Chamberlain's licensing restriction. By arranging to have his plays published, Shaw scored victories on three fronts: he helped to pioneer drama as a literary genre, an innovation that he used to his tremendous advantage throughout his career; he put *Mrs Warren's Profession* in front of at least a reading audience, who could judge for themselves its morality and the social hypocrisy it exposed; and he demonstrated the ultimate futility of a censorship that could keep audiences from seeing his play, but not reading it. Shaw and the Lord Chamberlain's office continued to battle over *Mrs Warren's Profession* for more than two decades before it was finally licensed for public production.

Shaw fared slightly better with productions for his next group of "pleasant" plays, scoring his first commercial audience hit with *Arms and the Man*, a comedy intended to expose idealistic illusions about war and heroism. What it exposed even more effectively was the difficulty audiences would have in seeing Shaw's serious ideas underneath the delightful comedy coating. He described the "curious experience of witnessing an apparently insane success" on the first night, "and of going before the curtain to tremendous applause, the only person in the theatre who knew that the whole affair was a ghastly failure." There must have been one other person in the theatre aware of the failure, as one lone "boo" apparently carried loudly over the audience applause. Quick-witted, Shaw immediately responded, "My dear fellow, I quite agree with you, but what are we two against so many?" (see Shaw's response to the first night of *Arms and the Man* in his letter to the booing heckler Reginald Golding Bright, page 78). But Shaw would continue to struggle throughout his long career with the challenge of audiences who failed to appreciate the seriousness of his comedies.

*Arms and the Man* represented Shaw's first popular audience success, but he couldn't live on audience admiration and the production had still lost money. Even though he couldn't give up his day job yet, he did give up music criticism at *The World* to become the dramatic critic for *The Saturday Review*. The weekly theatre columns Shaw contributed from 1895–98 still rank among the best bodies of dramatic criticism ever written. As a playwright who was actively and unabashedly involved in the productions of his own plays (see page 39 for Shaw's argument dismissing accusations that he created a conflict of interest by being both a playwright and a dramatic critic), Shaw could astutely differentiate between the merits of a play, production details, and the performances in it. His practical familiarity with so many individual playwrights and actors would make his dramatic criticism valuable enough as a veritable who's who of the plays and players that drew audiences into the theatres, but his exacting standards and keen attention to the details of staging, costume, and acting styles allowed him to sketch out an even richer picture of the theatrical experience they had there.

The dual role of critic-dramatist that Shaw played had real advantages for audiences, but it also admittedly had some advantages for him. He eventually recognized (see page 71) that he used his criticism to persuade audiences that what they actually wanted were the kinds of plays that he wanted to write. As Shaw the critic admitted, "I was accusing my opponents of failure because they were not doing what I wanted, whereas they were often succeeding very brilliantly in doing what they themselves wanted." Shaw the playwright claimed this advantage was ultimately cancelled out because "when my own turn came to be criticized, I also was attacked because I produced what I wanted to produce and not what some of my critics wanted me to produce." But Shaw wasn't necessarily as vulnerable to his critics as other playwrights had been to him: he often used the access that being a well-known critic and dramatist gave him to various publication platforms to refute or correct his critics, defending himself from those critical attacks more publicly than other playwrights could have defended themselves against him. Even after he gave up professional dramatic criticism, he continued to make sure he had the last word on the quality and value of his plays and their ideas when he felt that critics were failing to see them properly, circulating his own interpretations in newspaper and magazine articles, or in prefaces added to his play publications.

Like his plays, the columns Shaw wrote for *The Saturday Review* gave him a chance to unleash his wit and love of paradox in pursuit of a very serious goal: convincing audiences that the theatre they thought they enjoyed the most was actually the least enjoyable kind of theatre. Through his reviews, he always insisted that good theatre should entertain, but also educate audiences, challenge them and make them think. Hence his judgment on the première of a new play by Oscar Wilde: "I cannot say that I greatly cared for *The Importance of Being Earnest*. It amused me, of course; but unless comedy touches me as well as amuses me, it leaves me with a sense of having wasted my evening. I go to the theatre to be moved to laughter, not to be tickled or bustled into it; and that is why, though I laugh as much as anybody at a farcical comedy, I am out of spirits before the end of the second act, and out of temper before the end of the third..." Here was

Shaw, holding Wilde to the same standard of serious comedy that he practiced himself.

Behind Shaw's exacting critical judgments was his fundamental belief that the theatre was much more than an entertainment venue, it was the institution charged with the moral and spiritual improvement of the society around it, "a place 'where two or three are gathered together.'" He leveled some of his harshest criticisms at those he saw squandering that sacred trust, no matter how much audiences loved them. This often put him squarely at odds with the theatre culture in the late nineteenth century, which was organized around star actor-managers such as Henry Irving, who ran the Lyceum Theatre for two decades with his partner Ellen Terry. Irving was considered the foremost actor and Shakespearean of the time, and his fame and popularity ensured that audiences came mainly for the pleasure of seeing him act, preferably in the kinds of melodramatic, opulently staged productions he was famous for. It also meant that an actor-manager such as Irving was unlikely to be interested in staging plays that did not have the kind of major role for him that he knew his audiences expected to see. Shaw wanted theatre to be socially progressive and politically engaged, but male actor-managers were better served by dramatic worlds steeped in heroic idealism and the simplistic morality of melodrama. Shaw even predicted in a preface to William Archer's collected criticism (see page 232) that London theatre culture would continue to stagnate as long as the actor-managers were in charge, precisely because their theatrical success depended on keeping the outside world, where social and gendered hierarchies were breaking down, as far off the stage as possible. Instead, Shaw argued, the best hope likely lay with the "actress-manageress," who had much more to gain from a theatre like his that took the Woman Question and other social reforms from the street and reproduced them on the stage.

Shaw's dramatic focus on women's issues rather than heroic male characters meant that his plays offered better, more developed roles for actresses than most of his playwriting contemporaries, so he had a significant professional interest in wooing the promising actresses and actress-managers of the day. But with Shaw, the professional wooing crossed over into the personal with alarming frequency as he carried on—or at least attempted—passionate flirtations and romances, both on paper and in person, with most of the well-known actresses of the day. He wrote copious letters and in some cases wrote parts or entire plays specifically for them, flattered them shamelessly, critiqued them mercilessly, and generally tried to convert them to his own particular vision of theatre's mission. Occasionally, his tactics backfired, leaving him in difficult situations such as the one he dramatized at the beginning of The Philanderer, where a spurned woman violently barges in as he is wooing another, or the time the famous Ibsen actress Elizabeth Robins rejected his flirtatious advances by allegedly threatening to shoot him. He carried on an ardent, lifelong "paper courtship" with Ellen Terry, Henry Irving's partner at the Lyceum, that began during Shaw's years as a critic when Shaw often scolded her for letting Irving squander her talent with supporting roles that kept her in his shadow, and tried to persuade her that she would do better acting in his own plays. Many actresses became good friends with Shaw's wife, and only one ever seriously threatened his marriage: Mrs Patrick (Stella) Campbell, for whom Shaw wrote the part of Eliza Doolittle in Pygmalion.

In 1898, Shaw had married Charlotte Payne-Townshend, a wealthy Irish heiress; his wife's money, coupled with royalties that were starting to pour in from productions of a few early plays, allowed Shaw to give up paid journalism and, at the age of 42, finally begin his playwriting career in earnest. Over the next half century, he would add almost 40 more plays to the eight he had already written before his marriage. Shaw produced some of his best works—*Man and Superman, Major Barbara, Pygmalion, Heartbreak House,* and *Saint Joan*—between the ages of 50 and 75. He also received some of his most significant honors late in life. He was awarded the Nobel Prize for Literature for 1925, recognizing his body of work "which is marked by both idealism and humanity, its stimulating satire often being infused with a singular poetic beauty." In 1938, at the age of 82, he won an Academy Award for his original screenplay of *Pygmalion.* He wrote his final short play, *Why She Would Not,* at the age of 94, just a few months before the fall in his garden that precipitated his death, practicing his profession to the last.

As a professional playwright, Shaw matched his strong commitment to the ideological value of theatre with a keen understanding of its practical aspects. When he pitched his plays to theatre managers, he usually came prepared with a suggested casting list, compiled from his knowledge of each actor's capabilities, as well as their availability and affordability. In an era before the "director" was an established fixture of dramatic productions, Shaw took on the function himself, attending rehearsals, helping actors understand their characters and dialogue—sometimes speaking the speech himself so that actors could hear the musicality and rhythm of it—suggesting staging, and giving copious notes after the play opened. His "beginners' guide" on directing (see page 290), written the year before his death, is still an excellent primer of practical advice on how to put a cast together, how to run rehearsals and work respectfully with actors, the importance of understanding the material conditions of the stage, and other aspects of the director's role. His similar commitment to the practicalities of acting led to his involvement with the Academy of Dramatic Art (now the Royal Academy of Dramatic Art), a training school for actors established by Sir Herbert Beerbohm Tree in 1904. Shaw joined the Managing Council of the school in 1911, starting a strongly supportive relationship that lasted more than the rest of his life: in addition to almost immediately assigning the royalties from *Pygmalion* to the school (which would eventually include earnings from *My Fair Lady*), he also bequeathed RADA a third of his total royalties in his will.

While Shaw worked tirelessly to make sure production values were as good as he could make them, he also knew that no production was worth much if no one came to see it, and was always willing to do what he could to help generate publicity. He frequently wrote his own press, drafting interviews as if they had been conducted by some (nameless) reporter with the playwright on his new work. These fictionalized interviews allowed Shaw to present an exaggerated character version of himself, creating the mystique of "G.B.S." along with publicity for his plays. With *Mrs Warren's Profession*, *The Shewing-up of Blanco Posnet* (1909), and *Press Cuttings* (1909), there were battles fought in the public press and a parliamentary Commission over stage censorship. As Shaw's reputation grew and his name alone could attract attention for a production, paradoxical Shaw proved he could even generate publicity by explicitly not attaching his name to a play, premièring *Fanny's First Play* (1911) as the work of an anonymous author. The play pokes fun at drama critics (who bear a striking resemblance to Shaw's own contemporaries) who have to guess at the authorship of a play they watch about a young couple's emancipation from their parents' stifling social expectations. One of the critic characters even suggests Shaw as the likely author of the play before they learn it was written by Fanny O'Dowda, their host's daughter. Shaw did his best to keep people guessing about the authorship of *Fanny's First Play*, waging a coy campaign of denial and misdirection, and the publicity stunt helped keep *Fanny's First Play* running for over 600 performances.

Shaw clearly understood the value of his plays as well as the value of his celebrity, and he was an astute negotiator for production rights with theatre managers on both sides of the Atlantic. Some of Shaw's most lucrative early production partnerships were with Americans: he earned some of his first significant royalties from Richard Mansfield's New York productions of *Arms and the Man* and *The Devil's Disciple*, with Arnold Daly and Robert Loraine following after Mansfield to establish Shaw as a popular fixture in American theatre. At Mansfield's suggestion, Shaw had early on hired the formidable American theatre agent Elisabeth Marbury—"Rapacious Miss Marbury" he called her in an early letter—to manage his royalty and rights payments in America, and in Britain, where her office was eventually managed by Reginald Golding Bright. Shaw remained actively engaged in making sure his royalties were accurately collected and remitted, eventually bypassing agents altogether when he decided he could do the job just as well himself. And indeed, his correspondence with managers and theatre associates demonstrates that he often did know The Business of Theater rights better than they did.

Shaw's business acumen might have resulted from his early life of genteel poverty, where he learned the importance of having and managing money. He was acutely aware of how much it cost to produce plays and how theatre artists were paid, and repudiated the notion that anyone could or should be expected to work in theatre for love of art alone, or for less than a living wage. He objected to the growing trend of amateur theatre companies on the grounds that they undertook what was essentially professional work without treating the workers on professional terms. He objected even more strenuously when amateur theatricals were used to fundraise for civic projects, believing that it only let municipal governments renege on their fiscal responsibilities to their citizens. Any monies realized from amateur productions should be used to support other artistic endeavors; barring that, the players should be encouraged to get drunk on it, or anything but use it to fund social services the government should be funding.

As Shaw well knew, though, making money on theatre was an uncertain prospect for amateurs or professionals, as ticket sales could rarely keep pace with production costs. This was particularly true for the kind of socially relevant theatre that he believed in, which was less likely to appeal to mass audiences the way commercial farces or melodramas could. But the answer was not to expect those involved to work for less than a living wage—the theatre was not a sweatshop. A better solution was a subsidized, national theatre that would relieve theatre producers of their relentless financial pressures, which would in turn allow them to take some risks on more innovative or challenging dramas the way Vedrenne and Barker had done during their three seasons managing the Royal Court Theatre (1904–1907). Shaw's plays figured prominently during the Vedrenne-Barker seasons, and Shaw even made substantial personal contributions to financing the productions, but the project was ultimately not financially sustainable. Partly as a result of this experience, Shaw became an early member of the planning committee for a national theatre, and even worked on the acquisition of various sites designated for the project, but he never saw it actually materialize.

Shaw's plays chronicle the shifts from the Victorian to the atomic age, addressing issues as diverse as women's suffrage, marriage law reform, capitalism, class, religious idealism, medical ethics, science, evolution, governance, international relations, love, and sex. But Shaw's legacy to theatre is much more than just his plays, impressive as they are. In his nondramatic writings about theatre, Shaw demonstrates his ardent belief in the theatre as a vital social institution that needs to be nurtured both artistically and practically, the better to engage us in seeing ourselves honestly as we are and move us, with optimistic laughter, towards what we could be.

# Bernard Shaw and His Times: A Chronology

*[This chronology is common to all five volumes in the Critical Shaw series, and reflects the topics of the series: Politics, Theater, Literature, Music, and Religion. For a comprehensive and detailed chronology of Shaw's life and works, see A. M. Gibbs, A Bernard Shaw Chronology (Basingstoke: Palgrave, 2001).]*

1856   Shaw born in Dublin (26 July).

1859   Charles Darwin publishes *On the Origin of Species by Means of Natural Selection.*

1864   Herbert Spencer publishes *Principles of Biology* (and coins the phrase "survival of the fittest").

1865   The Salvation Army is founded by Methodist preacher William Booth.

1870   The doctrine of papal infallibility is defined as dogma at the First Vatican Council.

1876   Shaw moves from Dublin to London. He begins ghostwriting music reviews for Vandeleur Lee for *The Hornet.*

1879   Shaw begins writing music reviews for *The Saturday Musical Review, The Court Journal,* and other publications. He writes his first novel, *Immaturity,* quickly followed by four others: *The Irrational Knot* (1880), *Love Among the Artists* (1881), *Cashel Byron's Profession* (1882), and *An Unsocial Socialist* (1883).

1883  Shaw reads Karl Marx's *Das Kapital* (in a French translation) in the British Museum Reading Room.

1884  The Fabian Society is founded; Shaw joins in the same year. He publishes his first book review in *The Christian Scientist*.

1885  Shaw begins publishing book reviews regularly in *The Pall Mall Gazette*.

1886  Eleanor Marx, daughter of Karl Marx, organizes a reading of Ibsen's *A Doll's House*; Shaw reads the part of Krogstad.

1889  Having written music reviews for over a decade, Shaw becomes a full-time critic for *The Star*, and then (in 1890) *The World*.

1891  Shaw publishes *The Quintessence of Ibsenism* (revised and updated in 1922).

1892  Shaw's first play, *Widowers' Houses*, is performed.

1893  Founding of the Independent Labour Party, a socialist advocacy group.

1894  Shaw resigns from *The World* and henceforth writes only occasional music reviews. *Arms and the Man* is first performed. Shaw becomes acquainted with aspiring theatre critic Reginald Golding Bright.

1895  Shaw becomes full-time drama critic for *The Saturday Review*. He publishes a lengthy review column almost every week for the next two and a half years.

1897  Shaw is elected a member of the Vestry of the Parish of St Pancras (until 1903).

1898 Shaw marries Charlotte Payne-Townshend and resigns as *The Saturday Review* drama critic. He publishes
*The Perfect Wagnerite* and *Plays: Pleasant and Unpleasant*. One of the "unpleasant" plays, *Mrs Warren's Profession*, is refused a performance licence by the Lord
Chamberlain; the ban will stay in effect until 1924.

1901 *Caesar and Cleopatra* is first performed, with music
written by Shaw. Queen Victoria dies.

1904 J. E. Vedrenne and Harley Granville Barker begin their
management of the Court Theatre (until 1907), with
Shaw as a principal playwright. Eleven Shaw plays are
performed in three seasons.

1905 *Man and Superman* is first performed. Albert Einstein
publishes his theory of relativity.

1906 Founding of the Labour Party. *Major Barbara* and *The
Doctor's Dilemma* are first performed.

1908 *Der tapfere Soldat*, an unauthorized operetta loosely
based on *Arms and the Man*, with music by Oscar
Straus and libretto by Rudolf Bernauer and Leopold
Jacobson, is first performed in Vienna. It is later staged
(1910) in translation as *The Chocolate Soldier*.

1909 *The Shewing-up of Blanco Posnet* is refused a licence by
the Lord Chamberlain. W. B. Yeats and Lady Gregory
stage it at the Abbey Theatre in Dublin. Shaw appears
as a witness before the Joint Select Committee of the
House of Lords and the House of Commons on Stage
Plays (Censorship).

1911  Shaw joins the managing council of the Royal Academy of Dramatic Art. His strong support of RADA's programs will include bequeathing RADA a third of his royalties. Shaw writes an introduction for the Waverley edition of Dickens's *Hard Times*.

1913  *Pygmalion* is first performed.

1914  Beginning of the First World War. Shaw publishes *Common Sense About the War*.

1916  Easter Rising in Dublin against British rule of Ireland.

1917  The Russian Revolution overthrows the imperialist government and installs a communist government under Vladimir Ilyich Lenin. The United States joins the war against Germany. On 17 July Czar Nicholas II and his family are executed.

1918  Representation of the People Act gives the vote to all men over twenty-one, and to women over thirty if they meet certain qualifications (e.g., property owners, university graduates). End of the First World War.

1920  *Heartbreak House* is first performed. Shaw completes *Back to Methuselah*, a five-play cycle on evolutionary themes. League of Nations formed.

1921  The Irish Free State gains independence from Britain. Shaw writes the preface to *Immaturity*.

1922  Joseph Stalin becomes general secretary of the Communist Party Central Committee. Benito Mussolini becomes Italian prime minister.

1923  *Saint Joan* is first performed, with music written by Shaw.

1924  Ramsay MacDonald becomes the first Labour prime minister, in a Labour-Liberal coalition government.

1925 Adolf Hitler publishes *Mein Kampf* [*My Struggle*].

1926 General strike in Great Britain, 4–13 May. Shaw is awarded the 1925 Nobel Prize for Literature.

1928 Representation of the People (Equal Franchise) Act gives the vote to all women over twenty-one. Shaw publishes *The Intelligent Woman's Guide to Socialism and Capitalism*. *The Apple Cart* is first performed.

1929 The Wall Street Crash, 28–29 October, which signalled the beginning of the Great Depression. Shaw speaks as a delegate to the third International Congress of the World League for Sexual Reform. Sir Barry Jackson establishes the Malvern Festival, dedicated to Shaw's plays.

1931 Shaw visits Russia. He celebrates his seventy-fifth birthday on 26 July in Moscow's Concert Hall of Nobles with two thousand guests. He meets Stalin on 29 July.

1932 Unemployment reaches 3.5 million in Great Britain. South Wales and the industrial north experience mass unemployment and poverty. *Too True to Be Good* receives its English première at the Malvern Festival.

1933 Shaw makes his first visit to the United States. He speaks to an audience of thirty-five hundred at the Metropolitan Opera House (11 April). Hitler becomes German chancellor.

1934 *The Six of Calais* is first performed.

1936 Shaw makes his second (and last) visit to the United States. *The Millionairess* is first performed.

1938 *Geneva* is first performed. Shaw rejects a proposal from producer Gabriel Pascal for a musical version of *Pygmalion*.

1939 Beginning of the Second World War.

1941 The United States enters the Second World War.

1943 Charlotte Shaw dies.

1944 Shaw publishes *Everybody's Political What's What?*

1945 End of the Second World War. United Nations formed. The UK Labour Party wins its first majority government. Clement Atlee becomes prime minister. His government implements an extensive nationaliza-tion program of British industry and services.

1947 Discovery of the Dead Sea Scrolls in Qumran Caves, West Bank.

1948 World Council of Churches founded in Amsterdam.

1950 Shaw publishes his last book review in *The Observer* (26 March). He dies in Ayot St Lawrence, Hertford-shire (2 November).

# A Note on the Text

Sources for the selections of Shaw's theatrical writings are given in the heading for each selection. Full bibliographical details for the sources, when not included in the heading, are provided in Sources and Further Reading, where secondary sources on Shaw's theatrical writings are also listed. Shaw's original spelling and punctuation have been retained. All ellipses inserted in the text are editorial, unless otherwise noted. Brief explanatory notes are included in square brackets. In cases where there are multiple references to the same person or event, the note is given only for the first reference.

# Part I: Professional Critic

*Shaw is still studied as one of the most significant dramatic critics in the history of Western theatre; one of the most valuable features of his dramatic criticism stems from his refusal to confine his columns solely to the reviewing of specific plays and productions. Shaw had a very clear sense of what a theatre critic should be, even though it was a profession without formal training or credentials. As he explained in his "Author's Apology" for one of the collections of his dramatic criticism (see page 71), Shaw saw the column as his opportunity to advance his own agenda about what purpose theatre should serve, and to advocate in support of the innovative new types of social problem plays that would eventually replace the contrived and unrealistic melodramas and well-made plays that made up the repertoire of most actor-managers. And when he turned his attention to specific productions, Shaw's astonishing recall for details helped demonstrate how much he understood and respected the complexities of production and even the abilities and contributions of individual actors. He also had an uncanny eye for exceptional talent, as his notices of actors like Lillah McCarthy (see page 32) and Robert Loraine (see page 68) indicate.*

# 1. A New Lady Macbeth and a New Mrs Ebbsmith, 25 May 1895. [*Our Theatres in the Nineties*, vol. 1, pp. 126–33]

[The Notorious Mrs Ebbsmith *was playwright Arthur Wing Pinero's (1855–1934) attempt to follow up his very successful play* The Second Mrs Tanqueray. *The role of Mrs Ebbsmith had been originally played by Mrs Patrick Campbell (1865–1940), who had made her name by playing Paula Tanqueray in Pinero's earlier play. Shaw criticized both plays for their essentially conventional resolutions that required the "fallen women" to die or reform themselves. Here Shaw shows his ability to distinguish the actor from the role in his close analysis of a performance. He also shows his astute judge of talent in recognizing Lillah McCarthy, who would indeed become "a valuable recruit to the London stage," creating the role of Ann Whitefield in* Man and Superman *and becoming a well-known suffrage-era actress.*]

Last Saturday evening found me lurking, an uninvited guest, in an obscure corner of the Garrick Theatre, giving Mrs Ebbsmith another trial in the person of Miss Olga Nethersole [1867–1951]. This time I carefully regulated the dose, coming late for the preliminary explanations, and hurrying home at the end of the second act, when Mrs Ebbsmith had put her fine dress on, and was beginning to work up towards the stove. I cannot say I enjoyed myself very much; for the play bored me more than ever; but I perceived better than I did before that the fault was not altogether Mr Pinero's. The interest of the first act depends on Mrs Thorpe really affecting and interesting her audience in her scene with Agnes. Miss Ellice Jeffries [actress, dates unknown] fails to do this. I do not blame her, just as I should not blame Mr Charles Hawtrey [1858–1923, well-known farce and comedy actor] if he were cast for the ghost in *Hamlet* and played it somewhat disappointingly. On the contrary, I congratulate her on her hopeless incapacity to persuade us that she is the victim of an unhappy marriage, or that she lives in a dreary country rectory where she walks like a ghost about her dead child's room in the intervals of housekeeping for her parson brother. She has obviously not a scrap of anything of the kind in her whole disposition; and that Mr Pinero should have cast her for such business in a part on which his whole first act and a good deal of the rest of the play depends, suggests that his experience of the impossibility of getting all his characters fitted in a metropolis which has more theatres than companies is making him reckless. The impression left is that the scene between Agnes and Mrs Thorpe is tedious and colorless, and that between Agnes and the Duke biting and full of character. But really one scene is as good as the other; only Mr [John] Hare's [born Fairs, 1844–1921] Duke of St Olpherts is a consummate piece of acting, whilst Miss Jeffries' Mrs Thorpe is at best a graceful evasion of an impossible task. This was less noticeable before, because Mrs Patrick Campbell counted for so much in both scenes that the second factor in them mattered less. With Miss Nethersole, who failed to touch the character of Agnes at any point as far as I witnessed her performance, it mattered a great deal. I have no doubt that Miss Nethersole pulled the bible out of the stove, and played all the "emotional" scenes as well as Mrs Campbell or any one else could play them; but certainly in the first two acts, where Mrs Ebbsmith, not yet reduced to a mere phase of hysteria, is a self-possessed individual character, Miss Nethersole gave us nothing but the stage fashion of the day in a very accentuated and conscious manner. Mrs Campbell's extraordinary power of doing anything surely and swiftly with her hands whilst she is acting, preoccupation seeming an embarrassment unknown to her, is a personal peculiarity which cannot reasonably be demanded from her competitors. But Miss Nethersole seems to set a positive value on such preoccupation. When she pretends to darn a stocking she brings it down to the footlights, and poses in profile with the stockinged hand raised above the level of her head. She touches nothing without first poising her hand above it like a bird about to alight, or a pianist's fingers descending on a chord. She cannot even take up the box containing the rich dress to bundle it off into the next room, without disposing her hands round it with an unmistakeable reference to the conventional laws of grace. The effect in these first two acts, throughout which Mrs Ebbsmith is supposed to be setting Lucas Cleeve's teeth on edge at every turn by her businesslike ways, plain dress, and impatience of the effects that charm the voluptuary, may be imagined. The change of dress, with which Mrs Campbell achieved such a very startling effect, produced hardly any with Miss Nethersole, and would have produced none but for the dialogue; for Mrs Ebbsmith had been so obviously concerned all through with the effect of her attitudes, that one quite expected that she would not neglect herself when it came to dressing for dinner. The "Trafalgar Squaring" [being lectured at about social or political reform] of the Duke, a complete success on Mr Hare's part, was a complete failure on Miss Nethersole's. Mrs Campbell caught the right platform tone of political invective and contemptuous social criticism to perfection: Miss Nethersole made the speech an emotional outburst, flying out at the Duke exactly as, in a melodrama, she would have flown out at the villain who had betrayed her. My inference is that Miss Nethersole has force and emotion without sense of character. With force and emotion, and an interesting and plastic person, one can play "the heroine" under a hundred different names with entire success. But the individualized heroine is another matter; and that is where Mrs Patrick Campbell comes in.

It is usual to describe Mr Hare as an actor who does not do himself justice on first nights because he is nervous. His Duke of St Olpherts is certainly not an instance of this. It is still capital; but compared to his superb performance on the first night, it is minced in diction and almost off-hand in deportment. I have come to the conclusion that Mr [later Sir Johnston] Forbes Robertson [1853–1937, considered the greatest Hamlet of the nineteenth century] is only less out of place as Lucas Cleeve than Miss Jeffries as Mrs Thorpe. In contrast to the cool intensity of Mrs Campbell, his strong, resolute manner, slackened as much as he could slacken it, barely passed muster on the first night as the manner of the weak neurotic creature described by the Duke. But with Miss Nethersole, whose Mrs Ebbsmith is really not Mrs Ebbsmith at all, but a female Lucas Cleeve, even that faint scrap of illusion vanishes, and is replaced by a contrast of personal style in flat contradiction to the character relationship which is the subject of the drama. I still do not think *The Notorious Mrs Ebbsmith* could be made a good play by anything short of treating Agnes's sudden resolution to make Lucas fall in love with her as a comedy motive (as it essentially is), and getting rid of the claptrap about the bible, finishing the play with Lucas's discovery that his wife is quite as good a woman as he could stand life with, and possibly—though on this I do not insist—with Agnes's return to the political platform as the Radical Duchess of St Olpherts. But I am at least quite convinced now that the play as it stands would be much more interesting if the other characters were only half as appropriately impersonated as the Duke of St Olpherts is by Mr Hare, or as Mrs Ebbsmith was by Mrs Campbell....

Readers who have noticed the heading of this article may possibly want to know what Lady Macbeth has to do with it. Well, I have discovered a new Lady Macbeth. It is one of my eccentricities to be old-fashioned in my artistic tastes. For instance, I am fond—unaffectedly fond—of Shakespear's plays. I do not mean actor-managers' editions and revivals; I mean the plays as Shakespear wrote them, played straight through line by line and scene by scene as nearly as possible under the conditions of representation for which they were designed. I have seen the suburban amateurs of the Shakespear Reading Society, seated like Christy minstrels [popular blackface minstrel group] on the platform of the lecture hall at the London Institution, produce, at a moderate computation, about sixty-six times as much effect by reading straight through *Much Ado About Nothing* as Mr Irving with his expensively mounted and superlatively dull Lyceum version. When these same amateurs invited me to a regular stage performance of *Macbeth* in aid of the Siddons Memorial Fund, I went, not for the sake of Sarah the Respectable, whose great memory can take care of itself (how much fresher it is, by the way, than those of many writers and painters of her day, though no actor ever makes a speech without complaining that he is cheated out of the immortality every other sort of artist enjoys!), but simply because I wanted to see *Macbeth*. Mind, I am no admirer of the Elizabethan school. When Mr Henry Arthur Jones [1851–1929], whose collected essays on the English drama I am now engaged in reading, says: "Surely the crowning glory of our nation is our Shakespear; and remember he was one of a great school," I almost burst with the intensity of my repudiation of the second clause in that utterance. What Shakespear got from his "school" was the insane and hideous rhetoric which is all that he has in common with [Ben] Jonson [1572–1637], [John] Webster [c.1579–1630s], and the whole crew of insufferable bunglers and dullards whose work stands out as vile even at the beginning of the seventeenth century, when every art was corrupted to the marrow by the orgie called the Renaissance, which was nothing but the vulgar exploitation in the artistic professions of the territory won by the Protestant movement. The leaders of that great self-assertion of the growing spirit of man were dead long before the Elizabethan literary rabble became conscious that "ideas" were in fashion, and that any author who could gather a cheap stock of them from murder, lust, and obscenity, and formulate them in rhetorical blank verse, might make the stage pestiferous with plays that have no ray of noble feeling, no touch of faith, beauty, or even common kindness in them from beginning to end. I really cannot keep my temper over the Elizabethan dramatists and the Renaissance; nor would I if I could....

As to this performance of *Macbeth* at St George's Hall, of course it was, from the ordinary professional standpoint, a very bad one. I say this because I well know what happens to a critic when he incautiously praises an amateur. He gets by the next post a letter in the following terms: "Dear Sir,—I am perhaps transgressing the bounds of etiquette in writing privately to you; but I thought you might like to know that your kind notice of my performance as Guildenstern has encouraged me to take a step which I have long been meditating. I have resigned my position as Governor of the Bank of England with a view to adopting the stage as a profession, and trust that the result may justify your too favorable opinion of my humble powers." Therefore I desire it to be distinctly understood that I do not recommend any members of the *Macbeth* cast to go on the stage. The three witches... were as good as any three witches I ever saw; but the impersonation of witches, as a profession, is almost as precarious as the provision of smoked glasses for looking at eclipses through. Macduff was bad: I am not sure that with his natural advantages he could very easily have been worse; but still, if he feels himself driven to some artistic career by a radical aversion to earning an honest livelihood, and is prepared for a hard apprenticeship of twenty years in mastering the art of the stage—for that period still holds as good as when [François Joseph] Talma [1763–1826, famous French actor] prescribed it—he can become an actor if he likes. As to Lady Macbeth, she, too, was bad; but it is clear to me that unless she at once resolutely marries some rich gentleman who disapproves of the theatre on principle, she will not be able to keep herself off the stage. She is as handsome as Miss [Julia] Neilson [1868–1957, notable stage beauty]; and she can hold an audience whilst she is doing everything wrongly. The murder scene was not very good, because Macbeth belonged to the school of the Irish fiddler who, when Ole Bull asked him whether he played by ear or from notes, replied that he played "by main strength"; and you cannot get the brooding horror of the dagger scene by that method. Besides, Miss Lillah McCarthy—that is the lady's name as given in my program—is happily too young to conceive ambition and murder; or the temptation of a husband with a sickly conscience, as realities: they are to her delicious excitements of the imagination: with a beautiful, splendid terror about them, to be conveyed by strenuous pose, and flashing eye, and indomitable bearing. She went at them bravely in this spirit; and they came off more or less happily as her instinct and courage helped her, or her skill failed her. The banquet scene and the sleep-walking scene, which are the easiest passages in the part technically to a lady with the requisite pluck and personal fascination, were quite successful; and if the earlier scenes were immature, unskilful, and entirely artificial and rhetorical in their conception, still, they were very nearly thrilling. In short, I should like to see Miss Lillah McCarthy play again. I venture on the responsibility of saying that her Lady Macbeth was a highly promising performance, and that some years of hard work would make her a valuable recruit to the London stage. And with that very rash remark I will leave *Macbeth*, with a fervent wish that Mr Pinero, Mr [Sydney] Grundy [1848–1914, known for his adaptations of Scribe's plays], and Monsieur [Victorien] Sardou [1831–1908, writer of "well-made plays"], could be persuaded to learn from it how to write a play without wasting the first hour of the performance in tediously explaining its "construction." They really are mistaken in supposing that [Eugène] Scribe [1791–1861, credited with perfecting the "well-made play"] was cleverer than Shakespear.

## 2. The Case for the Critic-Dramatist, 16 November 1895. [*Our Theatres in the Nineties*, vol. 1, pp. 245–51]

*[The largely forgettable productions that Shaw was ostensibly reviewing in this column occupied only the final two, brief paragraphs. The rest of the column was given to his argument that a critic who was also a dramatist was actually better qualified to judge plays than a critic who was not. While Shaw was not the only dramatic critic who also wrote plays, he was certainly the most notorious by reputation both as a critic and playwright, and his relentless crusade for theatrical reform in both his plays and his columns easily opened him to personal criticism from other theatre personalities.]*

A discussion has arisen recently as to whether a dramatic critic can also be a dramatic author without injury to his integrity and impartiality. The feebleness with which the point has been debated may be guessed from the fact that the favorite opinion seems to be that a critic is either an honest man or he is not. If honest, then dramatic authorship can make no difference to him. If not, he will be dishonest whether he writes plays or not. This childish evasion cannot, for the honor of the craft, be allowed to stand. If I wanted to ascertain the melting-point of a certain metal, and how far it would be altered by an alloy of some other metal, and an expert were to tell me that a metal is either fusible or it is not—that if not, no temperature will melt it; and if so, it will melt anyhow—I am afraid I should ask that expert whether he was a fool himself or took me for one. Absolute honesty is as absurd an abstraction as absolute temperature or absolute value. A dramatic critic who would die rather than read an

American pirated edition of a copyright English book might be considered an absolutely honest man for all practical purposes on that particular subject—I say on that one, because very few men have more than one point of honor; but as far as I am aware, no such dramatic critic exists. If he did, I should regard him as a highly dangerous monomaniac. That honesty varies inversely with temptation is proved by the fact that every additional penny on the income-tax yields a less return than the penny before it, shewing that men state their incomes less honestly for the purposes of taxation at sevenpence in the pound than sixpence. The matter may be tested by a simple experiment. Go to one of the gentlemen whose theory is that a man is either honest or he is not, and obtain from him the loan of half a crown on some plausible pretext of a lost purse or some such petty emergency. He will not ask you for a written acknowledgment of the debt. Return next day and ask for a loan of £500 without a promissory note on the ground that you are either honest or not honest, and that a man who will pay back half a crown without compulsion will also pay back £500. You will find that the theory of absolute honesty will collapse at once.

Are we then to believe that the critic-dramatist who stands to make anything from five hundred to ten thousand pounds by persuading a manager to produce his plays, will be prevented by his honesty from writing about that manager otherwise than he would if he had never written a play and were quite certain that he never should write one? I can only say that people who believe such a thing would believe anything. I am myself a particularly flagrant example of the critic-dramatist. It is not with me a mere case of an adaptation or two raked up against me as incidents in my past. I have written half a dozen "original" plays, four of which have never been performed; and I shall presently write half a dozen more. The production of one of them, even if it attained the merest success of esteem, would be more remunerative to me than a couple of years of criticism. Clearly, since I am no honester than other people, I should be the most corrupt flatterer in London if there were nothing but honesty to restrain me. How is it, then, that the most severe criticisms of managers come from me and from my fellow critic-dramatists, and that the most servile puffery comes from writers whose every sentence proves that they have nothing to hope or fear from any manager? There are a good many answers to this question, one of the most obvious being that as the respect inspired by a good criticism is permanent, whilst the irritation it causes is temporary, and as, on the other hand, the pleasure given by a venal criticism is temporary and the contempt it inspires permanent, no man really secures his advancement as a dramatist by making himself despised as a critic. The thing has been tried extensively during the last twenty years; and it has failed. For example, the late Frank [Francis] Marshall [1840–89], a dramatist and an extravagantly enthusiastic admirer of Sir Henry Irving's [1838–1905, Lyceum Theatre manager and revered Shakespearean actor] genius, followed a fashion which at one time made the Lyceum Theatre a sort of court formed by a retinue of literary gentlemen. I need not question either their sincerity or the superiority of Canute [Shaw is comparing Irving to a powerful tenth-century Anglo-Danish king] to their idolatry; for Canute never produced their plays: *Robert Emmett* [play Marshall wrote for Irving, still unproduced] and the rest of their masterpieces remain unacted to this day. It may be said that this brings us back to honesty as the best policy; but honesty has nothing to do with it: plenty of the men who know that they can get along faster fighting than crawling, are no more honest than the first Napoleon [1769–1821, French conqueror-emperor] was. No virtue, least of all courage, implies any other virtue. The cardinal guarantee for a critic's integrity is simply the force of the critical instinct itself. To try to prevent me from criticizing by pointing out to me the superior pecuniary advantages of puffing is like trying to keep a young Irving from going on the stage by pointing out the superior pecuniary advantages of stockbroking. If my own father were an actor-manager, and his life depended on his getting favorable notices of his performance, I should orphan myself without an instant's hesitation if he acted badly. I am by no means the willing victim of this instinct. I am keenly susceptible to contrary influences—to flattery, which I swallow greedily if the quality is sufficiently good; to the need of money, to private friendship or even acquaintanceship, to the pleasure of giving pleasure and the pain of giving pain, to consideration for people's circumstances and prospects, to personal likes and dislikes, to sentimentality, pity, chivalry, pugnacity and mischief, laziness and cowardice, and a dozen other human conditions which make the critic vulnerable; but the critical instinct gets the better of them all. I spare no effort to mitigate its inhumanity, trying to detect and strike out of my articles anything that would give pain without doing any good. Those who think the things I say severe, or even malicious, should just see the things I do not say. I do my best to be partial, to hit out at remediable abuses rather than at accidental shortcomings, and at strong and responsible people rather than weak and helpless ones. And yet all my efforts do not alter the result very much. So stubborn is the critic within me, that with every disposition to be as good-natured and as popular an authority as the worst enemy of art could desire, I am to all intents and purposes incorruptible. And that is how the dramatist-critic, if only he is critic enough, "slates" the actor-manager in defiance of the interest he has in conciliating him. He cannot help himself, any more than the ancient mariner could help telling his story. And the actor-manager can no more help listening than the wedding guest could. In short, the better formula would have been, that a man is either a critic or not a critic; that to the extent to which he is one he will criticize the managers in spite of heaven or earth; and that to the extent to which he is not, he will flatter them anyhow, to save himself trouble.

The advantage of having a play criticized by a critic who is also a playwright is as obvious as the advantage of having a ship criticized by a critic who is also a master shipwright. Pray observe that I do not speak of the criticism of dramas and ships by dramatists and shipwrights who are not also critics; for that would be no more convincing than the criticism of acting by actors. Dramatic authorship no more constitutes a man a critic than actorship constitutes him a dramatic author; but a dramatic critic learns as much from having been a dramatic author as Shakespear or Mr Pinero from having been actors. The average London critic, for want of practical experience, has no real confidence in himself: he is always searching for an imaginary "right" opinion, with which he never dares to identify his own. Consequently every public man finds that as far as the press is concerned his career divides itself into two parts: the first, during which the critics are afraid to praise him; and the second, during which they are afraid to do anything else. In the first, the critic is uncomfortably trying to find faults enough to make out a case for his timid coldness: in the second, he is eagerly picking out excellences to justify his eulogies. And of course he blunders equally in both phases. The faults he finds are either inessential or are positive reforms, or he blames the wrong people for them: the triumphs of acting which he announces are stage tricks that any old hand could play. In criticizing actresses he is an open and shameless voluptuary. If a woman is pretty, well dressed, and self-satisfied enough to be at her ease on the stage, he is delighted; and if she is a walking monument of handsome incompetence, so much the better, as your voluptuary rarely likes a woman to be cleverer than himself, or to force him to feel deeply and think energetically when he only wants to wallow in her good looks. Confront him with an actress who will not condescend to attack him on this side—who takes her work with thorough seriousness and self-respect—and his resentment, his humiliation, his sense of being snubbed, break out ludicrously in his writing, even when he dare not write otherwise than favorably. A great deal of this nonsense would be taken out of him if he could only write a play and have it produced. No dramatist begins by writing plays merely as excuses for the exhibition of pretty women on the stage. He comes to that ultimately perhaps; but at first he does his best to create real characters and make them pass through three acts of real experiences. Bring a critic who has done this face to face with the practical question of selecting an actress for his heroine, and he suddenly realizes for the first time that there is not such a galaxy of talent on the London stage as he thought, and that the handsome walking ladies whom he always thought good enough for other people's plays are not good enough for his own. That is already an immense step in his education. There are other steps, too, which he will have taken before the curtain falls on the first public representation of his play; but they may be summed up in the fact that the author of a play is the only person who really wants to have it well done in every respect, and who therefore has every drawback brought fully home to him. The man who has had that awakening about one play will thenceforth have his eyes open at all other plays; and there you have at once the first moral with the first technical qualification of the critic—the determination to have every play as well done as possible, and the knowledge of what is standing in the way of that consummation. Those of our critics who, either as original dramatists or adapters and translators, have superintended the production of plays with paternal anxiety, are never guilty of the wittily disguised indifference of clever critics who have never seen a drama through from its first beginnings behind the scenes. Compare the genuine excitement of Mr Clement Scott [1841–1904], or the almost Calvinistic seriousness of Mr William Archer

[1856–1924], with the gaily easy what-does-it-matterness of Mr [Arthur Bingham] Walkley [1855–1926], and you see at once how the two critic-dramatists influence the drama, whilst the critic-playgoer only makes it a pretext for entertaining his readers. On the whole there is only as much validity in the theory that a critic should not be a dramatist, as in the theory that a judge should not be a lawyer nor a general a soldier. You cannot have qualifications without exp To J.E. Vedrenne, 19 July erience; and you cannot have experience without personal interest and bias. That may not be an ideal arrangement; but it is the way the world is built; and we must make the best of it.

*[Shaw concludes with two brief paragraphs largely dismissing the productions of* Merrifield's Ghost *by H.M. Paull (1854–1934), and George Alexander's production of* Liberty Hall *by R.C. Carton (1853–1928).]*

## 3. The Farcical Comedy Outbreak, 9 May 1896. [*Our Theatres in the Nineties*, vol. 2, pp. 118–24]

*[Shaw took comedy very seriously, and had little patience with plays that elicited laughter as an end in itself. His ability to separate the work of the actors from the futile characters they were forced to play shows his own strong understanding of acting as a profession and the capabilities of individual actors.]*

THE NEW BABY. A deception in three acts. Adapted by Arthur Bourchier from Der Rabensvater, by H. F. Fischer and J. Jarno. Royalty Theatre, 28 April 1896.
MONSIEUR DE PARIS. A play in one act. By Alicia Ramsey and Rudolph de Cordova. Royalty Theatre.
A NIGHT OUT. Farcical comedy in three acts. By Georges Feydeau and Maurice Desvallières. English version. Vaudeville Theatre, 29 April 1896.

One of the strongest objections to the institution of monogamy is the existence of its offspring, the conventional farcical comedy. The old warning, "Beware how you kiss when you do not love," ought to be paraphrased on the play-bills of all our lighter theatres as "Beware how you laugh when you do not enjoy." To laugh without sympathy is a ruinous abuse of a noble function; and the degradation of any race may be measured by the degree of their addiction to it. In its subtler forms it is dying very hard: for instance, we find people who would not join in the laughter of a crowd of peasants at the village idiot, or tolerate the public flogging or pillorying of a criminal, booking seats to shout with laughter at a farcical comedy, which is, at bottom, the same thing—namely, the deliberate indulgence of that horrible, derisive joy in humiliation and suffering which is the beastliest element in human nature. I make these portentous observations not by way of breaking a butterfly on a wheel, but in order to bring out with violent emphasis the distinction between the high and the base comedy of errors—between *Pink Dominos* [adapted from a French farce by James Albery, produced with great success by Charles Wyndham in 1877] and *Twelfth Night*.... To produce high art in the theatre, the author must create persons whose fortunes we can follow as those of a friend or enemy: to produce base laughter, it is only necessary to turn human beings on to the stage as rats are turned into a pit, that they may be worried for the entertainment of the spectators. Such entertainment is much poorer fun than most playgoers suspect. The critic, trained to analyse all his artistic sensations, soon gets cured of the public's delusion that everything that makes it laugh amuses it. You cannot impose on him by the mere galvanism of the theatre; for all its manifestations, from the brute laughter produced by an indecency or a bout of horseplay, to the tricks, familiar to old actors, by which worthless explosions of applause can be elicited with mechanical certainty at the end of a speech or on an exit, become so transparent to him that, instead of sharing the enthusiasm they excite, he measures merit by their absence. For example, one of the admirable points in Mrs Patrick Campbell's performance in *For the Crown* [by John Davidson, 1896] is the way in which, after her recitation of the butterfly poem, she avoids the round of clapping which any third-rate actress could get for it—however execrably it might be delivered—by simply finishing it with a swagger and waiting for the audience to make a fool of itself. I have no doubt that many old stagers regard this as the ineptitude of a novice letting a sure point go "for nothing" or "without a hand." But everybody remembers the recitation; everybody is struck by it; everybody is conscious of a spell which would be broken by any vulgar attempt to "bring down the house": the commercial result being that people go to see Mrs Campbell, whereas they stay at home when there is nothing to be enjoyed at the theatre except the galvanic tricks of the trade. If it could once be borne in upon the mental darkness of most of our public performers that the artists who draw best are not those who are fondest of making the noisy and hysterical section of the audience interrupt the play—that, in fact, applause in the middle of an act is not only discreditable on most occasions to both actor and audience but bad business as well—we should get vastly better work at the theatres.

I shall now, perhaps, be understood (if not, no matter) when I class the laughter produced by conventional farcical comedy as purely galvanic, and the inference drawn by the audience that since they are laughing they must be amused or edified or pleased, as a delusion. They are really being more or less worried and exhausted and upset by ill-natured cachinnation; and the proof is that they generally leave the theatre tired and out of humor with themselves and the world. Lest I should err here on the side of over-much righteousness, let me hasten to admit that a little galvanism may

THE CRITICAL SHAW: ON THEATER

be harmless and even beneficial in its effect on the lungs and liver; but three acts of it is too much. I first learnt the weariness of it from *Pink Dominos*, although that play had an excellent third act; and I have been wearied in the same way by every new version. For we have had it again and again under various titles. Act I, John Smith's home; Act II, the rowdy restaurant or casino at which John Smith, in the course of his clandestine spree, meets all the members of his household, including the schoolboy and the parlormaid; Act III, his house next morning, with the inevitable aftermath of the complications of the night before: who that has any theatrical experience does not know it all by heart? And now here it is again, with a fresh coat of paint on it, and as rotten as ever underneath.

But farcical comedy, like any other stage entertainment, may become artistically valuable, and even delightful, through fine execution. *Pink Dominos* is memorable, not for itself, but for the performances of Mr [Charles] Wyndham [1837–1919, comedy actor-manager] and [John] Clarke [c.1829–1879]. One remembers the charm of Miss [Mary] Eastlake [1856–1911] before she took up the heavy and violent work of supporting Mr Wilson Barrett [1846–1904] in tragic melodrama; and this generation, contemplating Sir Augustus Harris [1851–96, commercially successful impresario known for elaborate theatre and opera productions] with awe, little suspects how lighthearted he was as Harry Greenlanes [a character in *Pink Dominos*]. Since then, Mr Hawtrey, Mr [William Sydney] Penley [1851–1912], and Miss Lottie Venne [1852–1928] have managed to keep up the notion that farcical comedies are intrinsically amusing with considerable success. But the moment an attempt is made to run this sort of dramatic work on its own merits, its fundamental barrenness and baseness assert themselves and become intolerable. Therefore I shall make no pretence of discussing as drama the two specimens just produced at the Royalty and Vaudeville. Suffice it that the Royalty piece, *The New Baby*, is, from that point of view, so far beneath contempt that it never once rises to the point of even suggesting the disgust which its story would rouse in anyone who took it seriously; whilst *A Night Out*, at the Vaudeville, though a masterpiece of ingenuity and urbanity in comparison to the other, is essentially the same as previous nights out, from that in *Pink Dominos* downwards, and reproduces the stage arrangements of the second act of *Forbidden Fruit* [1876, by Dion Boucicault] pretty faithfully. But it is noteworthy that although *The New Baby* includes incest in its bewilderments, and one of the central incidents of *A Night Out* is the sudden retirement of a gentleman from a supper party on a pretext which [Tobias] Smollett [1721–71, Scottish satirist] might, and probably would, have employed, they are comparatively free from that detestable, furtive lubricity which was the rule twenty years ago. Farcical comedy used to have the manners of a pimp. It is now progressing upward towards the morals of Tom Jones [sexually adventurous title character of Henry Fielding's 1749 novel].

The question then being one of acting, we had better start by making certain allowances: First, for the absence from the cast of those light comedians who have been specially successful in this class of entertainment, and, second, for the homeliness of our English attempts to volatilize ourselves sufficiently to breathe that fantastic atmosphere of moral irresponsibility in which alone the hero of farcical comedy, like Pierrot or Harlequin [stock dramatic clown characters], can realize himself fully. On the understanding that these difficulties have not been surmounted, one may say that *A Night Out* is not in the main badly acted.... [*Shaw names and critiques the individual performers, generally positive on their acting, but not necessarily their stage movements.*] In this, and in such details as the crudity with which the second waiter keeps senselessly shouting Madame Paillard's name with an obvious consciousness of the mischief he is doing, not to mention the unnecessary noisiness of some of the scenes, one sees the chief fault of the production—puerility of stage management. Mr Seymour Hicks [1871–1949] has given way to his sense of fun, forgetting that a stage manager should have no sense of anything except fine art.

But if the management is immature at the Vaudeville, what is it at the Royalty? Alas! it is hardly to be described. Here is Mr [Arthur] Bourchier [1863–1927], a born actor—the likeliest successor, so far, to Mr Wyndham in light comedy—with a theatre of his own and an excellent company, the centre of which is well knit together by private as well as artistic ties, and with a handsome capital in personal popularity and good wishes to reinforce his cash balance, positively playing with his chances like an undergraduate. I protested mildly against the way in which *The Chili Widow* [1895, adapted from the French by Bourchier and Alfred Sutro] was romped through. No doubt it was jolly; but it was not artistic management, and it was hardly acting. But *The New Baby* is worse. Mr Bourchier has not only cast himself for an elderly part which he is physically unfit for—a part which might be played appropriately by James Lewis [1840–96, American comedy actor]—but he treats it as a pure lark from beginning to end, rattling along anyhow as if nothing mattered so long as his good humor and high spirits infected the audience sufficiently to keep them smiling. In desperation I ask Mr Bourchier, does he really think he is keeping himself up to his work at the Royalty? Would any other manager stand from him the happy-go-lucky playing he stands from himself with apparent complacency? Would any other author allow him to do so much less than his best at the very moment when he should be concentrating his intensest energy on the consolidation of his position? Does he expect me to pay him any higher compliment than to admit that his performance is at least good enough for the play he has selected? …But the play is too foolish to have much chance even of a success of folly.

The strongest part of the Royalty performance is a one-act drama, of exceptional merit as such things go, entitled *Monsieur de Paris* [1896, aka *The Executioner's Daughter*, by Alicia Ramsay and R. de Cordova], in which Miss Violet Vanbrugh [1867–1942, actress and Bourchier's wife], instead of trifling with her talent as she did in *The Chili Widow*, plays a purely romantic part with striking effect. The sanguinary ending of the play is as mechanical, obvious, and unimaginative as a Chicago pig-sticking; and Miss Vanbrugh, by overrating its value, attempts—what no thoroughly expert actress would attempt—a sustained and unvaried crescendo of forcible expression which only betrays the fact that it is her imagination and not her feeling that is at work; but the performance proves a great deal as to her remarkable qualifications for more serious work on the stage. May I add without offence that in the finest diction "crime," "quick," "true," and "heaven" are not vehemently dissyllabic?…

*[Shaw concludes by describing a celebration dinner he attended for theatre manager Charles Wyndham, "a wonderful occassion… owning the extremity of its huge success to its genuineness as a demonstration of admiration and regard for Mr Wyndham".]*

# 4. Blaming the Bard, 26 September 1896. [*Our Theatres in the Nineties*, vol. 2, pp. 195–202]

*[Henry Irving (later Sir Henry; in 1895, he became the first actor to be knighted) was already considered one of the outstanding actors of the nineteenth century when he took over as manager of the Lyceum Theatre in 1878. His leading lady at the Lyceum was Ellen Terry, (later Dame Ellen, 1847–1928), and together they were the most revered acting couple of the age, especially famous for their productions of Shakespeare's plays. Irving's lavish melodramatic style*

*was the opposite of the realism that Shaw advocated, and he was
relentlessly outspoken in his criticism of Irving and the Lyceum productions.]*

CYMBELINE. By Shakespeare. Lyceum Theatre, 22 Septem-
ber, 1896.

I confess to a difficulty in feeling civilized just at present.
Flying from the country, where the gentlemen of England are
in an ecstasy of chicken-butchering, I return to town to find
the higher wits assembled at a play three hundred years old,
in which the sensation scene exhibits a woman waking up to
find her husband reposing gorily in her arms with his head
cut off.

Pray understand, therefore, that I do not defend *Cymbeline*.
It is for the most part stagey trash of the lowest melodramatic
order, in parts abominably written, throughout intellectually
vulgar, and, judged in point of thought by modern intellectual standards, vulgar, foolish, offensive, indecent, and exasperating beyond all tolerance. There are moments when one
asks despairingly why our stage should ever have been cursed
with this "immortal" pilferer of other men's stories and ideas,
with his monstrous rhetorical fustian, his unbearable plati-
tudes, his pretentious reduction of the subtlest problems of
life to commonplaces against which a Polytechnic debating
club would revolt, his incredible unsuggestiveness, his sententious combination of ready reflection with complete intellectual sterility, and his consequent incapacity for getting
out of the depth of even the most ignorant audience, except
when he solemnly says something so transcendently plati-
tudinous that his more humble-minded hearers cannot bring
themselves to believe that so great a man really meant to
talk like their grandmothers. With the single exception of
Homer, there is no eminent writer, not even Sir Walter Scott
[1771–1832, author of popular historical fictions, including
*Ivanhoe*], whom I can despise so entirely as I despise Shake-

speare when I measure my mind against his. The intensity of my impatience with him occasionally reaches such a pitch, that it would positively be a relief to me to dig him up and throw stones at him, knowing as I do how incapable he and his worshippers are of understanding any less obvious form of indignity. To read *Cymbeline* and to think of [Johann Wolfgang von] Goethe [1749–1832, celebrated German author], of [Richard] Wagner [1813–83, German composer known for his innovative operas], of [Henrik] Ibsen [1828–1906, Norwegian realist playwright of social problem plays], is, for me, to imperil the habit of studied moderation of statement which years of public responsibility as a journalist have made almost second nature in me.

But I am bound to add that I pity the man who cannot enjoy Shakespeare. He has outlasted thousands of abler thinkers, and will outlast a thousand more. His gift of telling a story (provided some one else told it to him first); his enormous power over language, as conspicuous in his senseless and silly abuse of it as in his miracles of expression; his humor; his sense of idiosyncratic character; and his prodigious fund of that vital energy which is, it seems, the true differentiating property behind the faculties, good, bad, or indifferent, of the man of genius, enable him to entertain us so effectively that the imaginary scenes and people he has created become more real to us than our actual life—at least, until our knowledge and grip of actual life begins to deepen and glow beyond the common. When I was twenty I knew everybody in Shakespeare, from Hamlet to Abhorson, much more intimately than I knew my living contemporaries; and to this day, if the name of Pistol or Polonius catches my eye in a newspaper, I turn to the passage with more curiosity than if the name were that of—but perhaps I had better not mention any one in particular.

How many new acquaintances, then, do you make in reading *Cymbeline*, provided you have the patience to break your way into it through all the fustian, and are old enough to be free from the modern idea that Cymbeline must be the name of a cosmetic and Imogen of the latest scientific discovery in the nature of a hitherto unknown gas? Cymbeline is nothing; his queen nothing, though some attempt is made to justify her description as "a woman that bears all down with her brain"; Posthumus, nothing—most fortunately, as otherwise he would be an unendurably contemptible hound; Belarius, nothing—at least, not after Kent in *King Lear* (just as the Queen is nothing after Lady Macbeth); Iachimo, not much—only a *diabolus ex machina* [Latin term for an evil character who appears out of nowhere] made plausible; and Pisanio, less than Iachimo. On the other hand, we have Cloten, the prince of numbsculls, whose part, indecencies and all, is a literary masterpiece from the first line to the last; the two princes—fine presentments of that impressive and generous myth, the noble savage; Caius Lucius, the Roman general, urbane among the barbarians; and, above all, Imogen. But do, please, remember that there are two Imogens. One is a solemn and elaborate example of what, in Shakespeare's opinion, a real lady ought to be. With this unspeakable person virtuous indignation is chronic. Her object in life is to vindicate her own propriety and to suspect everybody else's, especially her husband's. Like Lothaw in the jeweller's shop in Bret Harte's burlesque novel [*Lothaw; or, The Adventures of a Young Gentleman in Search of a Religion*, 1892], she cannot be left alone with unconsidered trifles of portable silver without officiously assuring the proprietors that she has stolen naught, nor would not, though she had found gold strewed i' the floor. Her fertility and spontaneity in nasty ideas is not to be described: there is hardly a speech in her part that you can read without wincing. But this Imogen has another one tied to her with ropes of blank verse (which can fortunately be cut)—the Imogen of Shakespeare's genius, an enchanting person of the most delicate sensitiveness, full of sudden transitions from ecstasies of tenderness to transports of childish rage, and reckless of consequences in both, instantly hurt and instantly appeased, and of the highest breeding and courage. But for this Imogen, *Cymbeline* would stand about as much chance of being revived now as *Titus Andronicus* [early Shakespeare tragedy filled with gruesome deaths].

The instinctive Imogen, like the real live part of the rest of the play, has to be disentangled from a mass of stuff which, though it might be recited with effect and appropriateness by young amateurs at a performance by the Elizabethan Stage Society, is absolutely unactable and unutterable in the modern theatre, where a direct illusion of reality is aimed at, and where the repugnance of the best actors to play false passages is practically insuperable. For the purposes of the Lyceum, therefore, *Cymbeline* had to be cut, and cut liberally. Not that there was any reason to apprehend that the manager would flinch from the operation: quite the contrary. In a true republic of art Sir Henry Irving would ere this have expiated his acting versions on the scaffold. He does not merely cut plays: he disembowels them. In *Cymbeline* he has quite surpassed himself by extirpating the antiphonal third verse of the famous dirge. A man who would do that would do anything—cut the coda out of the first movement of Beethoven's Ninth Symphony, or shorten one of [Diego] Velasquez's Philips [series of portraits depicting Philip IV of Spain] into a kitcat [a portrait approximately half-length] to make it fit over his drawing-room mantelpiece. The grotesque character tracery of Cloten's lines, which is surely not beyond the appreciation of an age educated by [Robert Louis] Stevenson [1850–94, Scottish novelist best known for *Treasure Island*], is defaced with Cromwellian ruthlessness [Oliver Cromwell, 1599–1658, ruled brutally as Lord Protector of England after the execution of Charles I]; and the patriotic scene, with the Queen's great speech about the natural bravery of our isle, magnificent in its *Walkürenritt* [Wagner's *Ride of the Valkyries*] swing, is shorn away, though it might easily have been introduced in the Garden scene. And yet, long screeds of rubbish about "slander, whose edge is sharper than the sword," and so on, are preserved with superstitious veneration.

This curious want of connoisseurship in literature would disable Sir Henry Irving seriously if he were an interpretative actor. But it is, happily, the fault of a great quality—the creative quality. A prodigious deal of nonsense has been written about Sir Henry Irving's conception of this, that, and the other Shakespearean character. The truth is that he has never in his life conceived or interpreted the characters of any author except himself. He is really as incapable of acting another man's play as Wagner was of setting another man's libretto; and he should, like Wagner, have written his plays for himself. But as he did not find himself out until it was too late for him to learn that supplementary trade, he was compelled to use other men's plays as the framework for his own creations. His first great success in this sort of adaptation was with the *Merchant of Venice*. There was no question then of a bad Shylock or a good Shylock: he was simply not Shylock at all; and when his own creation came into conflict with Shakespeare's, as it did quite openly in the Trial scene, he simply played in flat contradiction of the lines, and positively acted Shakespeare off the stage. This was an original policy, and an intensely interesting one from the critical point of view; but it was obvious that its difficulty must increase with the vividness and force of the dramatist's creation. Shakespeare at his highest pitch cannot be set aside by any mortal actor, however gifted; and when Sir Henry Irving tried to interpolate a most singular and fantastic notion of an old man between the lines of a fearfully mutilated acting version of *King Lear*, he was smashed. On the other hand, in plays by persons of no importance, where the dramatist's part of the business is the merest trash, his creative activity is unhampered and uncontradicted; and the author's futility is the opportunity for the actor's masterpiece. Now I have already described Shakespeare's Iachimo as little better than any of the lay figures in *Cymbeline*—a mere *diabolus ex machina*. But Irving's Iachimo is a very different affair. It is a new and independent creation. I knew Shakespeare's play inside and out before last Tuesday; but this Iachimo was quite fresh and novel to me. I witnessed it with unqualified delight: it was no vulgar bagful of "points," but a true impersonation, unbroken in its life-current from end to end, varied on the surface with the finest comedy, and without a single lapse in the sustained beauty of its execution. It is only after such work that an artist can with perfect naturalness and dignity address himself to his audience as "their faithful and loving servant"; and I wish I could add that the audience had an equal right to offer him their applause as a worthy acknowledgment of his merit. But when a house distributes its officious first-night plaudits impartially between the fine artist and the blunderer who roars a few lines violently and rushes off the stage after compressing the entire art of How Not to Act into five intolerable minutes, it had better be told to reserve its impertinent and obstreperous demonstrations until it has learnt to bestow them with some sort of discrimination. Our first-night people mean well, and will, no doubt, accept my assurance that they are donkeys with all possible good humor; but they should remember that to applaud for the sake of applauding, as schoolboys will cheer for the sake of cheering, is to destroy our own power of complimenting those who, as the greatest among us, are the servants of all the rest.

Over the performances of the other gentlemen in the cast let me skate as lightly as possible. Mr. Norman Forbes's [1858–1932, brother of Johnston Forbes-Robertson] Cloten, though a fatuous idiot rather than the brawny "beefwitted" fool whom Shakespeare took from his own Ajax in *Troilus and Cressida*, is effective and amusing, so that one feels acutely the mangling of his part, especially the cutting of that immortal musical criticism of his upon the serenade. Mr. [Edward] Gordon Craig [1872–1966, son of Ellen Terry, who is best known as a modernist director and designer] and Mr. [Ben] Webster [1864–1947] are desperate failures as the two noble savages. They are as spirited and picturesque as possible; but every pose, every flirt of their elfin locks, proclaims the wild freedom of Bedford Park [a west London suburb]. They recite the poor maimed dirge admirably, Mr. Craig being the more musical of the twain; and Mr. Webster's sword-and-cudgel fight with Cloten is very lively; but their utter deficiency in the grave, rather sombre, uncivilized primeval strength and Mohican dignity so finely suggested by Shakespeare, takes all the ballast out of the fourth act, and combines with the inappropriate prettiness and sunniness of the landscape scenery to most cruelly handicap Miss Ellen Terry in the crucial scene of her awakening by the side of the flower-decked corpse—a scene which, without every accessory to heighten its mystery, terror, and pathos, is utterly and heart-breakingly impossible for any actress, even if she were [Eleanora] Duse [1858–1924], [Adelaide] Ristori [1822–1906], Mrs. [Sarah] Siddons [1755–1831], and Miss Terry [these are considered among the greatest actresses of all time] rolled into one. When I saw this gross and palpable oversight, and heard people talking about the Lyceum stage management as superb, I with difficulty restrained myself from tearing out my hair in handfuls and scattering it with imprecations to the four winds. That cave of the three mountaineers wants nothing but a trellised porch, a bamboo bicycle, and a nice little bed of standard roses, to complete its absurdity.

With Mr. Frederic Robinson [1832–1912] as Belarius, and Mr. [Frank] Tyars [1848–1918] as Pisanio, there is no reasonable fault to find, except that they might, perhaps, be a little brighter with advantage; and of the rest of their male colleagues I think I shall ask to be allowed to say nothing at all, even at the cost of omitting a tribute to Mr. Fuller Mellish's [1865–1936] discreet impersonation of the harmless necessary Philario. There remains Miss [later Dame] Genevieve Ward [1837–1922], whose part, with the Neptune's park speech lopped off, was not worth her playing, and Miss Ellen Terry, who invariably fascinates me so much that I have not the smallest confidence in my own judgment respecting her. There was no Bedford Park about the effect she made as she stepped into the King's garden; still less any of the atmosphere of ancient Britain. At the first glance, we were in the Italian fifteenth century; and the house, unversed in the *cinquecento* [Italian for fifteenth century], but dazzled all the same, proceeded to roar until it stopped from exhaustion. There is one scene in *Cymbeline*, the one in which Imogen receives the summons to "that same blessed Milford," which might have been written for Miss Terry, so perfectly does its innocent rapture and frank gladness fit into her hand. Her repulse of Iachimo brought down the house as a matter of course, though I am convinced that the older Shakespeareans present had a vague impression that it could not be properly done except by a stout, turnip-headed matron, with her black hair folded smoothly over her ears and secured in a classic bun. Miss Terry had evidently cut her own part; at all events the odious Mrs. Grundyish ["Mrs Grundy" is a figurative term for restrictive conservatism] Imogen had been dissected out of it so skilfully that it went without a single jar. The circumstances under which she was asked to play the fourth act were, as I have explained, impossible. To wake up in the gloom amid the wolf and robber-haunted mountain gorges which formed the Welsh mountains of Shakespeare's imagination in the days before the Great Western existed is one thing: to wake up at about three on a nice Bank-holiday afternoon in a charming spot near the valley of the Wye is quite another. With all her force, Miss Terry gave us faithfully the whole process which Shakespeare has presented with such dramatic cunning—Imogen's bewilderment, between dream and waking, as to where she is; the vague discerning of some strange bedfellow there; the wondering examination of the flowers with which he is so oddly covered; the frightful discovery of blood on the flowers, with the hideous climax that the man is headless and that his clothes are her husband's; and it was all ruined by that blazing, idiotic, prosaic sunlight in which everything leapt to the eye at once, rendering the mystery and the slowly growing clearness of perception incredible and unintelligible, and spoiling a scene which, properly stage-managed, would have been a triumph of histrionic intelligence. Cannot somebody be hanged for this?—men perish every week for lesser crimes. What consolation is it to me that Miss Terry, playing with infinite charm and delicacy of appeal, made up her lost ground in other directions, and had more than as much success as the roaring gallery could feel the want of?

A musical accompaniment to the drama has been specially composed; and its numbers are set forth in the bill of the play, with the words "LOST PROPERTY" in conspicuous red capitals in the margin. Perhaps I can be of some use in restoring at least some of the articles to their rightful owner. The prelude to the fourth act belongs to Beethoven—first movement of the Seventh Symphony. The theme played by "the ingenious instrument" in the cave is Handel's, and is familiar to lovers of Judas Maccabeus as O never bow we down to the rude stock or sculptured stone. J.F.R. [Johnston Forbes-Robertson] will, I feel sure, be happy to carry the work of identification further if necessary.

Sir Henry Irving's next appearance will be on Bosworth Field [i.e. Shakespeare's *Richard III*]. He was obviously astonished by the startling shout of approbation with which the announcement was received. We all have an old weakness for Richard. After that *Madame Sans-Gêne*, with Sardou's

*Napoleon* [both popular French melodramas, "well-made plays," by Sardou].

## 5. The Theatres, 16 October 1897. [*Our Theatres in the Nineties*, vol. 3, pp. 215–21]

[*Charles Frohman (1856–1915) was one of the founders of the Theatrical Syndicate, an organization of theatre managers that exercised a virtual monopoly on theatre production in the United States around the turn of the twentieth century. Richard Mansfield (1854–1907), the actor-manager responsible for Shaw's first successful American productions, staunchly opposed the Theatrical Syndicate's control. Frohman successfully produced shows in New York and London until his death on the Lusitania in 1915. This review shows Shaw mixing a lecture about theatrical form and production methods with the specific reviews of plays and actors. He once again shows his keen eye for talent in singling out Robert Loraine (1876–1935), the handsome actor-aviator who would produce Shaw's* Arms and the Man *on Broadway in 1905.*]

NEVER AGAIN. A farcical comedy in three acts. By Maurice Desvallières and Antony Mars. Vaudeville Theatre, 11 October 1897.
ONE SUMMER'S DAY. A love story in three acts. By H. V. Esmond. Comedy Theatre.
THE WHITE HEATHER. By Cecil Raleigh and Henry Hamilton. Drury Lane Theatre.

I can hardly estimate offhand how many visits to *Never Again* at the Vaudeville would enable an acute acrostician to unravel its plot. Probably not less than seventeen. It may be that there is really no plot, and that the whole bewildering tangle of names and relationships is a sham. If so, it shews how superfluous a real plot is. In this play everyone who opens a door and sees somebody outside it utters a yell of dismay and slams the door to as if the fiend in person had knocked at it. When anybody enters a room, he or she is received with a roar of confusion and terror, and frantically ejected by bodily violence. The audience does not know why; but as each member of it thinks he ought to, and believes that his neighbor does, he echoes the yell of the actor with a shout of laughter; and so the piece "goes" immensely. It is, to my taste, a vulgar, stupid, noisy, headachy, tedious business. One actor, Mr Ferdinand Gottschalk [1858–1944], shews remarkable talent, both as actor and mimic, in the part of a German musician; but this character is named Katzenjammer [colloquial German term for confused uproar or hangover headache], which can produce no effect whatever on those who do not know what it means, and must sicken those who do. There is of course a Shakespearean precedent in *Twelfth Night*; but even in the spacious times of great Elizabeth they did not keep repeating Sir Toby's surname all over the stage, whereas this play is all Katzenjammer: the word is thrown in the face of the audience every two or three minutes. Unfortunately this is only part of the puerile enjoyment of mischief and coarseness for their own sakes which is characteristic not so much of the play as of the method of its presentation. And as that method is aggressively American, and is apparently part of a general design on Mr Charles Frohman's part to smarten up our stage habits by Americanizing them, it raises a much larger question than the merits of an insignificant version of a loose French farce.

I need hardly point out to intelligent Americans that any difference which exists between American methods and English ones must necessarily present itself to the American as an inferiority on the part of the English, and to the Englishman as an inferiority on the part of the Americans; for it is obvious that if the two nations were agreed as to the superiority of any particular method, they would both adopt it, and the difference would disappear, since it can hardly be seriously contended that the average English actor cannot, if he chooses, do anything that the average American actor can do, or vice versa. Consequently nothing is more natural and inevitable than that Mr Frohman, confronted with English stage business, should feel absolutely confident that he can alter it for the better. But it does not at all follow that the English public will agree with him. For example, if in a farcical comedy a contretemps is produced by the arrival of an unwelcome visitor, and the English actor extricates himself from the difficulty by half bowing, half coaxing the intruder out, it may seem to Mr Frohman much funnier and livelier that he should resort to the summary and violent methods of a potman [a server in a pub], especially if the visitor is an elderly lady. Now I do not deny that Mr Frohman may strike on a stratum of English society which will agree with him, nor even that for twenty years to come the largest fortunes made in theatrical enterprise may be made by exploiting that stratum; but to English people who have learnt the art of playgoing at our best theatres, such horseplay is simply silly. Again, it may seem to Mr Frohman, as it did once (and probably does still) to Mr Augustin Daly [1838–1899, American theatre manager, director, playwright], that the way to work every act of a comedy up to a rattling finish is to upset chairs, smash plates, make all the women faint and all the men tumble over one another. But in London we are apt to receive that sort of thing so coldly even in its proper place in the rallies of a harlequinade that there is no temptation to West End managers to condescend to it. The truth is, all this knockabout stuff, these coarse pleasantries about women's petticoats, Katzenjammer, and so forth, belong, not to American civilization, but to American barbarism. It converts what might be, at worst, a wittily licentious form of comedy for licentiously witty people into a crude sort of entertainment for a crude sort of audience. The more it tries to hustle and bustle me into enjoying myself, the more does it put me on my most melancholy dignity, and set me reflecting funereally on the probable future of a race nursed on such amusements. To save myself from pessimism I have to remind myself that neither in America nor here is the taste for them a mature taste, and that the Americans in particular are so far from being its partisans that they rate English acting and English methods far higher than we do ourselves.

There is, however, a heavy account on the other side. The routine of melodrama and farcical comedy is not a fine art: it is an industry; and in it the industrial qualities of the Americans shine out. Their companies are smarter, better drilled, work harder and faster, waste less time, and know their business better than English companies. They do not select duffers when they can help it; and though the duffer may occasionally get engaged *faute de mieux* [French for "in the absence of better alternatives"], as a dog gets eaten during a siege, he does not find that there is a living for him in melodrama, and so gets driven into the fashionable drama of the day, in which he will easily obtain engagements if he convinces the manager that he is a desirable private acquaintance. A good deal of the technique acquired by American actors no doubt makes one almost long for the famous complacency of the British "walker-on"; but still it is at least an accomplishment which raises its possessor above the level of an unskilled laborer; and the value of a well-directed systematic cultivation of executive skill will be appreciated by anyone who compares the speech of Miss Maud Jeffries [1869–1946, American actress famous for her voice and physical grace] and the physical expertness of Miss Fay Davis [1873–1945, American actress known for her oratory] with those of English actresses of their own age and standing. Now in so far as Mr Frohman's Americanizations tend to smarten the organization of English stage business, and to demand from every actor at least some scrap of trained athleticism of speech and movement, they are welcome. So far, too, as the influence of a bright, brainy people, full of fun and curiosity, can wake our drama up from the half-asleep, half-drunk delirium of brainless sentimentality in which it is apt to wallow, it will be a good influence. But in so far as it means mechanical horseplay, prurient pleasantries, and deliberate nastinesses of the Katzenjammer order, it is our business to reform the Americans, not theirs to reform us. When it comes to the stupidities, follies, and grossnesses of the stage, we may safely be left to our native resources, which have never yet failed us in such matters.

The only notable addition to the Vaudeville company is Mr Allan Aynesworth [1864–1959], who keeps up the fun with an unsparing devotion to a bad play which must be extremely touching to the author. I do not believe he understands the plot, because no man can do what is impossible; but he quite persuades the audience that he does.

*One Summer's Day* at the Comedy Theatre is a play written by Mr [Henry V.] Esmond [1869–1922] to please himself. Some plays are written to please the author; some to please the actor-manager (these are the worst); some to please the public; and some—my own, for instance—to please nobody. Next to my plan, I prefer Mr Esmond's; but it undoubtedly leads to self-indulgence. When Mr Esmond, in the third act of a comedy, slaughters an innocent little boy to squeeze two pennorth [pennies worth] of sentiment out of his mangled body, humanity protests. If Mr Esmond were hard to move, one might excuse him for resorting to extreme measures. But he is, on the contrary, a highly susceptible man. He gets a perfect ocean of sentiment out of Dick and Dick's pipe. If you ask who Dick was, I reply that that is not the point. It is in the name Dick—in its tender familiarity, its unaffected good-nature, its modest sincerity, its combination of womanly affectionateness with manly strength, that the charm resides. If you say that the name Dick does not convey this to you, I can only say that it does to Mr Esmond when associated with a pipe; and that if your imagination is too sluggish or prosaic to see it, then that is your misfortune and not Mr Esmond's fault. He cherishes Dick more consistently than [satirist William Makepeace] Thackeray [1811–63] cherished Colonel Newcome [main character in Thackeray's 1855 novel *The Newcomes*]; for he tells you nothing unpleasant, and indeed nothing credible, about him; whereas Thackeray, being daimonic as well as sentimental, must paint his Colonel remorselessly as a fool, humbug, and swindler with one hand, whilst vainly claiming the world's affection for him with the other. Dick's drawbacks are not hinted at. Provided you take him on trust, and Maysie on trust, and indeed everybody else on trust, *One Summer's Day* is a quite touching play. Mr Hawtrey has finally to dissolve in tears, like the player in *Hamlet*; and he does it like a true comedian: that is, in earnest, and consequently almost distressingly. That is the penalty of comedianship: it involves humanity, which forbids its possessor to enjoy grief. Your true pathetic actor is a rare mixture of monstrous callousness and monstrous vanity. To him suffering means nothing but a bait to catch sympathy. He enjoys his malingering; and so does the audience. Mr Hawtrey does not enjoy it; and the result is an impression of genuine grief, which makes it seem quite brutal to stare at him. Fortunately, this is only for a moment, at the end of the play, just after Mr Esmond's massacre of the innocent. For the rest, he is as entertaining as ever, and happily much smoother, pleasanter, sunnier, and younger than Mr Esmond evidently intended Dick to be. I really could not have stood Dick if he had gone through with the Dobbin-Newcome formula, and robbed good-nature of grace and self-respect. The comic part of the play has a certain youthfully mischievous quality, which produces good entertainment with a lovesick schoolboy... [*Shaw briefly comments on several cast members*]. Miss Eva Moore's [1868–1955, wife of H.V. Esmond] Maysie secures the success of the piece, though the part is not difficult enough to tax her powers seriously.

The Drury Lane play proves Mr Arthur [Pelham] Collins [1864–1932] to be every whit as competent a manager of Harrisian drama as the illustrious founder of that form of art was himself. In fact, Mr Collins, as a younger man, with a smarter and more modern standard, does the thing rather better. Sir Augustus [Harris], lavish as to the trappings and suits of his fashionable scenes, was reckless as to the presentability of their wearers. Compare Mr Collins's cycling parade in Battersea Park, for instance, with Sir Augustus's church parade in Hyde Park! There is no reason to suppose that Battersea has cost a farthing more; yet it is ten times more plausible. It is not given to all "extra ladies" to look ladylike in proportion to the costliness of their attire: on the contrary, many of them have the gift of looking respectable in the uniform of a parlormaid, or even in a shawl, gown, apron, and ostrich-feathered hat, but outrageous and disreputable in a fashionable frock confected by an expensive *modiste*. Now whether Sir Augustus knew the difference, and cynically selected the disreputable people as likely to be more attractive to the sailorlike simplicity of the average playgoer, or whether he had a bad eye for such distinctions, just as some people have a bad ear for music, there can be no doubt that not even the Vicar of Wakefield [title character of Oliver Goldsmith's 1766 novel, known for his unsophisticated, trusting nature] could have been imposed on by his fashionable crowds. Mr Collins is much more successful in this respect. As I saw *The White Heather* from a rather remote corner of the stalls, distance may have lent my view some enchantment; but as far as I could see, Mr Collins does not, if he can help it, pay an extravagant sum for a dress, and then put it on the back of a young lady who obviously could not have become possessed of it by ladylike means. His casting of principal parts is also much better: he goes straight to the mark with Mrs John Wood [1831–1915, actress-manager born Matilda Charlotte Vining] where Sir Augustus would have missed it with

Miss Fanny Brough [1852–1914] (an habitually underparted tragi-comic actress); and he refines the whole play by putting Miss Kate Rorke [1866–1945] and Miss Beatrice Lamb [1866–?] into parts which would formerly have been given respectively to a purely melodramatic heroine and villainess. Indeed he has in one instance overshot the mark in improving the company; for though he has replaced the usual funny man with a much higher class of comedian in Mr [Herman] De Lange [1851–1929], the authors have abjectly failed to provide the actor with anything better than the poorest sort of clowning part; and as Mr De Lange is not a clown, he can only help the play, at a sacrifice of "comic relief," by virtually suppressing the buffoonery with which the authors wanted to spoil it. In short, everything is improved at Drury Lane except the drama, which, though very ingeniously adapted to its purpose, and not without flashes of wit (mostly at its own expense), remains as mechanical and as void of real dramatic illusion as the equally ingenious contrivances of the lock up the river, the descent of the divers and their combat under the sea, the Stock Exchange, and the reproduction of the costume ball at Devonshire House [the posh London residence of the Duke of Devonshire].

Naturally, though there is plenty of competent acting that amply fulfils the requirements of the occasion, the principals have nothing to do that can add to their established reputations. Mr Robert Loraine as Dick Beach was new to me; but he played so well that I concluded that it was I, and not Mr Loraine, who was the novice in the matter.

# 6. "Valedictory," 21 May 1898. [*Our Theatres in the Nineties*, vol. 3, pp. 384–86]

[*Between the gathering momentum of his playwriting career and his marriage to wealthy Irish heiress Charlotte Payne-Townshend,*

*Shaw no longer needed the income from his job as dramatic critic for* The Saturday Review. *Suffering from exhaustion and necrosis in his foot (which ultimately required surgery), he resigned his column and christened his successor, essayist and caricaturist Max Beerbohm (1872–1956) with the lasting epithet, "the incomparable Max."]*

As I lie here, helpless and disabled, or, at best, nailed by one foot on the floor like a doomed Strasburg goose, a sense of injury grows on me. For nearly four years—to be precise, since New Year 1895—I have been the slave of the theatre. It has tethered me to the mile radius of foul and sooty air which has its centre in the Strand, as a goat is tethered in the little circle of cropped and trampled grass that makes the meadow ashamed. Every week it clamors for its tale of written words; so that I am like a man fighting a windmill: I have hardly time to stagger to my feet from the knock-down blow of one sail, when the next strikes me down. Now I ask, is it reasonable to expect me to spend my life in this way? For just consider my position. Do I receive any spontaneous recognition for the prodigies of skill and industry I lavish on an unworthy institution and a stupid public? Not a bit of it; half my time is spent in telling people what a clever man I am. It is no use merely doing clever things in England. The English do not know what to think until they are coached, laboriously and insistently for years, in the proper and becoming opinion. For ten years past, with an unprecedented pertinacity and obstination, I have been dinning into the public head that I am an extraordinarily witty, brilliant, and clever man. That is now part of the public opinion of England; and no power in heaven or on earth will ever change it. I may dodder and dote; I may potboil and platitudinize; I may become the butt and chopping-block of all the bright, original spirits of the rising generation; but my reputation shall not suffer: it is built up fast and solid, like Shakespear's, on an impregnable basis of dogmatic reiteration.

Unfortunately, the building process has been a most painful one to me, because I am congenitally an extremely modest man. Shyness is the form my vanity and self-consciousness take by nature. It is humiliating, too, after making the most dazzling displays of professional ability, to have to tell people how capital it all is. Besides, they get so tired of it, that finally, without dreaming of disputing the alleged brilliancy, they begin to detest it. I sometimes get quite frantic letters from people who feel that they cannot stand me any longer.

Then there are the managers. Are *they* grateful? No: they are simply forbearing. Instead of looking up to me as their guide, philosopher, and friend, they regard me merely as the author of a series of weekly outrages on their profession and their privacy. Worse than the managers are the Shakespeareans. When I began to write, William was a divinity and a bore. Now he is a fellow-creature; and his plays have reached an unprecedented pitch of popularity. And yet his worshippers overwhelm my name with insult.

These circumstances will not bear thinking of. I have never had time to think of them before; but now I have nothing else to do. When a man of normal habits is ill, everyone hastens to assure him that he is going to recover. When a vegetarian is ill (which fortunately very seldom happens), everyone assures him that he is going to die, and that they told him so, and that it serves him right. They implore him to take at least a little gravy, so as to give himself a chance of lasting out the night. They tell him awful stories of cases just like his own which ended fatally after indescribable torments; and when he tremblingly inquires whether the victims were not hardened meat-eaters, they tell him he must not talk, as it is not good for him. Ten times a day I am compelled to reflect on my past life, and on the limited prospect of three weeks or so of

lingering moribundity which is held up to me as my probable future, with the intensity of a drowning man. And I can
never justify to myself the spending of four years on dramatic
criticism. I have sworn an oath to endure no more of it. Never
again will I cross the threshold of a theatre. The subject is exhausted; and so am I.

Still, the gaiety of nations must not be eclipsed. The long
string of beautiful ladies who are at present in the square
without, awaiting, under the supervision of two gallant po-
licemen, their turn at my bedside, must be reassured when
they protest, as they will, that the light of their life will go
out if my dramatic articles cease. To each of them I will present the flower left by her predecessor, and assure her that
there are as good fish in the sea as ever came out of it. The
younger generation is knocking at the door; and as I open it
there steps spritely in the incomparable Max.

For the rest, let Max speak for himself. I am off duty for
ever, and am going to sleep.

# 7. The Author's Apology, 1906, 1931. [*Our Theatres in the Nineties*, vol. 1, pp. v–viii]

*[Less than a decade after Shaw signed off forever as* The Saturday
Review's *dramatic critic, American critic James Huneker
(1857–1921) convinced him to write a preface for a selection of Shaw's
theatre criticism that he edited. This "Apology" and its Postscript
show Shaw reflecting with a great deal of self-awareness about not
just his critical principles but his clear reformist agenda.]*

In justice to many well-known public persons who are handled rather recklessly in the following pages, I beg my readers
not to mistake my journalistic utterances for final estimates
of their worth and achievements as dramatic artists and authors. It is not so much that the utterances are unjust; for I
have never claimed for myself the divine attribute of justice.

But as some of them are hardly even reasonably fair I must honestly warn the reader that what he is about to study is not a series of judgments aiming at impartiality, but a siege laid to the theatre of the XIXth Century by an author who had to cut his own way into it at the point of the pen, and throw some of its defenders into the moat.

Pray do not conclude from this that the things hereinafter written were not true, or not the deepest and best things I knew how to say. Only, they must be construed in the light of the fact that all through I was accusing my opponents of failure because they were not doing what I wanted, whereas they were often succeeding very brilliantly in doing what they themselves wanted. I postulated as desirable a certain kind of play in which I was destined ten years later to make my mark (as I very well foreknew in the depth of my own unconsciousness); and I brought everybody: authors, actors, managers and all, to the one test: were they coming my way or staying in the old grooves?

Sometimes I made allowances for the difference in aim, especially in the case of personal friends. But as a rule I set up my own standard of what the drama should be and how it should be presented; and I used all my art to make every deviation in aiming at this standard, every recalcitrance in approaching it, every refusal to accept it seem ridiculous and old-fashioned. In this, however, I only did what all critics do who are worth their salt. The critics who attacked Ibsen and defended Shakespear whilst I was defending Ibsen and attacking Shakespear; or who were acclaiming the reign of Irving at the Lyceum Theatre as the Antonine age of the Shakespearean drama whilst I was battering at it in open preparation for its subsequent downfall, were no more impartial than I. And when my own turn came to be criticized, I also was attacked because I produced what I wanted to produce and not what some of my critics wanted me to produce.

Dismissing, then, the figment of impartiality as attainable only through an indifference which would have prevented me from writing about the theatre at all, or even visiting it, what merit have these essays to justify their republication? Well, they contain something like a body of doctrine, because when I criticized I really did know definitely what I wanted. Very few journalistic critics do. When they attack a new man as Ibsen was attacked, they are for the most part only resisting a change which upsets their habits, the proof being that when they get the sort of play they blame the innovator for not producing, they turn up their noses at it, yawn over it, even recommend the unfortunate author to learn from the new-comer how to open his eyes and use his brains. Weariness of the theatre is the prevailing note of London criticism. Only the ablest critics believe that the theatre is really important: in my time none of them would claim for it, as I claimed for it, that it is as important as the Church was in the Middle Ages and much more important than the Church was in London in the years under review. A theatre to me is a place "where two or three are gathered together." The apostolic succession from Eschylus [525–456 BCE, ancient Greek dramatist] to myself is as serious and as continuously inspired as that younger institution, the apostolic succession of the Christian Church.

Unfortunately this Christian Church, founded gaily with a pun, has been so largely corrupted by rank Satanism that it has become the Church where you must not laugh; and so it is giving way to that older and greater Church to which I belong: the Church where the oftener you laugh the better, because by laughter only can you destroy evil without malice, and affirm good fellowship without mawkishness. When I wrote, I was well aware of what an unofficial census of Sunday worshippers presently proved: that churchgoing in London has been largely replaced by playgoing. This would be a very good thing if the theatre took itself seriously as a factory of thought, a prompter of conscience, an elucidator of social conduct, an armory against despair and dullness, and a temple of the Ascent of Man. I took it seriously in that way, and preached about it instead of merely chronicling its news and alternately petting and snubbing it as a licentious but privileged form of public entertainment. This, I believe, is why my sermons gave so little offence, and created so much interest. The artists of the theatre, led by Sir Henry Irving, were winning their struggle to be considered ladies and gentlemen, qualified for official honors. Now for their gentility and knighthoods I cared very little: what lay at the root of my criticism was their deeper claim to be considered, not merely actors and actresses, but men and women, not hired buffoons and posturers, however indulged, but hierophants of a cult as eternal and sacred as any professed religion in the world. And so, consciously or unconsciously, I was forgiven when many of my colleagues, less severe because less in earnest on the subject, gave deadly offence.

POSTSCRIPT, 1931. The foregoing was prefaced to a reprint of a selection from my criticisms entitled *Dramatic Opinions and Essays*, edited in America by the late James Huneker. Let me add now what I should have added then: that a certain correction should be made, especially in reading my onslaught on Shakespear, but also in valuing my vigorous slating of my contemporaries, for the devastating effect produced in the nineties by the impact of Ibsen on the European theatre. Until then Shakespear had been conventionally ranked as a giant among psychologists and philosophers. Ibsen dwarfed him so absurdly in those aspects that it became impossible for the moment to take him seriously as an intellectual force. And if this was Shakespear's fate what could the others expect? The appearanTce of a genius of the first order is always hard on his competitors. Salieri said of Mozart "If this young man goes on what is to become of us?" and was actually accused of poisoning him. And certainly no one has since been just to Salieri. If my head had not been full of Ibsen and Wagner in the nineties I should have been kinder and more reasonable in my demands. Also, perhaps, less amusing. So forgive; but make the necessary allowances.

G. B. S.

# Part II: Advice on Seeing and Producing Shaw's Plays

*As a dramatic critic, Shaw's job was to expertly advise audiences about the merits of the plays he saw, a job that he argued benefitted greatly from his own experience as a playwright (see page 39). When it came to the critical reception of his own plays, however, Shaw rarely trusted to the expertise of his fellow critics to understand them properly. To a certain extent this was justified, as critics trained to appreciate the conventions of nineteenth century melodrama were not necessarily well-equipped to judge Shaw's pioneering efforts in the modern, realist problem play. Shaw could hardly write his own actual reviews (although he frequently did write his own interviews and publicity), but he could take advantage of his access to a variety of publication platforms to correct critical misconceptions about his plays. While he no doubt hoped it would help win audiences for his own plays, Shaw was also motivated by a desire to educate audiences, critics, actors and directors in the value of theatre as serious art, rather than just a casual leisure activity.*

# 1. "There is no way of becoming a dramatic critic," a letter to Reginald Golding Bright, 30 April 1894. [*Bernard Shaw: Collected Letters 1874–1897*, pp. 423–4]

*[Reginald Golding Bright (1875–1941) was an office clerk and aspiring journalist when he made Shaw's acquaintance after the opening of Shaw's play* Arms and the Man. *Golding Bright disrupted the audience's enthusiastic applause with loud booing, famously leading Shaw to address the heckler with "My dear fellow, I quite agree with you, but what are we two against so many?" Golding Bright would eventually become a successful theatrical agent, who counted Shaw among his impressive clientele. This early letter shows Shaw both encouraging Golding Bright's ambition and defending his own position.]*

Dear Sir,

Your letter has only just reached me. They did not forward it from the theatre, expecting a visit from me every day. There is no way of becoming a dramatic critic. It happens by accident. For instance, I have never been offered a post of the kind, though I should have been quite willing to take it any time these last 18 years. But when the accident happens, it happens to a journalist. It is to men who are already in the profession, and known as men who can write and who know the ways of papers, that editors turn when a vacancy occurs. If you work for a paper as a reporter or paragraphist, and are keen on theatres, you can generally do a stray notice on an emergency which makes you known to the editor as having a turn that way. Then, if the dramatic critic dies, or goes on another paper, or drops journalism, you have your chance of succeeding him, if you have shown the requisite capacity. That is the regular way. But you may induce some friend who starts a paper, or becomes the editor of one, to give you a trial straight off; but that is a matter of pure luck, with, of course, the skill to take the luck when it comes. Remember, to be a critic, you must be not only a bit of an expert in your subject, but you must also have literary skill, and trained critical skill too—the power of analysis, comparison &c. I have had to go through years of work as a reviewer of books, a critic of pictures, a writer on political & social questions, and a musical critic, in order to qualify myself for the post I now hold on the staff of *The World*. You must not think that because you only heard of me for the first time the other day or thereabouts that I got such reputation as I have cheaply. I came to London in 1876, and have been fighting for existence ever since. Even my little platform performance at the Playgoers' Club [founded in 1884 for critical discussion and debate about drama; Shaw lectured on "Criticism, Corruption, and its Cure" at the April 1894 meeting] was the result of about fifteen years practice of public speaking, mostly under the humblest of circumstances. I tell you this lest you should be discouraged and embittered by thinking that you are meeting with exceptional and unfair difficulties. In London all beginners are forty, with twenty years of obscure hard work behind them; and, believe me, those obscure twenty years are not the worst part of one's life nor need you nor anyone be afraid to face them.

I still hold to it that a man who thinks a dramatic performance worth waiting at the pit door all day for is a lunatic [reference to a statement from his Playgoers' Club speech]. The front row of the pit is worth something; but it is not worth that. However, I only give you my own valuation. If your enthusiasm makes it worth the trouble to you, I have no right to object.

All the views which you attribute to me concerning Mr. [Henry] Irving and Mr. [Herbert Beerbohm] Tree [1852–1917] and the "new school" have, if you will excuse me saying so, been put into your mind by newspaper paragraphs written by people who have not the slightest knowledge of me or my views. There is nothing that annoys me more than all this nonsense about new schools & the new drama & the rest of it. I suffer from it considerably, as it leads people to construe purely dramatic passages in my plays as interpolations of what are supposed to be my political views. But even if the play did contain any such interpolation, I should not admit your right to make a disturbance on the head of it. If the Fabians in the gallery were enjoying my play, as I am glad to say that the gallery still does now that there are no longer any Fabians in it, why did you carry your disapproval of a purely imaginary allusion to the Royal Family to the point of making them lose patience with you? Have they ever disturbed you in the enjoyment of the patriotic and loyal sentiments with which popular melodramas are freely spiced? We have been present, I have no doubt, at first nights of plays containing a good deal that is exceedingly repugnant to my political & moral opinions. I don't think you have ever found me interrupting an actor or annoying my neighbours on that account. I simply do not go to the sort of plays I dislike.

In conclusion, let me assure you that I did my best to put before you a true picture of what a brave soldier who knows his business really is. I heartily wish you could bring me an audience of veterans—of men who know what it is to ride a bolting horse in a charge, or to trust to the commissariat for food during a battle, or to be under fire for two or three days: they would not have taken my chocolate &c &c for silly jokes, as I feel a good many of the audience did.

## 2. From "A Dramatic Realist to His Critics," *The New Review* XI, July 1894. [*The Bodley Head Bernard Shaw: Collected Plays with their Prefaces,* vol. 1, pp. 485–511]

[*Shaw published this response to objections from theatre critics that he portrayed soldiers disrespectfully and unrealistically in* Arms and the Man, *a play set in the aftermath of the 1885 Serbo-Bulgarian War. In the opening scene of that play, a retreating Swiss mercenary confesses he always carries chocolate instead of ammunition, and is on the verge of crying from exhaustion, while the Bulgarian forces are shown to be naïve and inept about military strategy.*]

I think very few people know how troublesome dramatic critics are. It is not that they are morally worse than other people; but they know nothing. Or, rather, it is a good deal worse than that: they know everything wrong. Put a thing on the stage for them as it is in real life, and instead of receiving it with the blank wonder of plain ignorance, they reject it with scorn as an imposture, on the ground that the real thing is known to the whole world to be quite different. Offer them Mr Crummles's real pump and tubs [refers to a discussion about real items as theatre props from Dickens's *Nicholas Nickleby*], and they will denounce both as spurious on the ground that the tubs have no handles, and the pump no bung-hole.

I am, among other things, a dramatist; but I am not an original one, and so have to take all my dramatic material either from real life at first hand, or from authentic documents. The more usual course is to take it out of other dramas, in which case, on tracing it back from one drama to another, you finally come to its origin in the inventive imagination of some original dramatist. Now a fact as invented by a dramatist differs widely from the fact of the same name as it exists or occurs objectively in real life. Not only stage pumps and tubs, but (much more) stage morality and stage human nature differ from the realities of these things. Consequently to a man who derives all his knowledge of life from witnessing plays, nothing appears more unreal than objective life. A dramatic critic is generally such a man; and the more exactly I reproduce objective life for him on the stage, the more certain he is to call my play an extravaganza.

It may be asked here whether it is possible for one who every day contemplates the real world for fourteen of his waking hours, and the stage for only two, to know more of the stage world than the real world. As well might it be argued that a farmer's wife, churning for only two hours a week, and contemplating nature almost constantly, must know more about geology, forestry, and botany than about butter. A man knows what he works at, not what he idly stares at. A dramatic critic works at the stage, writes about the stage, thinks about the stage, and understands nothing of the real life he idly stares at until he has translated it into stage terms. For the rest, seeing men daily building houses, driving engines, marching to the band, making political speeches, and what not, he is stimulated by these spectacles to imagine what it is to be a builder, an engine-driver, a soldier, or a statesman. Of course, he imagines a stage builder, engine-driver, soldier, and so on, not a real one. Simple as this is, few dramatic critics are intelligent enough to discover it for themselves. No class is more idiotically confident of the reality of its own unreal knowledge than the literary class in general and dramatic critics in particular.

We have, then, two sorts of life to deal with: one subjective or stagey, the other objective or real. What are the comparative advantages of the two for the purposes of the dramatist? Stage life is artificially simple and well understood by the masses; but it is very stale; its feeling is conventional; it is totally unsuggestive of thought because all its conclusions are foregone; and it is constantly in conflict with the real knowledge which the separate members of the audience derive from their own daily occupations. For instance, a naval or military melodrama only goes down with civilians. Real life, on the other hand, is so ill understood, even by its clearest observers, that no sort of consistency is discoverable in it; there is no "natural justice" corresponding to that simple and pleasant concept, "poetic justice"; and, as a whole, it is unthinkable. But, on the other hand, it is credible, stimulating, suggestive, various, free from creeds and systems—in short, it is real.

This rough contrast will suffice to show that the two sorts of life, each presenting dramatic potentialities to the author, will, when reproduced on the stage, affect different men differently. The stage world is for the people who cannot bear to look facts in the face, because they dare not be pessimists, and yet cannot see real life otherwise than as the pessimist sees it. It might be supposed that those who conceive all the operations of our bodies as repulsive, and of our minds as sinful, would take refuge in the sects which abstain from playgoing on principle. But this is by no means what happens. If such a man has an artistic or romantic turn, he takes refuge, not in the conventicle, but in the theatre, where, in the contemplation of the idealized, or stage life, he finds some relief from his haunting conviction of omnipresent foulness and baseness. Confront him with anything like reality, and his chronic pain is aggravated instead of relieved; he raises a terrible outcry against the spectacle of cowardice, selfishness, faithlessness, sensuality—in short, everything that he went to the theatre to escape from. This is not the effect on those pessimists who dare face facts and profess their own faith. They are great admirers of the realist playwright, whom they embarrass greatly by their applause. Their cry is "Quite right: strip off the whitewash from the sepulchre; expose human nature in all its tragi-comic baseness; tear the mask of respectability from the smug bourgeois, and show the liar, the thief, the coward, the libertine beneath."

Now to me, as a realist playwright, the applause of the conscious, hardy pessimist is more exasperating than the abuse of the unconscious, fearful one. I am not a pessimist at all. It does not concern me that, according to certain ethical systems, all human beings fall into classes labelled liar, coward, thief, and so on. I am myself, according to these systems, a liar, a coward, a thief, and a sensualist; and it is my deliberate, cheerful, and entirely self-respecting intention to continue to the end of my life deceiving people, avoiding danger, making my bargains with publishers and managers on principles of supply and demand instead of abstract justice, and indulging all my appetites, whenever circumstances commend such actions to my judgment. If any creed or system deduces from this that I am a rascal incapable on occasion of telling the truth, facing a risk, foregoing a commercial advantage, or resisting an intemperate impulse of any sort, then so much the worse for the creed or system, since I have done all these things, and will probably do them again. The saying "All have sinned," is, in the sense in which it was written, certainly true of all the people I have ever known. But the sinfulness of my friends is not unmixed with saintliness: some of their actions are sinful, others saintly. And here, again, if the ethical system to which the classifications of saint and sinner belong, involves the conclusion that a line of cleavage drawn between my friends' sinful actions and their saintly ones will coincide exactly with one drawn between their mistakes and their successes (I include the highest and widest sense of the two terms), then so much the worse for the system; for the facts contradict it. Persons obsessed by systems may retort; "No; so much the worse for your friends"—implying that I must move in a circle of rare blackguards; but I am quite prepared not only to publish a list of friends of mine whose names would put such a retort to open shame, but to take any human being, alive or dead, of whose actions a genuinely miscellaneous unselected dozen can be brought to light, to show that none of the ethical systems habitually applied by dramatic critics (not to mention other people) can verify their inferences. As a realist dramatist, therefore, it is my business to get outside these systems. For instance, in the play of mine which is most in evidence in London just now, the heroine [Raina in *Arms and the Man*] has been classified by critics as a minx, a liar, and a *poseuse*. I have nothing to do with that: the only moral question for me is, does she do good or harm? If you admit that she does good, that she generously saves a man's life and wisely extricates herself from a false position with another man, then you may classify her as you please—brave, generous, and affectionate; or artful, dangerous, faithless—it is all one to me: you can no more prejudice me for or against her by such artificial categorizing than you could have made [French playwright and actor Jean-Baptiste Poquelin] Molière [1622–1673] dislike Monsieur Jourdain [main character in Molière's *Le Bourgeois Gentilhomme*] by a lecture on the vanity and pretentiousness of that amiable "bourgeois gentilhomme." The fact is, though I am willing and anxious to see the human race improved, if possible, still I find that, with reasonably sound specimens, the more intimately I know people the better I like them; and when a man concludes from this that I am a cynic, and that he, who prefers stage monsters—walking catalogues of the systematized virtues—to his own species, is a person of wholesome philanthropic tastes, why, how can I feel towards him except as an Englishwoman feels towards the Arab who, faithful to *his* system, denounces her indecency in appearing in public with her mouth uncovered?

The production of *Arms and the Man* at the Avenue Theatre, about nine weeks ago, brought the misunderstanding between my real world and the stage world of the critics to a climax, because the misunderstanding was itself, in a sense, the subject of the play. I need not describe the action of the piece in any detail: suffice it to say that the scene is laid in Bulgaria in 1885-6, at a moment when the need for repelling the onslaught of the Servians made the Bulgarians for six months a nation of heroes. But as they had only just been redeemed from centuries of miserable bondage to the Turks, and were, therefore, but beginning to work out their own redemption from barbarism—or, if you prefer it, beginning to contract the disease of civilization—they were very ignorant heroes, with boundless courage and patriotic enthusiasm, but with so little military skill that they had to place themselves under the command of Russian officers. And their attempts at Western civilization were much the same as their attempts at war—instructive, romantic, ignorant. They were a nation of plucky beginners in every department. Into their country comes, in the play, a professional officer from the high democratic civilization of Switzerland—a man completely acquainted by long, practical experience with the realities of war. The comedy arises, of course, from the collision of the knowledge of the Swiss with the illusions of the Bulgarians. In this dramatic scheme Bulgaria may be taken as symbolic of the stalls on the first night of a play. The Bulgarians are dramatic critics; the Swiss is the realist playwright invading their realm; and the comedy is the comedy of the collision of the realities represented by the realist playwright with the preconceptions of stageland. ...

The extent to which the method brought me into conflict with the martial imaginings of the critics is hardly to be conveyed by language. The notion that there could be any limit to a soldier's courage, or any preference on his part for life and a whole skin over a glorious death in the service of his country, was inexpressibly revolting to them. Their view was simple, manly, and straightforward, like most impracticable views. A man is either a coward or he is not. If a brave man, then he is afraid of nothing. If a coward, then he is no true

soldier; and to represent him as such is to libel a noble profession.

The tone of men who know what they are talking about
is remarkably different. ... [*Shaw quotes at length from several
articles about warfare written by experienced military officers that
describe conditions very similar to the ones in his play.*]

In *Arms and the Man*, this very simple and intelligible picture is dramatized by the contrast between the experienced
Swiss officer, with a high record for distinguished services,
and the Bulgarian hero who wins the battle by an insanely
courageous charge for which the Swiss thinks he ought to be
court-martialled. Result: the dramatic critics pronounce the
Swiss "a poltroon." ...

[*Shaw compares the romanticized, heroic accounts of the Battle of
Balaclava (1854) in Tennyson's "The Charge of the Light Brigade"
to reports of the actual orders given to "Keep back" and other actions taken to avoid unnecessary risk.*]

The stage hero finds in death the supreme consolation of being able to get up and go home when the curtain falls; but
the real soldier, even when he leads Balaclava charges under conditions of appalling and prolonged danger, does not
commit suicide for nothing. The fact is, Captain Bluntschli's
description of the cavalry charge is taken almost verbatim
from an account given privately to a friend of mine by an officer who served in the Franco-Prussian war [1870–71]. I am well
aware that if I choose to be guided by men grossly ignorant of
dramatic criticism, whose sole qualification is that they have
seen cavalry charges on stricken fields, I must take the consequences. Happily, as between myself and the public, the consequences have not been unpleasant; and I recommend the
experiment to my fellow dramatists with every confidence.

But great as has been the offence taken at my treating a soldier as a man with no stomach for unnecessary danger, I have

given still greater by treating him as a man with a stomach for necessary food. Nature provides the defenders of our country with regular and efficient appetites. The taxpayer provides, at considerable cost to himself, rations for the soldier which are insufficient in time of peace and necessarily irregular in time of war. The result is that our young, growing soldiers sometimes go for months without once experiencing the sensation of having had enough to eat. ...In the field the matter is more serious. It is a mistake to suppose that in a battle the waiters come round regularly with soup, fish, an entrée, a snack of game, a cut from the joint, ice pudding, coffee and cigarettes, with drinks at discretion. When battles last for several days, as modern battles often do, the service of food and ammunition may get disorganized or cut off at any point; and the soldier may suffer exceedingly from hunger in consequence. To guard against this the veteran would add a picnic hamper to his equipment if it were portable enough and he could afford it, or if Fortnum and Mason [store known for its gourmet food hampers] would open a shop on the field. As it is, he falls back on the cheapest, most portable, and most easily purchased sort of stomach-stayer, which, as every cyclist knows, is chocolate. This chocolate, which so shocks Raïna in the play—for she, poor innocent, classes it as "sweets"—and which seems to so many of my critics to be the climax of my audacious extravagances, is a commonplace of modern warfare. I know of a man who lived on it for two days in the Shipka Pass [site of several major battles during the Russo-Turkish War (1877–78)].

By the way, I have been laughed at in this connection for making my officer carry an empty pistol, preferring chocolate to cartridges. But I might have gone further and represented him as going without any pistol at all. Lord [Garnet Joseph] Wolseley [1833–1913; Commander-in-Chief of the Forces 1895–1900] mentions two officers who seldom carried any weapons. One of them had to defend himself by shying

stones when the Russians broke into his battery at Se-
bastopol. The other was [Sir John William] Gordon
[1805?–70].

The report that my military realism is a huge joke has once
or twice led audiences at the Avenue Theatre to laugh at certain grim touches which form no part of the comedy of dis-
illusionment elsewhere so constant between the young lady
and the Swiss. Readers of General [Baron de] Marbot's
[1782–1854] *Memoirs* will remember his description of how,
at the battle of Wagram, the standing corn was set on fire
by the shells and many of the wounded were roasted alive.
"This often happens," says Marbot, coolly, "in battles fought
in summer." The Servo-Bulgarian war was fought in winter;
but Marbot will be readily recognized as the source of the
incident of Bluntschli's friend Stolz, who is shot in the hip
in a wood-yard and burnt in the conflagration of the timber
caused by the Servian shells. ...

I might considerably multiply my citations of documents;
but the above will, I hope, suffice to show that what struck
my critics as topsy-turvy extravaganza, having no more relation to real soldiering than Mr Gilbert's [H.M.S.] *Pinafore* has
to real sailoring, is the plainest matter-of-fact. There is no
burlesque: I have stuck to the routine of war, as described
by real warriors, and avoided such farcical incidents as Sir
William Gordon defending his battery by throwing stones, or
General [Horace] Porter's [1837–1921] story of the two generals
who, though brave and capable men, always got sick under
fire, to their own great mortification. I claim that the dramatic effect produced by the shock which these realities give
to the notions of romantic young ladies and fierce civilians
is not burlesque, but legitimate comedy, none the less pun-
gent because, on the first night at least, the romantic young
lady was on the stage and the fierce civilians in the stalls. And
since my authorities, who record many acts almost too brave
to make pleasant reading, are beyond suspicion of that cyn-

ical disbelief in courage which has been freely attributed to me, I would ask whether it is not plain that the difference between my authenticated conception of real warfare and the stage conception lies in the fact that in real warfare there is real personal danger, the sense of which is constantly present to the mind of the soldier, whereas in stage warfare there is nothing but glory? Hence Captain Bluntschli, who thinks of a battlefield as a very busy and very dangerous place, is incredible to the critic who thinks of it only as a theatre in which to enjoy the luxurious excitements of patriotism, victory, and bloodshed without risk or retribution. ...

I have been much lectured for my vulgarity in introducing certain references to soap and water in Bulgaria: I did so as the shortest and most effective way of bringing home to the audience the stage of civilization in which the Bulgarians were in 1885, when, having clean air and clean clothes, which made them much cleaner than any frequency of ablution can make us in the dirty air of London, they were adopting the washing habits of big western cities as pure ceremonies of culture and civilization, and not on hygienic grounds. I had not the slightest intention of suggesting that my Bulgarian major, who submits to a good wash for the sake of his social position, or his father, who never had a bath in his life, are uncleanly people, though a cockney, who by simple exposure to the atmosphere becomes more unpresentable in three hours than a Balkan mountaineer in three years, may feel bound to pretend to be shocked at them, and to shrink with disgust from even a single omission of the daily bath which, as he knows very well, the majority of English, Irish, and Scotch people do not take, and which the majority of the inhabitants of the world do not even tell lies about. Major Petkoff is quite right in his intuitive perception that soap, instead of being the radical remedy for dirt, is really one of its worst consequences. And his remark that the cultus of soap comes from the English because their climate makes them

exceptionally dirty, is one of the most grimly and literally accurate passages in the play, as we who dwell in smoky towns
know to our cost. However, I am sorry that my piece of realism should have been construed as an insult to the Bulgarian
nation; and perhaps I should have hesitated to introduce it
had I known that a passionate belief in the scrupulous clean-
liness of the inhabitants of the Balkan peninsula is a vital part
of Liberal views on foreign policy [see page 143]. But what is
done is done. ...

I am afraid most of my critics will receive the above explanations with an indulgent sense of personal ingratitude on
my part. The burden of their mostly very kind notices has
been that I am a monstrously clever fellow, who has snatched
a brilliant success by amusingly whimsical perversions of
patent facts and piquantly cynical ridicule of human nature.
I hardly have the heart to turn upon such friendly help with
a cold-blooded confession that all my audacious originalities
are simple liftings from stores of evidence which is ready to
everybody's hand. Even that triumph of eccentric invention
which nightly brings down the house, Captain Bluntschli's
proposal for the hand of Raïna, is a paraphrase of an actual
proposal made by an Austrian hotel proprietor for the hand
of a member of my own family. To that gentleman, and to him
alone, is due the merit of the irresistible joke of the four thousand tablecloths and the seventy equipages of which twenty-
four will hold twelve inside. I have plundered him as I have
plundered Lord Wolseley and General Porter and everyone
else who had anything that was good to steal. I created nothing; I invented nothing; I imagined nothing; I perverted nothing; I simply discovered drama in real life.

I now plead strongly for a theatre to supply the want of
this sort of drama. I declare that I am tired to utter disgust
of imaginary life, imaginary law, imaginary ethics, science,
peace, war, love, virtue, villainy, and imaginary everything
else, both on the stage and off it. I demand respect, interest,

affection for human nature as it is and life as we must still live it even when we have bettered it and ourselves to the utmost. If the critics really believe all their futile sermonizing about "poor humanity" and the "seamy side of life" and meanness, cowardice, selfishness, and all the other names they give to qualities which are as much and as obviously a necessary part of themselves as their arms and legs, why do they not shoot themselves like men instead of coming whimpering to the dramatist to pretend that they are something else? I, being a man like to themselves, know what they are perfectly well; and as I do not find that I dislike them for what they persist in calling their vanity, and sensuality, and mendacity, and dishonesty, and hypocrisy, and venality, and so forth; as furthermore, they would not interest me in the least if they were otherwise, I shall continue to put them on the stage as they are to the best of my ability, in the hope that some day it may strike them that if they were to try a little self-respect, and stop calling themselves offensive names, they would discover that the affection of their friends, wives, and sweethearts for them is not a reasoned tribute to their virtues, but a human impulse towards their very selves. When Raïna says in the play, "Now that you have found me out, I suppose you despise me," she discovers that that result does not quite follow in the least, Captain Bluntschli not being quite critic enough to feel bound to repudiate the woman who has saved his life as "a false and lying minx," because, at twenty-three, she has some generous illusions which lead her into a good deal of pretty nonsense.

I demand, moreover, that when I deal with facts into which the critic has never inquired, and of which he has had no personal experience, he shall not make his vain imaginations the criterion of my accuracy. I really cannot undertake, every time I write a play, to follow it up by a textbook on mortgages, or soldiering, or whatever else it may be about, for the instruction of gentlemen who will neither accept the result of my study of the subject (lest it should destroy their cherished ideals), nor undertake any study on their own account. When I have written a play the whole novelty of which lies in the fact that it is void of malice to my fellow creatures, and laboriously exact as to all essential facts, I object to be complimented on my "brilliancy" as a fabricator of cynical extravaganzas. Nor do I consider it decent for critics to call their own ignorance "the British public," as they almost invariably do....

### 3. From the Preface to *Major Barbara*, 1906. [*The Bodley Head Bernard Shaw: Collected Plays with their Prefaces*, vol. 3, pp. 15–63]

[*Major Barbara dramatizes the debate between Barbara Undershaft, an enthusiastic major in the Salvation Army, and her father Andrew Undershaft, a wealthy arms dealer, over whose religious principles offer the better opportunity for salvation. Shaw greatly admired the Salvation Army's exuberance and its work among London's poorest neighborhoods, but most professional critics accused him of mocking the Salvation Army in his play because Barbara and her fiancé ultimately recognize that the munitions works do more widespread good than the Salvation Army. Shaw responded to this fundamental misreading with an essay on his dramatic and economic philosophy, which he added as a preface when he published the play.*]

### First Aid to Critics

Before dealing with the deeper aspects of *Major Barbara*, let me, for the credit of English literature, make a protest against an unpatriotic habit into which many of my critics have fallen. Whenever my view strikes them as being at all outside the range of, say, an ordinary suburban churchwarden, they conclude that I am echoing [German philosopher Arthur] Schopenhauer [1788–1860], [German philosopher Friedrich] Nietzsche [1844–1900], Ibsen, [Swedish playwright

Johan August] Strindberg [1849–1912], [Russian novelist Leo] Tolstoy [1828–1910], or some other heresiarch in northern or eastern Europe.

I confess there is something flattering in this simple faith in my accomplishment as a linguist and my erudition as a philosopher. But I cannot tolerate the assumption that life and literature is so poor in these islands that we must go abroad for all dramatic material that is not common and all ideas that are not superficial. I therefore venture to put my critics in possession of certain facts concerning my contact with modern ideas.

About half a century ago, an Irish novelist, Charles Lever [1806–72], wrote a story entitled *A Day's Ride: A Life's Romance*. It was published by Charles Dickens [1812–70] in *Household Words*, and proved so strange to the public taste that Dickens pressed Lever to make short work of it. I read scraps of this novel when I was a child; and it made an enduring impression on me. The hero was a very romantic hero, trying to live bravely, chivalrously, and powerfully by dint of mere romance-fed imagination, without courage, without means, without knowledge, without skill, without anything real except his bodily appetites. Even in my childhood I found in this poor devil's unsuccessful encounters with the facts of life, a poignant quality that romantic fiction lacked. The book, in spite of its first failure, is not dead: I saw its title the other day in the catalogue of Tauchnitz [German publisher of inexpensive paperback reprints].

Now why is it that when I also deal in the tragi-comic irony of the conflict between real life and the romantic imagination, no critic ever affiliates me to my countryman and immediate forerunner, Charles Lever, whilst they confidently derive me from a Norwegian author of whose language I do not know three words, and of whom I knew nothing until years after the Shavian *Anschauung* [German for "outlook"] was already unequivocally declared in books full of what came, ten years later, to be perfunctorily labelled Ibsenism. I was not Ibsenist even at second hand; for Lever, though he may have read Henri Beyle, alias Stendhal [1783–1842], certainly never read Ibsen. Of the books that made Lever popular, such as *Charles O'Malley* and *Harry Lorrequer*, I know nothing but the names and some of the illustrations. But the story of the day's ride and life's romance of Potts (claiming alliance with [Corsican diplomat Charles-André, Comte] Pozzo di Borgo [1768–1842]) caught me and fascinated me as something strange and significant, though I already knew all about Alnaschar [over-imaginative, failed hero of fable] and Don Quixote [heroically delusional title character of Cervantes's *Don Quixote*] and Simon Tappertit [boastful character from Dickens's *Barnaby Rudge*] and many another romantic hero mocked by reality. From the plays of Aristophanes [ancient Greek playwright] to the tales of Stevenson that mockery has been made familiar to all who are properly saturated with letters. ...

*[Shaw argues that Lever, like Shakespeare with* Hamlet, *suggested that "lunacy may be inspiration in disguise," and forced audiences to recognize something of themselves in the character depicted as mad.]*

Another mistake as to my literary ancestry is made whenever I violate the romantic convention that all women are angels when they are not devils; that they are better looking than men; that their part in courtship is entirely passive; and that the human female form is the most beautiful object in nature. Schopenhauer wrote a splenetic essay ["On Woman," 1851] which, as it is neither polite nor profound, was probably intended to knock this nonsense violently on the head. A sentence denouncing the idolized form as ugly has been largely quoted. The English critics have read that sentence; and I must here affirm, with as much gentleness as the implication will bear, that it has yet to be proved that they have dipped any deeper. At all events, whenever an English playwright represents a young and marriageable woman as being anything but a romantic heroine, he is disposed of without further thought as an echo of Schopenhauer. My own case is a specially hard one, because, when I implore the critics who are obsessed with the Schopenhaurian formula to remember that playwrights, like sculptors, study their figures from life, and not from philosophic essays, they reply passionately that I am not a playwright and that my stage figures do not live. But even so, I may and do ask them why, if they must give the credit of my plays to a philosopher, they do not give it to an English philosopher? Long before I ever read a word by Schopenhauer, or even knew whether he was a philosopher or a chemist, the Socialist revival of the eighteen-eighties brought me into contact, both literary and personal, with Mr Ernest Belfort Bax [1854–1926], an English Socialist and philosophic essayist, whose handling of modern feminism would provoke romantic protests from Schopenhauer himself, or even Strindberg. As a matter of fact I hardly noticed Schopenhauer's disparagements of women when they came under my notice later on, so thoroughly had Mr Bax familiarized me with the homoist attitude, and forced me to recognize the extent to which public opinion, and consequently legislation and jurisprudence, is corrupted by feminist sentiment.

But Mr Bax's essays were not confined to the Feminist question. He was a ruthless critic of current morality. Other writers have gained sympathy for dramatic criminals by eliciting the alleged "soul of goodness in things evil"; but Mr Bax would propound some quite undramatic and apparently shabby violation of our commercial law and morality, and not merely defend it with the most disconcerting ingenuity, but actually prove it to be a positive duty that nothing but the certainty of police persecution should prevent every right-minded man from at once doing on principle. The Socialists were naturally shocked, being for the most part morbidly moral people; but at all events they were saved later on from the delusion that nobody but Nietzsche had ever challenged our mercanto-Christian morality....

*[Shaw summarizes ideas that he first encountered in the works of British philosophers Captain Frederick Wilson (economist and Comprehensionist philosopher, dates unknown) and John Stuart-Glennie (1841–1910), which critics subsequently credited to Nietzsche and Marx.]*

## The Gospel of St. Andrew Undershaft

It is this credulity that drives me to help my critics out with *Major Barbara* by telling them what to say about it. In the millionaire Undershaft I have represented a man who has become intellectually and spiritually as well as practically conscious of the irresistible natural truth which we all abhor and repudiate: to wit, that the greatest of evils and the worst of crimes is poverty, and that our first duty—a duty to which every other consideration should be sacrificed—is not to be poor. "Poor but honest," "the respectable poor," and such phrases are as intolerable and as immoral as "drunken but amiable," "fraudulent but a good after-dinner speaker," "splendidly criminal," or the like. Security, the chief pretence of civilization, cannot exist where the worst of dangers, the danger of poverty, hangs over everyone's head, and where the alleged protection of our persons from violence is only an accidental result of the existence of a police force whose real business is to force the poor man to see his children starve whilst idle people overfeed pet dogs with the money that might feed and clothe them. ...

Undershaft, the hero of *Major Barbara*, is simply a man who, having grasped the fact that poverty is a crime, knows that when society offered him the alternative of poverty or a lucrative trade in death and destruction, it offered him, not a choice between opulent villainy and humble virtue, but between energetic enterprise and cowardly infamy.... To be wealthy, says Undershaft, is with me a point of honor for which I am prepared to kill at the risk of my own life. This preparedness is, as he says, the final test of sincerity. Like [Jean] Froissart's [1337–1410] medieval hero [see page 113], who saw that "to rob and pill was a good life," he is not the dupe of that public sentiment against killing which is propagated and endowed by people who would otherwise be killed themselves, or of the mouth-honor paid to poverty and obedience by rich and insubordinate do-nothings who want to rob the poor without courage and command them without superiority. Froissart's knight, in placing the achievement of a good life before all the other duties—which indeed are not duties at all when they conflict with it, but plain wickednesses—behaved bravely, admirably, and, in the final analysis, public-spiritedly. Medieval society, on the other hand, behaved very badly indeed in organizing itself so stupidly that a good life could be achieved by robbing and pilling. If the knight's contemporaries had been all as resolute as he, robbing and pilling would have been the shortest way to the gallows, just as, if we were all as resolute and clearsighted as Undershaft, an attempt to live by means of what is called "an independent income" would be the shortest way to the lethal chamber. But as, thanks to our political imbecility and personal cowardice (fruits of poverty both), the best imitation of a good life now procurable is life on an independent income, all sensible people aim at securing such an income, and are, of course, careful to legalize and moralize both it and all the actions and sentiments which lead to it and support it as an institution. What else can they do? They know, of course, that they are rich because others are poor. But they cannot help that: it is for the poor to repudiate poverty when they have had enough of it. The thing can be done easily enough: the demonstrations to the contrary made by the economists, jurists, moralists and

sentimentalists hired by the rich to defend them, or even doing the work gratuitously out of sheer folly and abjectness,
impose only on the hirers....

*[Shaw continues to develop his argument that poverty is the greatest
evil and that the "crying need of the nation is... simply for enough
money." He claims that his greatest dramatic innovation in the play
"is that article in Undershaft's religion which recognizes in Money
the first need and in poverty the vilest sin of man and society."]*

This dramatic conception has not, of course, been attained
*per saltum* [Latin for "all at once"]. Nor has it been borrowed
from Nietzsche or from any man born beyond the Channel.
The late Samuel Butler [1835–1902], in his own department the
greatest English writer of the latter half of the XIX century,
steadily inculcated the necessity and morality of a conscientious Laodiceanism [lukewarm indifference] in religion and
of an earnest and constant sense of the importance of money.
It drives one almost to despair of English literature when
one sees so extraordinary a study of English life as Butler's
posthumous *Way of All Flesh* making so little impression that
when, some years later, I produce plays in which Butler's extraordinarily fresh, free and future-piercing suggestions have
an obvious share, I am met with nothing but vague cack-
lings about Ibsen and Nietzsche, and am only too thankful
that they are not about [French Romantic writers] Alfred de
Musset [1810–57] and Georges Sand [pseudonym of Amantine
Aurore Lucile Ducet, 1804–76]. Really, the English do not
deserve to have great men. They allowed Butler to die practically unknown, whilst I, a comparatively insignificant Irish
journalist, was leading them by the nose into an advertisement of me which has made my own life a burden. In Sicily
there is a Via Samuele Butler. When an English tourist sees
it, he either asks "Who the devil was Samuele Butler?" or

wonders why the Sicilians should perpetuate the memory of the author of *Hudibras*.

Well, it cannot be denied that the English are only too anxious to recognize a man of genius if somebody will kindly point him out to them. Having pointed myself out in this manner with some success, I now point out Samuel Butler, and trust that in consequence I shall hear a little less in future of the novelty and foreign origin of the ideas which are now making their way into the English theatre through plays written by Socialists. There are living men whose originality and power are as obvious as Butler's; and when they die that fact will be discovered. Meanwhile I recommend them to insist on their own merits as an important part of their own business.

## The Salvation Army

When *Major Barbara* was produced in London, the second act was reported in an important northern newspaper as a withering attack on the Salvation Army, and the despairing ejaculation of Barbara deplored by a London daily as a tasteless blasphemy. And they were set right, not by the professed critics of the theatre, but by religious and philosophical publicists like Sir Oliver Lodge [1850–1940] and Dr Stanton Coit [1857–1944], and strenuous Nonconformist journalists like Mr William Stead [1849–1912], who not only understood the act as well as the Salvationists themselves, but also saw it in its relation to the religious life of the nation, a life which seems to lie not only outside the sympathy of many of our theatre critics, but actually outside their knowledge of society. Indeed nothing could be more ironically curious than the confrontation *Major Barbara* effected of the theatre enthusiasts with the religious enthusiasts. On the one hand was the playgoer, always seeking pleasure, paying exorbitantly for it, suffering unbearable discomforts for it, and hardly ever getting it. On the other hand was the Salvationist, repudiating gaiety and courting effort and sacrifice, yet always in the wildest spirits, laughing, joking, singing, rejoicing, drumming, and tambourining: his life flying by in a flash of excitement, and his death arriving as a climax of triumph. And, if you please, the playgoer despising the Salvationist as a joyless person, shut out from the heaven of the theatre, self-condemned to a life of hideous gloom; and the Salvationist mourning over the playgoer as over a prodigal with vine leaves in his hair, careering outrageously to hell amid the popping of champagne corks and the ribald laughter of sirens! Could misunderstanding be more complete, or sympathy worse misplaced?

Fortunately, the Salvationists are more accessible to the religious character of the drama than the playgoers to the gay energy and artistic fertility of religion. They can see, when it is pointed out to them, that a theatre, as a place where two or three are gathered together, takes from that divine presence an inalienable sanctity of which the grossest and profanest farce can no more deprive it than a hypocritical sermon by a snobbish bishop can desecrate Westminster Abbey. But in our professional playgoers this indispensable preliminary conception of sanctity seems wanting. They talk of actors as mimes and mummers, and, I fear, think of dramatic authors as liars and pandars, whose main business is the voluptuous soothing of the tired city speculator when what he calls the serious business of the day is over. Passion, the life of drama, means nothing to them but primitive sexual excitement: such phrases as "impassioned poetry" or "passionate love of truth" have fallen quite out of their vocabulary and been replaced by "passional crime" and the like. They assume, as far as I can gather, that people in whom passion has a larger scope are passionless and therefore uninteresting. Consequently they come to think of religious people as people who are not interesting and not amusing. And so, when Barbara cuts the regular Salvation Army jokes, and snatches a kiss from her lover across his drum, the devotees of the theatre think they ought to appear shocked, and conclude that the whole play is an elaborate mockery of the Army. And then either hypocritically rebuke me for mocking, or foolishly take part in the supposed mockery!

Even the handful of mentally competent critics got into difficulties over my demonstration of the economic deadlock in which the Salvation Army finds itself. Some of them thought that the Army would not have taken money from a distiller and a cannon founder: others thought it should not have taken it: all assumed more or less definitely that it reduced itself to absurdity or hypocrisy by taking it. On the first point the reply of the Army itself was prompt and conclusive. As one of its officers said, they would take money from the devil himself and be only too glad to get it out of his hands and into God's. They gratefully acknowledged that publicans not only give them money but allow them to collect it in the bar—sometimes even when there is a Salvation meeting outside preaching teetotalism. In fact, they questioned the verisimilitude of the play, not because Mrs Baines took the money, but because Barbara refused it.

On the point that the Army ought not to take such money, its justification is obvious. It must take the money because it cannot exist without money, and there is no other money to be had. Practically all the spare money in the country consists of a mass of rent, interest, and profit, every penny of which is bound up with crime, drink, prostitution, disease, and all the evil fruits of poverty, as inextricably as with enterprise, wealth, commercial probity, and national prosperity. The notion that you can earmark certain coins as tainted is an unpractical individualist superstition. None the less the fact that all our money is tainted gives a very severe shock to earnest young souls when some dramatic instance of the taint first makes them conscious of it. When an enthusiastic young clergyman of the Established Church first realizes that the Ecclesiastical Commissioners receive the rents of sport-

ing public houses, brothels, and sweating dens; or that the
most generous contributor at his last charity sermon was an
employer trading in female labor cheapened by prostitution
as unscrupulously as a hotel keeper trades in waiters' labor
cheapened by tips, or commissionaire's labor cheapened by
pensions; or that the only patron who can afford to rebuild
his church or his schools or give his boys' brigade a gymna-
sium or a library is the son-in-law of a Chicago meat King,
that young clergyman has, like Barbara, a very bad quarter
hour. But he cannot help himself by refusing to accept money
from anybody except sweet old ladies with independent incomes and gentle and lovely ways of life. He has only to follow up the income of the sweet ladies to its industrial source,
and there he will find Mrs Warren's profession [reference to
Shaw's play *Mrs Warren's Profession* about a brothel owner]
and the poisonous canned meat [reference to Upton Sin-
clair's *The Jungle*] and all the rest of it. His own stipend has
the same root. He must either share the world's guilt or go to
another planet. He must save the world's honor if he is to save
his own. This is what all the Churches find just as the Salvation Army and Barbara find it in the play. Her discovery that
she is her father's accomplice; that the Salvation Army is the
accomplice of the distiller and the dynamite maker; that they
can no more escape one another than they can escape the
air they breathe; that there is no salvation for them through
personal righteousness, but only through the redemption of
the whole nation from its vicious, lazy, competitive anarchy:
this discovery has been made by everyone except the Phar-
isees and (apparently) the professional playgoers, who still
wear their Tom Hood shirts [reference to a song by Thomas
Hood (1799–1845) about sweated labor] and underpay their
washerwomen without the slightest misgiving as to the elevation of their private characters, the purity of their private
atmospheres, and their right to repudiate as foreign to themselves the coarse depravity of the garret and the slum. Not

that they mean any harm: they only desire to be, in their little private way, what they call gentlemen. They do not understand Barbara's lesson because they have not, like her, learnt it by taking their part in the larger life of the nation....

## 4. The Court Theatre, 1907. [*Platform and Pulpit*, pp. 36–41]

*[Shaw gave this speech in reply to a toast by the Earl of Lytton at a dinner honoring J.E. Vedrenne (1867–1930) and Harley Granville Barker (1877–1941) for their management of the Court Theatre from 1904–7. The dinner took place at the Criterion Restaurant in London on 7 July 1907. The Vedrenne-Barker seasons at the Court Theatre represented an important experiment in repertory and ensemble theatre, and provided important production opportunities for emerging modernist playwrights, including Granville Barker and especially Shaw, whose reputation as an important dramatist was largely made through the Court Theatre productions.]*

A good deal has been said here tonight as to how much our guests of the evening owe to me. My lord, ladies and gentlemen, I assure you they owe me nothing. They are perfectly solvent. The success, such as it is, has been a perfectly genuine one. There are plenty of managements who will make a brilliant show of success if you give them a sufficiently large subsidy to spend. Vedrenne and Barker have had no subsidy. They have paid me my fees to the uttermost farthing, and they have had nothing else to pay or repay me. This does not mean that the highest theatrical art is independent of public support, moral and financial. The Court Theatre has had to cut its coat according to its cloth, and It has never really had cloth enough. But it has paid its way and made a living wage for its workers, and it has produced an effect on dramatic art and public taste in this country which is out of all proportion to the mere physical and financial bulk of its achievements.

PART II: ADVICE ON SEEING AND PRODUCING SHAW'S
PLAYS

I am glad to have the honor of speaking here for the Court
Theatre authors, because if they had to answer for themselves they would be prevented from doing themselves justice by their modesty. Modesty, fortunately, is not in my line;
and if it were, I should follow the precept offered by Felix
Drinkwater to Captain Brassbound [characters in Shaw's
play *Captain Brassbound's Conversion* (1899)], and be modest
on my own account, not on theirs. As a matter of fact, I am
overrated as an author: most great men are. We have, I think,
proved that there is in this country plenty of dramatic faculty—faculty of the highest order too—only waiting for its
opportunity; and it is the supreme merit of our guests this
evening that they have provided that opportunity. You may
say that genius does not wait for its opportunity: it creates it.
But that is not true of any particular opportunity when there
are alternatives open. Men of genius will not become the
slaves of the ordinary fashionable theatres when they have
the alternative of writing novels. The genius of Dickens, who
at first wanted to write for the theatre, was lost to it because
there was no theatre available in which his art could have
breathed. I have myself tried hard to tempt Mr [H. G.] Wells
[1866–1946], Mr [Rudyard] Kipling [1865–1936], Mr [Joseph]
Conrad [1857–1924], and Mr Maurice Hewlett [1861–1923] to
leave their safe and dignified position as masters of the art
of fiction, and struggle with new difficulties and a new technique—though the technical difficulties are absurdly exaggerated—for the sake of redeeming the British drama from
banality. But it was too much to ask. They all knew the story
of the manager who, after receiving favorably a suggestion of
a play by Stevenson, drew back in disgust on learning that
the author question was not what he called "*the* Stephenson,"
meaning the librettist of a well-known light opera, but one
Robert Louis Stevenson, of whom he had never heard.

If Mr Maurice Hewlett was persuaded at last to make an experiment at the Court Theatre, it was because he knew that

Vedrenne and Barker would know his worth and respect his commanding position in literature. Without that no alliance between literature and the theatre is possible—for it is hard enough to make one reputation and conquer one eminence without having to set to again as a stranger and a beginner on the stage. If Mr [John] Galsworthy [1867–1933], after winning his spurs as one of the finest of the younger novelists, brought to the stage in *The Silver Box* that penetrating social criticism, and that charm of wonderfully fastidious and restrained art which makes me blush for the comparative blatancy of my own plays, it is because there was at last a stage for him to bring them to, and that stage was the Court stage, the creation of Vedrenne and Barker.

Barker, by the way, was not, like Vedrenne, wholly disinterested in the matter for he, too, is a Court author, and he, too, produces work whose delicacy and subtlety require exquisite handling. It is Vedrenne's just boast that he has produced Barker. The same thing is true of all the Court authors, more or less. Mr St John Hankin [1869–1909], the Mephistopheles of the new Comedy, would have been suspected by an old-fashioned manager—and suspected very justly—of laughing at him. Mr [Robert] Vernon Harcourt [politician and playwright, 1878–1962] and Mr [Laurence] Housman [1865–1959], whose charm is so much a charm of touch, would not have had much more chance than Mr Henry James [novelist and unsuccessful playwright, 1843–1916] has had on the long-run system. Literary is like the bloom on fine wall-fruit: the least roughness of handling knocks it off; and in our ordinary theatres literary plays are handled much as American trunks are handled at the boat trains. Mr Gilbert Murray [1866–1957] has not merely translated Euripides—many fools have done that, and only knocked another nail into the coffin of a dead language—he has reincarnated Euripides and made him a living poet in our midst. But Vedrenne and Barker made a Court author of him when no other managers dared touch him.

The difficulties of the enterprize have been labors of love, except in one unfortunately very trying respect. There has been no sort of satisfaction in the unremitting struggle with the London Press, which from first to last has done what in it lay to crush the enterprize. I know this uncompromising statement will surprise some of you, because in every newspaper you see praises of Vedrenne and Barker, ecstasies over the Court Theatre acting, paragraphs about the most frequently played Court author, and so forth. That has become the fashion, and the indiscriminate way in which it is done shews that it is done as a matter of fashion rather than of real appreciation. But if you turn back from this new convention to the points at which newspaper notices really help or hinder management—to the first-night notices of the first productions—you will see what I mean. There you will find a chronicle of failure, a sulky protest against this new and troublesome sort of entertainment that calls for knowledge and thought instead of for the usual *clichés*.

Take, for example, the fate of Mr [John] Masefield [1878–1967]. Mr Masefield's *Campden Wonder* is the greatest work of its kind that has been produced in an English theatre within the recollection—I had almost said within the reading—of any living critic. It has that great literary magic of a ceaseless music of speech—of haunting repetitions that play upon the tragic themes and burn them into the imagination. Its subject is one of those perfect simplicities that only a master of drama thinks of. Greater hate hath no man than this, that he lay down his life to kill his enemy: that is the theme of the *Campden Wonder*; and a wonder it is—of literary and dramatic art. And what had the press to say? They fell on it with howls of mere Philistine discomfort, and persuaded the public that it was a dull and disgusting failure. They complained of its horror, as if Mr Masefield had not known how to make that horror bearable, salutary, even fascinating by the enchantments of his art—as if it was not their business to face horror on the tragic stage as much as it is a soldier's business to face danger in the field. They ran away shamelessly, whining for happy endings and the like, blind and deaf to the splendid art of the thing, complaining that Mr Masefield had upset their digestion, and the like.

And what they did brutally to the *Campden Wonder* they did more or less to every other play. As we rehearsed our scenes and rejoiced in the growing interest and expectancy of our actors as they took the play in, we knew that no matter how enthusiastic our audience on the first night would be, no matter how triumphant the success of our actors, the next day—always a day of reaction at the best of times—would bring down on them all a damp cloud of grudging, petulant, ill-conditioned disparagement, suggesting to them that what they had been working so hard at was not a play at all, but a rather ridiculous experiment which was no credit to anybody connected with it. The mischief done was very considerable in the cases of new authors; and the discouragement to our actors must have had its effect, bravely as they concealed it.

Now, we were all—we authors—very much indebted to our actors, and felt proportionately disgusted at the way in which they were assured that they were wasting their time on us. I should like to make my personal acknowledgments to all of them, but that is a duty reserved for a later speaker; so I will only give, as an instance, the fact that my own play, *John Bull's Other Island*, failed as completely in America without Mr Louis Calvert [1859–1923] as Broadbent as it succeeded here, where it was carried on his massive shoulders. The success was his, not mine: I only provided the accessories. Well, you will say, but did not the press acknowledge this? is not the play always spoken of as a masterpiece? is not Mr Calvert's Broadbent as famous as [James] Quin's [1693–1766] Falstaff? Yes, it is—*now*. But turn back to the first-night notices, and you will learn that the masterpiece is not a play at all, and that Mr Calvert only did the best he could with an impossible part. It was not until *Man and Superman* followed that the wonderful qualities of *John Bull* were contrasted with the emptiness and dulness of its successor. It was not until *Major Barbara* came that the extinction of all the brilliancy that blazed through *Man and Superman* was announced. And not until *The Doctor's Dilemma* had been declared my Waterloo was it mentioned that *Major Barbara* had been my Austerlitz.

Now, I want to make a suggestion to the press. I don't ask them to give up abusing me, or declaring that my plays are not plays and my characters not human beings. Not for worlds would I deprive them of the inexhaustible pleasure these paradoxes seem to give them. But I do ask them, for the sake of the actors and of Vedrenne and Barker's enterprize, to reverse the order of their attacks and their caresses. In the future, instead of abusing the new play and praising the one before, let them abuse the one before and praise the new one. Instead of saying that *The Doctor's Dilemma* shews a sad falling-off from the superb achievement of *Major Barbara*, let them say that *The Doctor's Dilemma* is indeed a welcome and delightful change from the diseased trash which they had to endure last year from this most unequal author. That will satisfy their feelings just as much as the other plan, and will be really helpful to us. It is not the revivals that we want written up: the revivals can take care of themselves. Praise comes too late to help plays that have already helped themselves. If the press wishes to befriend us, let it befriend us in need, instead of throwing stones at us whilst we are struggling in the waves and pressing life-belts on us when we have swum to shore.

# 5. Statement to New York Theatre Audiences, 1924. [*The Bodley Head Bernard Shaw: Collected Plays with their Prefaces*, vol. 6, pp. 209–12]

*[This statement was written in January 1924 (but not published until 1951) for the Theatre Guild of New York, where Saint Joan had its world premiere in December 1923 with Winifred Lenihan (1898–1964) in the title role. The play concludes with an epilogue in which Joan reappears after her burning, a scene that Shaw saw as crucial to the story, but which often bewilders directors and audiences, especially coming at the end of an already long play. The Guild expressed concern about the play's length, asking Shaw to cut and revise it so that audiences could still catch the last train to their suburban homes. Shaw cabled his now-famous reply: "BEGIN AT EIGHT OR RUN LATER TRAINS."]*

As there seems to be some misunderstanding in the New York press of my intention in writing *Saint Joan*, I had better make myself quite clear. I am supposed to have set myself the task of providing the playgoing public with a pleasant theatrical entertainment whilst keeping the working hours of the professional critics within their customary limits; and it is accordingly suggested that I can improve the play vastly by cutting off a sufficient length from it to enable the curtain to rise at half past eight and descend finally at ten minutes to eleven. Certainly nothing could be easier. In the popular entertainment business, if your cradle is too short for your baby, you can always cut down your baby to fit the cradle.

But I am not in the popular entertainment business. The sort of entertainment provided by the fate of Joan of Arc seems to be quite sufficiently looked after in the United States by the Ku Klux Klan, and is all the more entertaining for being the real thing instead of a stage show.

As to the grievance of the professional critics, I, as an ex-critic, understand it only too well. It is a hideous experience for a critic, when at half past ten he has all the material for a good long notice, and is longing to get back to his newspaper office and write it at comparative leisure, to be forced to sit for another hour by that rival artist the author, until all the leisure is gone and nothing but a hurried scramble to feed the clamoring compositors is possible. But the remedy for that is, not to demand that the play shall be mutilated for the convenience of a score or two of gentlemen who see it as their breadwinning job on the first night only but to combine as other professional men do, and establish the custom of beginning plays of full classical length an hour earlier on the first night.

So much for the negative side of the situation. As to the positive side, I am, like all educated persons, intensely interested, and to some extent conscience stricken, by the great historical case of Joan of Arc. I know that many others share that interest and that compunction, and that they would eagerly take some trouble to have it made clear to them how it all happened. I conceive such a demonstration to be an act of justice for which the spirit of Joan, yet incarnate among us, is still calling. Every step in such a demonstration is intensely interesting to me; and the real protagonists of the drama, the Catholic Church, the Holy Roman Empire, and the nascent Reformation, appeal to my imagination and my intellect with a grip and fascination far beyond those of Dick Dudgeon and General Burgoyne [characters in *The Devil's Disciple* by Shaw]. When in the face of that claim of a great spirit for justice, and of a world situation in which we see whole peoples perishing and dragging us towards the abyss which has swallowed them all for want of any grasp of the political forces that move civilizations, I am met with peevish complaints that three hours or so is too long, and with petitions to cut the cackle and come to the burning, and promises that if I adapt the play to the outlook and tastes and capacities of the purblind people who have made the word suburban a derisive epithet, it will run for eighteen months and make a fortune for me and the Theatre Guild, the effect is to make me seem ten feet high and these poor people ten inches, which is bad for my soul, and not particularly healthy for theirs.

In theatres as elsewhere, people must learn to know their places. When a man goes to church and does not like the service nor understand the doctrine, he does not ask to have it changed to suit him: he goes elsewhere until he is suited. When he goes to a classical concert and is bored by Beethoven, he does not scream to the conductor for a fox trot, and suggest that Beethoven should introduce a saxophone solo into the Ninth Symphony: he goes to the nearest hall where a jazz band is at work. I plead for equally reasonable behaviour in the theatre. *Saint Joan* is not for connoisseurs of the police and divorce drama, or of the languors and lilies and roses and raptures of the cinema; and it is not going to be altered to suit them. It is right over their heads, and they must either grow up to it or let it alone. Fortunately for me, it interests and even enthralls serious people who would not enter an ordinary theatre if they were paid to, and draws novices who have never crossed the threshold of a theatre in their lives, and were taught by their parents that it is the threshold of hell. And the class of intelligent and cultivated playgoers whose neglected needs have brought the Theatre Guild into existence, naturally jump at it.

However, even at the risk of a comprehensive insult to the general public of New York, I must add that the limitation of the audience to serious, intelligent, and cultivated Americans means that *Saint Joan* must be regarded for the present as an Exceptional Play for Exceptional People. It has cost a good deal to produce it for them, and is costing a good deal to keep the opportunity open. This will not matter if they seize the opportunity promptly with a sense that if they do not, they will miss it, and discourage the Guild from future public spirited enterprises of this sort. The solvency of a play depends not only on the number of persons who pay to witness it, but on the length of time over which their attendances are spread. Even a million enthusiasts will not help if they arrive at the rate of ten per week. A thousand can do a great deal if they do it in two days. *Saint Joan's* present prosperity cannot in the nature of things last many months. Those who come early and come often are the pillars of the sort of play that gives you something to take home with you.

## 6. Prefatory Note to *The Six of Calais*, 1935. [*The Bodley Head Bernard Shaw: Collected Plays with their Prefaces*, vol. 6, pp. 973–75]

[*Shaw wrote* The Six of Calais, *a minor one-act play, over three days in May 1934. It was first performed at the Open Air Theatre in London's Regent's Park on 17 July 1934. The play was inspired by Auguste Rodin's sculpture* The Burghers of Calais *and more directly by the historical account from* The Chronicles of Froissart, *which were begun in the late fourteenth century and record the historical military events of the century. Shaw frequently claimed that his historical plays were more accurate and realistic than others' accounts, as he does here in claiming that the play improves on Froissart's romanticized version of the historical events.*]

The most amusing thing about the first performance of this little play was the exposure it elicited of the quaint illiteracy of our modern London journalists. Their only notion of a king was a pleasant and highly respectable gentleman in a bowler hat and Victorian beard, shaking hands affably with a blushing football team. To them a queen was a dignified lady, also Victorian as to her coiffure, graciously receiving bouquets from excessively washed children in beautiful new clothes. Such were their mental pictures of Great Edward's grandson and his queen Philippa [of Hainault, 1314–69]. They were hurt, shocked, scandalized at the spectacle of a medieval soldier monarch publicly raging and cursing, crying and laughing, asserting his authority with thrasonic ferocity and the next moment blubbering like a child in his wife's lap or snarling like a savage dog at a dauntless and defiant tradesman: in short behaving himself like an unrestrained human being in a very trying situation instead of like a modern constitutional monarch on parade keeping up an elaborate fiction of living in a political vacuum and moving only when his ministers pull his strings. Edward Plantagenet the Third [1312–77] had to pull everybody else's strings and pull them pretty hard, his father having been miserably killed for taking his job too lightly. But the journalist critics knew nothing of this. A King Edward who did not behave like the son of King Edward the Seventh [1841–1910] seemed unnatural and indecent to them, and they rent their garments accordingly.

They were perhaps puzzled by the fact that the play has no moral whatever. Every year or so I hurl at them a long play full of insidious propaganda, with a moral in every line. They never discover what I am driving at: it is always too plainly and domestically stated to be grasped by their subtle and far flung minds; but they feel that I am driving at something: probably something they had better not agree with if they value their livelihoods. A play of mine in which I am not driving at anything more than a playwright's direct business is as inconceivable by them as a medieval king.

Now a playwright's direct business is simply to provide the theatre with a play. When I write one with the additional attraction of providing the twentieth century with an up-to-date religion or the like, that luxury is thrown in gratuitously; and the play, simply as a play, is not necessarily either the better or the worse for it. What, then, is a play simply as a play?

Well, it is a lot of things. Life as we see it is so haphazard that it is only by picking out its key situations and arranging them in their significant order (which is never how they actually occur) that it can be made intelligible. The highbrowed dramatic poet wants to make it intelligible and sublime. The farce writer wants to make it funny. The melodrama merchant wants to make it as exciting as some people find the police news. The pornographer wants to make it salacious. All interpreters of life in action, noble or ignoble, find their instrument in the theatre; and all the academic definitions of a play are variations of this basic function.

Yet there is one function hardly ever alluded to now, though it was made much too much of from Shakespear's time to the middle of the nineteenth century. As I write my plays it is continually in my mind and very much to my taste. This function is to provide an exhibition of the art of acting. A good play with bad parts is not an impossibility; but it is a monstrosity. A bad play with good parts will hold the stage and be kept alive by the actors for centuries after the obsolescence of its mentality would have condemned it to death without them. A great deal of the British Drama, from Shakespear to [Edward] Bulwer Lytton [1803–73], is as dead as mutton, and quite unbearable except when heroically acted; yet *Othello* and *Richelieu* can still draw hard money into the pay boxes; and *The School For Scandal* revives again and again with unabated vigor. Rosalind can always pull *As You Like It* through in spite of the sententious futility of the melancholy Jaques; and Millamant, impossible as she is, still produces the usual compliments to the wit and style of [William] Congreve [1670–1729], who thought that syphilis and cuckoldry and concupiscent old women are things to be laughed at.

*The Six of Calais* is an acting piece and nothing else. As it happened, it was so well acted that in the eighteenth century all the talk would have been about [Sarah] Siddons [1755–1831] as Philippa. But the company got no thanks except from the audience: the critics were prostrated with shock, damn their eyes!

I have had to improve considerably on the story as told by that absurd old snob Froissart, who believed that "to rob and pill was a good life" if the robber was at least a baron (see page 93). He made a very poor job of it in my opinion.

# Part III: Theater and Social Reform

*Throughout his prolific career as a critic and dramatist, Shaw's main guiding principle was his belief that theatre had a sacred function to fulfill in helping society to achieve self-awareness and enlightenment. He compared the theatre to the church in terms of both mission and method, and feared that the public had fallen into the bad habit of not taking the theatre any more seriously than it bothered to take the church anymore. Shaw championed the plays of Ibsen and Brieux because they presented audiences with realistic representations of the ethical dilemmas and social injustices that existed off the stage. His own plays grappled with the urgent social problems of rampant poverty (see page 93), gender inequality, and sexual morality, but his irrepressible tendency towards dramatic comedy may have undermined the seriousness of his social critique. As he admitted to biographer Archibald Henderson, "I have produced no permanent impression because nobody has ever believed me."*

# 1. Acting, by one who does not believe in it, 1889.
## [*Platform and Pulpit*, pp. 12–23]

[*Shaw himself drafted this report of his talk given at a meeting of the Reverend Stewart D. Headlam's Church and Stage Guild, London in February 1889. Headlam (1847–1924), a controversial Christian Socialist, founded the Guild of St Matthew, a socialist fellowship of clergy and laity. Headlam disagreed with the church's anti-theatre stance, and founded the Church and Stage Guild after he was dismissed from St Matthew's parish, to teach clergy about the value of theatre, a mission clearly aligned with Shaw's belief about theatre's significance. Here Shaw argues for a new mode of acting that would better serve the realism required by social problem plays like those of Ibsen.*]

At the meeting of the Guild on the afternoon of 5 February, Mr Bernard Shaw read a paper entitled "Acting, by one who does not believe in it; or the place of the Stage in the Fools' Paradise of Art." After a characteristic prelude on the Guild work generally, Mr Shaw began to work up to his point, thus:

One of the questions I come here to ask is: "Would the Church and Stage Guild be satisfied if it could bring the whole nation, including the Bishop of London [Frederick Temple, 1821–1902] and his Puritanic following, into the same frame of mind with the theatre-loving folk?" If so, then certainly it does not take itself so seriously as I take it; for my own feeling is that the attitude of the Puritan towards the actor is to be preferred to that of the "first-nighter" by just as much as superstitious horror is easier to bear than contempt....

The ground of this contempt is obvious. The dramatic critic believes in acting, and regards the man on the stage as an actor. In English, acting means shamming. The critic, then, despises the stage as a sham, and the actor as a wretched impostor, disguised in the toga of Caesar, and spouting the words of Shakespear—a creature with the trappings and the language of a hero, but with the will of a vain mummer—a fellow that fights without courage, dares without danger, is eloquent without ideas, commands without power, suffers without self-denial, loves without passion, and comes between the author and the stalls much as a plaster of colored earths and oil comes between Raphael [Renaissance Italian painter, 1483–1520] and the Cook's tourist [*Cook's Travellers Handbooks* were aimed at relatively unsophisticated, middle-class audiences].

Now, even if the actor admitted that he is no more than this, which no actor does, he could retort with terrible effect on his literary censor. "Granted," he might say, "that I am incapable of doing the deeds I play at, pray do you practise what you write about? If it takes no real courage to fight a duel on the stage, does it take any more to write the scene in which that duel occurs, or to criticize my fencing? If I have not the will of Caesar, had Shakespear, or have you? Is the inventor of the sham scene, or the actor, or the delighted spectator the most futile and ridiculous from your point of view? Are the real virtues and the real trials of the actor at all different from those of the men who condemn him without being intelligent enough to see that they must plead guilty themselves to every count of their indictment?" The reason that this retort is not actually made is that it satisfies neither the enthusiastic actor, who generally does suppose that he only needs opportunity to become all that he pretends to be on the stage, nor even the cynical actor, who at least knows that, in proportion to the opportunities, competent actors of Caesar are much scarcer than real Caesars, the inevitable conclusion being that, for any given man whatsoever, it is much easier to be Caesar than to act Caesar. And, indeed, if we consider how the achievements for which we honor Caesar are really the achievements of many thousands typified in one; if we could subtract from his reputation the fame of the things he never did, and of those which fell out quite otherwise than he intended them; if we make due allowance, in calculating his stature, for the height of the wave of fortune on whose crest he came to his throne, then, considering on the other hand how absolutely individual and unaided is the task of the great actor, we begin to perceive why no actor has any consciousness of paradox when he hears it claimed that the first Napoleon was a commonplace person in comparison with Talma. I might go on to make some amends to the critic by pointing out that he may with some color claim to be the rarest of all species in his highest development, but such a process would be endless and idle. I have said enough to bear the trite moral that the contempt of one for another, whether it be the contempt of the historian for the statesman, the critic for the actor, or the virtuous person for the vicious, is as a hood to the eyes and a wired lawn to the feet of the seeker for justice.

But there is a contempt that is harder to escape than any of these—the contempt of a man for himself. The most terrible doubt that can come into the mind of a man is a doubt as to the utility of his profession. No class of men—not even doctors—can be more subject to that sort of doubt than artists. All art is play; and all play is make-believe. How, then, be an artist without being a rogue and a vagabond? Make a few thousand a year and the thing is done, as far as the opinion of others is concerned. But self-opinion, what of that? Must the novelist know himself a liar, the sculptor an image-man, the actor an illusion, a simulacrum, a glittering sword that will not cut, a burnished hydrant that will not extinguish anything? The eternal cry of the artist's soul is for salvation in this matter: the claim which he most vehemently urges is the claim for the reality of what he plays at....

[Shaw compares the statements by two famous actors, Signor Tommaso Salvini (1829–1915) and M. Benoît Constant Coquelin

*(1841–1909), about their working methods: Salvini claims he must genuinely feel emotions and characters to act them convincingly, while Coquelin prides himself on being a skilled craftsman who can convincingly animate characters no matter how little they resemble him personally. Shaw refuses to accept Coquelin's explanation because it reduces the brilliant actor to "a contemptibly shiftless and limited automaton."]*

The truth is, of course, that M. Coquelin is less an actor than any other comedian on the stage. So far from being a mere mask with no individuality, to be put on by Shakespear, Molière, or any other author, he is one of the few points in the human mass at which individuality is concentrated, fixed, gripped in one exceptionally gifted man, who is, consequently, what we call a personality, a man pre-eminently himself, impossible to disguise, the very last man who could under any circumstances be an actor. Yet this is just what makes him the stage-player par excellence. We go to see him because we know he will always be Coquelin, because every new part he plays will be some new side of Coquelin or some new light on a familiar side of him, because his best part will be that which shews all sides of him and realizes him wholly to us and to himself. If no such part exists in dramatic literature, then the want of it is the great sorrow and unfulfilment of his life. If he finds such a part, he seizes on it as oxygen seizes on certain metallic bases. In it he becomes for the first time completely real: he has achieved the aspiration of the hero of Ibsen's fantastic play [Peer Gynt] and become himself at last. This is not acting: it is the final escape from acting, the ineffable release from the conventional mask which must be resumed as the artist passes behind the wing, washes off the paint, and goes down into the false lights and simulated interests and passions of the street.

At this point there was a general suspicion that Mr Shaw was going to evaporate in a neat paradox of the stage being the real world, and off-the-stage the unreal one, thus turning inside out Shakespear's fancy about all the world being a stage. But he went on to shew that kindred self "realizations" were being constantly sought and sometimes achieved in ordinary life.... Then, harking back to the stage, he went on:

Let us take another instance. A man has a strong sense of mischievous humor, and a certain mercurial vivacity and agility which make rapid and riotous movement essential to his complete satisfaction. His sense of the ludicrous feeds on his veneration and eats it up. Nevertheless, he is a goodnatured man and possibly a timid one. When he sees a cripple painfully traversing the streets, he is sorry for him, but cannot resist laughing at the notion of knocking his crutches from under him and flying, pursued by a policeman, only to lie down unexpectedly in his pursuer's path, and upset him, too, in the mud. But he does not do these things, because the cripple would be hurt, and the policeman would make him pay too dearly for his jest. In order to give the fullest expression to the craving of his whimsical side for action and exhibition, he must find a scene where these restraining conditions do not exist. He finds it on the stage or in the circus ring as a clown. This instance is an extremely improbable one, because although to a schoolboy of twelve a career of mischievous trickery without moral responsibility or ulterior risk may seem the fullest self-realization, to an adult man, with his passions and ambitions, it appeals very feebly and intermittently.... Still, we all have a clown in us somewhere; and [playwright and actor David] Garrick's [1717–79] Petruchio [title character of *Catherine and Petruchio*, Garrick's adaptation of Shakespeare's *Taming of the Shrew*], [Frédérick] Lemaître's [1800–76] Macaire [subversively satirical character famously created by Lemaître], and Mr Irving's Jingle and Jeremy Diddler [farcical buffoon characters famously played by Irving] may be regarded as the outcome of the impulse felt by these actors to realize for a moment the clown in themselves. This, of course, is a realization of only a side of themselves; but there are very few parts in drama which will hold an entire man or woman....

This was practically the end of Mr Shaw's exposition of acting as metaphysical self-realization rather than shamming.... Then came the explanation of the mysterious phrase, "Fool's Paradise of Art," in the title of the paper.

But the main thing was that this cloud of silly illusions which I supposed to be Art was still my refuge from real life, my asylum from the squalor and snobbery outside, from the bewilderment of a world in which, as in church, everybody was pretending to enjoy what he disliked, and praising one course of conduct whilst pursuing another; above all, from the irksomeness of the struggle for bread and butter. When at last I made a plunge into London, I soon found out that the artistic people were the shirkers of the community. They ran away from their political duties to portfolios of etchings; from their social duties to essays on the delicacies of their culture; and from their religious duties to the theatre. They were doing exactly what I had done myself, in short—keeping up a Fool's Paradise in order to save themselves the trouble of making the real world any better. Naturally, they hated reality; and this involved some awkward consequences for them. For since the climaxes of Art are brought about by the successful effort of some powerful individuality or idea to realize itself in an act of some kind, whether picture, book, or stage impersonation, these artistic skulkers had to be continually dodging great works of art, or else devising ways of discussing and enjoying their accidental methods, conditions, and qualities so as to ward off their essential purpose and meaning. And they, or rather we, did this so effectually that I might have remained in my Fool's Paradise of Art with the other fools to this day, had I not, to preserve myself from the dry rot of idleness, attempted to realize myself in works of Art.

These works of art were Mr Shaw's novels, which he described as "bad sermons, which failed because I, thanks to skulking in picture galleries, was a nonentity; and the realization of a nonentity in a novel is not interesting." He gave up novel-writing, and pursued the Real by way of the incessant lecturing on Socialism which distinguishes his present phase of self-realization. "As it happens," he remarked, "I have an incorrigible propensity for preaching. In conversation this did not make me so unpopular as might have been expected; for I have some unconscious and unintentional infirmity of expression which often leads people to doubt whether I am serious in my sermons." Socialist propaganda brought Mr Shaw into contact with Mr Stewart Headlam:

He, not being a dramatic critic, saw what none of the dramatic critics could see, that the world behind the footlights was a real world, peopled with men and women instead of with despicable puppets. He proclaimed the solidarity of the stage with the stalls by founding the Church and Stage Guild. The critics stared, laughed, and promptly set up a convention that the Guild was ludicrous combination of parson and ballet. Mr Headlam affected them just on one point. He disclosed to them the fact that the ballet is the richest mine of idiotic conventions that exists: it is practically dying of them. The critics are now eagerly learning the jargon of these conventions, in order that their minds, hitherto a blank on the subject of dancing, may be filled with a basketful of irrelevancies to it.

As to any chance of reforming these gentlemen, or obtaining help from them in reforming the drama, I am inclined to think it would be less trouble to undertake the work without them. They never learn anything, never discuss anything, never believe anything, never doubt that they are heading the march that is really leaving them almost out of sight. They cannot tell you anything about a play or an actor that is of the smallest consequence, though they will tell you a dozen things that are quite beside the point. They can write as good a notice of a perfectly hollow play as it is worth; but confront them with a great piece of acting and they will astonish you by the ingenuity with which they will evade the main point, and, like cuttlefish, conceal their bonelessness in a cloud of ink....

*[Shaw claims that the great French actress Madame Sarah Bern-hard (1844–1923) was ultimately degraded and vulgarized by re-peatedly performing the emotionally overwhelming parts that play-wright Victorien Sardou wrote for her, and argues that critics failed to realize that would happen "because the whole affair was not real enough to be worth troubling about. After all, the play was a sham, the woman a puppet: why should you expect a cultivated man to make a fuss about these things, and incidentally to make himself ridiculous?"]*

I do not propose to bring further evidence against the critics now: they will perhaps supply it themselves in the course of the discussion. I have said enough to make myself thoroughly misunderstood; and I will conclude by restating the views upon which I base my respect for the actor and the stage, and my despair of the critics.

1. That acting, in the common use of the word, is self-falsification, forgery, and fraud.

2. That the true goal of the stage-player is self-realization, expression, and exhibition.

3. That the drama can only progress by making higher and higher demands on the players' powers of self-development and realization.

4. That the critic who rejects this view lapses into a vicious contempt for the player, and, having no valid standard, is compelled to coin conventions which will not circulate any-where outside his own circle of accomplices....

## 2. Church and Stage, 1898. [*Our Theatres in the Nineties*, vol. 3, pp. 292–97]

*[Under the guise of reviewing* The Conversion of England *by the Rev. Henry Cresswell, Shaw argues with evangelical zeal for audiences and critics to recognize the affinities that church and theatre have as pulpits for social reform. With typical Shavian paradox, Shaw warns that audiences will abandon theatres in favor of churches unless theatre managers begin to take the drama more seriously.]*

It has come at last. Again and again in these columns I have warned the managers—or rather the syndicates: a manager nowadays is only the man in possession—that they would be supplanted by the parsons if they did not take their business a little more seriously. I meant no more by this than that the modern Church, with its attractive musical services carefully advertised in the hall of the local hotel side by side with the pantomimes, would finally be discovered by the playgoer as a much pleasanter, cheaper, wholesomer, restfuller, more recreative place to spend a couple of hours in than a theatre. But now the parson has carried the war into the enemy's country. He has dramatized the lessons of the Church, and is acting them with scenery, costumes, limelight, music, processions, and everything complete in Church House great halls which hold £200 easily. Not that he charges for admission: such worldliness is as far from him as from the Independent Theatre when it performs Ibsen's *Ghosts*. But just as the Independent Theatre encourages the New Drama by inviting those who subscribe to it to witness *Ghosts*; so the charitable persons who subscribe to the Waifs and Strays Society, to the building of St Peter's Church, South Tottenham, or the parish of St Ann, South Lambeth, receive, to their surprise and delight, a reserved seat or seats for the performance of *The Conversion of England*, in positions which, by a remarkable coincidence, are spectatorially favorable in proportion to the number of half-sovereigns, crowns, or half-crowns contained in the subscription. And the view is not obstructed by *matinée* hats; for before the performance a clergyman, clad with the whole authority of the Church of England, steps before the curtain and orders those hats to come off. What is more, they actually do come off, except in those desperate cases in which the hat and the hair, all in one piece, are equally foreign to the wearer. There is no band to play the overture to *Mireille* [1864 opera by Gounod] and Mr [Edward] German's [1862–1936] Lyceum dances [popular incidental music composed for productions at the Lyceum Theatre] for the 735th time: instead, the choir sings a hymn, and the audience may stand up and join in it if it likes. Further, the scenery consists of pictures, with all the capacity of pictures for beauty and poetry. Unroll one painted cloth and you are in Rome: unroll another and you are in Britain. This may seem a small matter to people who have no eye for pictures, and who love nothing better than a built-in stage drawing room full of unquestionable carpets and curtains and furniture from Hampton's and Maple's, not to mention a Swan & Edgar [London department stores] windowful of costumes. But if these worthy people only knew how much of the dullness and monotony of modern fashionable drama is produced by the fact that on the stage nowadays "three removes are as bad as a fire," [proverb meaning that changing something three times essentially destroys it] and how much livelier the old adventurous plays, with a change of scene every ten minutes, were than the modern drama chained for forty-five minutes at a time to the impedimenta of Jack Hinton's Rooms in Whitehall Court [reference to *The Guardsman*, a play by Charles Lever] and the like, they would understand what a formidable rival the miracle play in ten short scenes may prove to fixture plays in three long ones by any but the ablest hands.

There is another point on which, in the present excited state of public feeling on the question of actors' morals, I touch with trembling. To say that the clergymen who enact the miracle plays speak better than actors is nothing; for at present all the professions and most of the trades can make the same boast. But the difference is something more than a technical one. The tone of a man's voice is the tone of his life. The average clergyman's utterance betrays his ignorance, his conceit, his class narrowness, his snobbery, and his conception of religion as an official authorization of all these offences so unmistakeably that in a lawless community he would be shot at sound as a mad dog is shot at sight. But the clergymen who are coming into the field against the managers are not average clergymen. *The Conversion of England* on their playbills means something more than the title of an entertainment; and that something is not the conversion of England's follies and vices into box-office returns. At the Westminster performance last Saturday the actors spoke as men speak in the presence of greater matters than their own personal success. You may go to the theatre for months without hearing that particular dramatic effect. The men who can make it will finally play the men who cannot make it off the stage, in spite of the hankering of the public after the vulgarities which keep its own worst qualities in countenance. I should add, by the way, that the applause which our actors declare they cannot do without was excommunicated in the Church House like the hats, and that the effect on the performance was highly beneficial.

As to Mr Cresswell's drama, I cannot speak with any confidence. I came to it from a round of duties which included such works as *Never Again* [author unknown] at the Vaudeville; so that the mere force of contrast made it perfectly enthralling to me. When the British Bishop, objecting to the Roman missionaries, exclaimed "The whole world is heretic! There is no knowledge of the truth anywhere except at Bangor," I shrieked with laughter. No doubt it was not a first-class joke; but after the dreary equivoques of the farcical comedians it was as manna in the wilderness. Indeed, I suspect Mr Cresswell of being more of a humorist than he pretends. I dare not flatly assert that his sketch of Bertha, the Christian Queen of Kent, is a lively caricature of some Mrs Proudie who oppressed him in his early curacies; but I will quote a sample of the lady and leave my readers to draw their own conclusions. Sebba, the priest of Woden ("pagan, I regret to say," as Mr Pecksniff observed), tells the pious princess that the gods have declared a certain fact by an oracle. Here is her reply, to be delivered, according to the stage directions, with an incredulous smile. "Ah!—*your* gods, Sebba! They must be very clever gods to be able to tell you what they do not know themselves. [*Aside*] I scarcely dare to interfere. These people are so attached to their superstitions. Poor souls, they know no better!"

*The Conversion of England* evades censorship by not taking money at the doors. Otherwise the Lord Chamberlain would probably suppress it, unless Mr Cresswell consented to cut out the religious passages, and assimilate the rest to Gentleman Joe and Dandy Dan [popular musicals by Walter Slaughter and Basil Hood].

The controversy about the morality of the stage has been stabbed stone dead by an epigram. Mr [Robert] Buchanan's [1841–1901, poet and playwright] "Thousands of virtuous women on the stage, but only six actresses!" is so irresistible that it is exceedingly difficult to say anything more without anti-climax. Nevertheless there are one or two points that had better be clearly understood. First, that there has been no genuine moral discussion. In England there never is. Our habit of flooding the newspapers with prurient paragraphs about women, whether actresses or duchesses matters not a rap, is not a habit of threshing out moral questions. But even on this trivial ground Mr Clement Scott's position remains entirely unshaken. He made his charge in terms of the perfectly well-understood marriage morality on which, to cite a leading case, [Charles Stewart] Parnell [1846–91, MP and leader of the Irish National League who was implicated in an adultery and divorce scandal] was driven out of public life and a great political combination wrecked. The theatrical profession may profess that morality or it may repudiate it. When Ibsen, following the footsteps of the great hierarchy of illustrious teachers who have made war on it, attacked it with intense bitterness in *Ghosts*, those who supported him were vilified in terms compared to which Mr Clement Scott's strictures are enthusiastic eulogies. The issue between natural human morality and the mechanical character tests of Mr Stead was then vehemently raised in the theatrical world by Mr Scott himself. Its leaders, I am sorry to say, ranged themselves on the side of Mr Stead with sanctimonious promptitude. The rod they helped to pickle then, and which they laid so zealously on Ibsen's back, has now been laid on their own; and I should be more than human if I did not chuckle at their shrieks of splendid silence. Mr Buchanan, whilst chivalrously refusing to join in the cowardly rush which has been made at Mr Scott under the very mistaken impression that he is down, declares that a profession that can boast such names as those of—he mentions six leading actors and actresses—should surely disdain to defend itself against Mr Scott's charges. As to that, I beg to point out remorselessly that at least three out of the six are artists whose characters on the point at issue must notoriously stand or fall with that of Parnell, and that these very three are the most admired, the most respected, the most unshamed and unashamed, the most publicly and privately honored members of their profession. What should we think of them if they were to burst into frenzied accusations of falsehood and calumny against Mr Scott, and exculpatory asserverations of their own perfect conformity to Mr Stead's ideal? They would at once put themselves in the wrong, not only from the point of view of Mr Stead and of a devout Roman Catholic critic bound by his Church to regard even the marriage of divorced persons as a deadly sin, but from any point of view that discountenances flagrant and cowardly hypocrisy. The gentlemen who are just now so busily claiming Mr Stead's certificate of "purity" for our most esteemed English actresses had better ask those ladies first whether they would accept it if it were offered to them.

Do not let it be supposed, however, that the hypocrisy is all on one side. I have before me a pile of press cuttings from such papers as *Great Thoughts*, the *Christian Commonwealth*, the *Christian Million*, and the *British Weekly*, from which I learn that I am held to have testified, with Mr Clement Scott, that the theatre is so evil a place and its professors so evil a people, that "so long as women are exposed to such temptations and perils as Mr Clement Scott describes, no man who reverences woman as Christ reverenced her can possibly support the stage." These are the words of Mr Hugh Price Hughes [Methodist clergyman, 1847–1902]. I am sorry we have led Mr Hughes to deceive himself in this matter. The only authority I have at hand as to Christ's view of the subject is the Bible; and I do not find there that in his reverence for humanity he drew Mr Stead's line at publicans or sinners, or accepted the marriage laws of his time as having any moral authority. Indeed, I gather that his object was to discredit legal tests of conduct, and that he would not have objected to go to the theatre on Sunday with Mary Magdalene if Jerusalem had been Paris. However, I will not rest my case on these pious claptraps. Mr Price Hughes knows as well as I do that women are employed in the manufacture of sacred books on terms which make the prostitution of a certain percentage of them virtually compulsory. He knows that no actress is trampled into the gin-sodden degradation of the wretched laundresses who provide the whited walls of starched shirt that make his congregation look so respectable on Sunday. He knows that many a church and chapel in this country would fall into ruin without the conscience money of traders who pay girls from five to seven shillings a week to exhaust in their shops and factories the strength nourished on the contributions of their sweethearts. And he ought to know that the stage, of which neither I nor Mr Clement Scott has said the worst, is nevertheless, from the point of view of the consideration shewn to women on it, and the wages paid to them, much more worthy of his support than any other commercially supported English institution whatsoever, the Methodist churches not excepted. And so, reverend gentlemen, do not give sceptical persons like myself occasion to scoff by an outburst of Pharisaism [self-righteous hypocrisy]. Never mind the mote in the actor's eye: you will find plenty of beams behind the spectacles of your own congregations.

## 3. From the Preface to *Plays Pleasant*, 1898. [*The Bodley Head Bernard Shaw: Collected Plays with their Prefaces*, vol. 1, pp. 371–85]

[*By 1897, Shaw had written seven plays but their subject matter and style made it difficult for him to get them produced. At the time, drama was not a popular publication genre, but Shaw took his cue from Ibsen's plays, which were more readily accessible in print than in performance, and published his* Plays: Unpleasant and Pleasant *with Grant Richards, including a Preface for each volume. In a letter to Reginald Golding Bright, Shaw explained, "I am not a disappointed dramatist.... But in the present condition of the theatre it is evident that a dramatist like Ibsen, who absolutely disregards the conditions which managers are subject to, and throws himself on the reading public, is taking the only course in which any serious advance is possible...." Shaw had an astute understanding of the conditions of theatrical production, and recognized that publishing*

*his plays was a strategic way of developing audiences for their even-*
*tual performance (see also page 231).]*

Readers of the discourse with which the preceding volume
commences will remember that I turned my hand to playwriting when a great deal of talk about "the New Drama,"
followed by the actual establishment of a "New Theatre" (the
Independent), threatened to end in the humiliating discovery
that the New Drama, in England at least, was a figment of the
revolutionary imagination. This was not to be endured. I had
rashly taken up the case; and rather than let it collapse I manufactured the evidence.

Man is a creature of habit. You cannot write three plays
and then stop. Besides, the New movement did not stop. In
1894, Florence Farr [1860–1917, actress and one of Shaw's love
interests], who had already produced Ibsen's *Rosmersholm*,
was placed in command of the Avenue Theatre in London
for a season on the new lines by Miss A. E. F. [Annie Elizabeth Fredericka] Horniman [1860–1937, wealthy tea heiress]
who had family reasons for not yet appearing openly as a
pioneer-manageress. There were, as available New Dramatists, myself, discovered by the Independent Theatre (at my
own suggestion); Dr John Todhunter [1839–1916], who had
been discovered before (his play *The Black Cat* had been one
of the Independent's successes); and Mr W. B. Yeats
[1865–1939, founder of the Abbey Theatre in Ireland], a genuine discovery. Dr Todhunter supplied *A Comedy of Sighs*: Mr
Yeats, *The Land of Heart's Desire*. I, having nothing but unpleasant plays in my desk, hastily completed a first attempt at
a pleasant one, and called it *Arms and the Man*, taking the title from the first line of Dryden's [translation of the ancient
epic *Aeneid* by] Virgil. It passed for a success, the applause on
the first night being as promising as could be wished; and it
ran from the 21st of April to the 7th of July. To witness it the
public paid £1777:5:6, an average of £23:2:5 per representation

(including nine matinées). A publisher receiving £1700 for a book would have made a satisfactory profit: experts in West End theatrical management will contemplate that figure with a grim smile.

In the autumn of 1894 I spent a few weeks in Florence, where I occupied myself with the religious art of the Middle Ages and its destruction by the Renascence. From a former visit to Italy on the same business I had hurried back to Birmingham to discharge my duties as musical critic at the Festival there. On that occasion a very remarkable collection of the works of our British "pre-Raphaelite" painters [group of artists and authors founded in 1848 to revive a detailed style of art that realistically represented nature] was on view. I looked at these, and then went into the Birmingham churches to see the windows of William Morris [1834–96, publisher, artist, social reformer] and [Edward] Burne-Jones [1833–98]. On the whole, Birmingham was more hopeful than the Italian cities; for the art it had to shew me was the work of living men, whereas modern Italy had, as far as I could see, no more connection with Giotto [1266–1337, Italian painter] than Port Said [modern Egyptian city] has with Ptolemy [100–70 CE, Greco-Egyptian astronomer]. Now I am no believer in the worth of any mere taste for art that cannot produce what it professes to appreciate. When my subsequent visit to Italy found me practising the playwright's craft, the time was ripe for a modern pre-Raphaelite play. Religion was alive again, coming back upon men, even upon clergymen, with such power that not the Church of England itself could keep it out. Here my activity as a Socialist had placed me on sure and familiar ground. To me the members of the Guild of St Matthew (see page 118) were no more "High Church clergymen," Dr [John] Clifford [1836–1923] no more "an eminent Nonconformist divine," than I was to them "an infidel." There is only one religion, though there are a hundred versions of it. We all had the same thing to say; and though some of us cleared our throats to say it by singing revolutionary lyrics and republican hymns, we thought nothing of singing them to the music of [Arthur] Sullivan's *Onward Christian Soldiers* or Haydn's *God Preserve the Emperor*.

Now unity, however desirable in political agitations, is fatal to drama; for every drama must present a conflict. The end may be reconciliation or destruction; or, as in life itself, there may be no end; but the conflict is indispensable: no conflict, no drama. Certainly it is easy to dramatize the prosaic conflict of Christian Socialism with vulgar Unsocialism: for instance, in *Widowers' Houses*, the clergyman, who does not appear on the stage at all, is the real antagonist of the slum landlord. But the obvious conflicts of unmistakeable good with unmistakeable evil can only supply the crude drama of villain and hero, in which some absolute point of view is taken, and the dissentients are treated by the dramatist as enemies to be piously glorified or indignantly vilified. In such cheap wares I do not deal. Even in my unpleasant propagandist plays I have allowed every person his or her own point of view, and have, I hope, to the full extent of my understanding of him, been as sympathetic with Sir George Crofts [a character in *Mrs Warren's Profession*] as with any of the more genial and popular characters in the present volume.

*[Shaw explains that art helps "the common man" understand his spiritual evolutionary purpose, but the artists who create it can't explain their genius other than through their art.]*

...Let Ibsen explain, if he can, why the building of churches and happy homes is not the ultimate destiny of Man, and why, to thrill the unsatisfied younger generations, he must mount beyond it to heights that now seem unspeakably giddy and dreadful to him, and from which the first climbers must fall and dash themselves to pieces. He cannot explain it: he can only shew it to you as a vision in the magic glass of his artwork; so that you may catch his presentiment and make what you can of it. And this is the function that raises dramatic art above imposture and pleasure hunting, and enables the playwright to be something more than a skilled liar and pandar.

Here, then, was the higher but vaguer and timider vision, the incoherent, mischievous, and even ridiculous unpracticalness, which offered me a dramatic antagonist for the clear, bold, sure, sensible, benevolent, salutarily shortsighted Christian Socialist idealism. I availed myself of it in *Candida*, the drunken scene in which has been much appreciated, I am told, in Aberdeen. I purposely contrived the play in such a way as to make the expenses of representation insignificant; so that, without pretending that I could appeal to a very wide circle of playgoers, I could reasonably sound a few of our more enlightened managers as to an experiment with half a dozen afternoon performances. They admired the play generously: indeed I think that if any of them had been young enough to play the poet, my proposal might have been acceded to, in spite of many incidental difficulties. Nay, if only I had made the poet a cripple, or at least blind, so as to combine an easier disguise with a larger claim for sympathy, something might have been done. Richard Mansfield [1854–1907, English actor-manager who emigrated to America], who had, with apparent ease, made me quite famous in America by his productions of my plays, went so far as to put the play actually into rehearsal before he would confess himself beaten by the physical difficulties of the part. But they did beat him; and *Candida* did not see the footlights until my old ally the Independent Theatre, making a propagandist tour through the Provinces with *A Doll's House*, added *Candida* to its repertory, to the great astonishment of its audiences.

In an idle moment in 1895 I began the little scene called *The Man of Destiny*, which is hardly more than a bravura piece to display the virtuosity of the two principal performers.

In the meantime I had devoted the spare moments of 1896 to the composition of two more plays, only the first of which appears in this volume. *You Never Can Tell* was an attempt to comply with many requests for a play in which the much paragraphed "brilliancy" of *Arms and the Man* should be tempered by some consideration for the requirements of managers in search of fashionable comedies for West End theatres. I had no difficulty in complying, as I have always cast my plays in the ordinary practical comedy form in use at all the theatres; and far from taking an unsympathetic view of the popular preference for fun, fashionable dresses, a little music, and even an exhibition of eating and drinking by people with an expensive air, attended by an if-possible-comic waiter, I was more than willing to shew that the drama can humanize these things as easily as they, in the wrong hands, can dehumanize the drama. But as often happens it was easier to do this than to persuade those who had asked for it that they had indeed got it. A chapter in Cyril Maude's [1862–1951, English actor-manager] history of the Haymarket Theatre records how the play was rehearsed there, and why I withdrew it. And so I reached the point at which, as narrated in the preface to the *Unpleasant* volume, I resolved to avail myself of my literary expertness to put my plays before the public in my own way.

It will be noticed that I have not been driven to this expedient by any hostility on the part of our managers. I will not pretend that the modern actor-manager's talent as player can in the nature of things be often associated with exceptional critical insight. As a rule, by the time a manager has experience enough to make him as safe a judge of plays as a Bond Street [expensive London shopping district] dealer is of pictures he begins to be thrown out in his calculations by the slow but constant change of public taste, and by his own growing conservatism. But his need for new plays is so great, and the few accredited authors are so little able to keep pace with their commissions, that he is always apt to over-rate rather than to underrate his discoveries in the way of new pieces by new authors. An original work by a man of genius like Ibsen may, of course, baffle him as it baffles many professed critics; but in the beaten path of drama no unacted works of merit, suitable to his purposes, have been discovered; whereas the production, at great expense, of very faulty plays written by novices (not "backers") is by no means an unknown event. Indeed, to anyone who can estimate, even vaguely, the complicated trouble, the risk of heavy loss, and the initial expense and thought, involved by the production of a play, the ease with which dramatic authors, known and unknown, get their works performed must needs seem a wonder.

Only, authors must not expect managers to invest many thousands of pounds in plays, however fine (or the reverse), which will clearly not attract perfectly commonplace people. Playwriting and theatrical management, on the present commercial basis, are businesses like other businesses, depending on the patronage of great numbers of very ordinary customers. When the managers and authors study the wants of these customers, they succeed: when they do not, they fail. A public-spirited manager, or an author with a keen artistic conscience, may choose to pursue his business with the minimum of profit and the maximum of social usefulness by keeping as close as he can to the highest marketable limit of quality, and constantly feeling for an extension of that limit through the advance of popular culture. An unscrupulous manager or author may aim simply at the maximum of profit with the minimum of risk. These are the opposite poles of our system, represented in practice by our first rate managements at the one end, and the syndicates which exploit pornographic farces at the other. Between them there is plenty of room for most talents to breathe freely: at all events there is a career, no harder of access than any cognate career, for all qualified playwrights who bring the manager what his customers want and understand, or even enough of it to induce them to swallow at the same time a great deal that they neither want nor understand; for the public is touchingly humble in such matters.

For all that, the commercial limits are too narrow for our social welfare. The theatre is growing in importance as a social organ. Bad theatres are as mischievous as bad schools or bad churches; for modern civilization is rapidly multiplying the class to which the theatre is both school and church. Public and private life become daily more theatrical: the modern Kaiser, Dictator, President or Prime Minister is nothing if not an effective actor; all newspapers are now edited histrionically; and the records of our law courts shew that the stage is affecting personal conduct to an unprecedented extent, and affecting it by no means for the worse, except in so far as the theatrical education of the persons concerned has been romantic: that is, spurious, cheap, and vulgar. The truth is that dramatic invention is the first effort of man to become intellectually conscious. No frontier can be marked between drama and history or religion, or between acting and conduct, nor any distinction made between them that is not also the distinction between the masterpieces of the great dramatic poets and the commonplaces of our theatrical seasons. When this chapter of science is convincingly written, the national importance of the theatre will be as unquestioned as that of the army, the fleet, the Church, the law, and the schools.

For my part, I have no doubt that the commercial limits should be overstepped, and that the highest prestige, with a financial position of reasonable security and comfort, should be attainable in theatrical management by keeping the public in constant touch with the highest achievements of dramatic art. Our managers will not dissent to this: the best of them are so willing to get as near that position as they can without ruining themselves, that they can all point to honorable losses incurred through aiming "over the heads of the public," and will no doubt risk such loss again, for the sake of their reputation as artists, as soon as a few popular successes enable them to afford it. But even if it were possible for them to educate the nation at their own private cost, why should they be expected to do it? There are much stronger objections to the pauperization of the public by private doles than were ever entertained, even by the Poor Law Commissioners of 1834 [in a report to British Parliament on the state of public charity in Britain], to the pauperization of private individuals by public doles. If we want a theatre which shall be to the drama what the National Gallery and British Museum are to painting and literature, we can get it by endowing it in the same way. In the meantime there are many possibilities of local activity. Groups of amateurs can form permanent societies and persevere until they develop into professional companies in established repertory theatres. In big cities it should be feasible to form influential committees, preferably without any actors, critics, or playwrights on them, and with as many persons of title as possible, for the purpose of approaching one of the leading local managers with a proposal that they shall, under a guarantee against loss, undertake a certain number of afternoon performances of the class required by the committee, in addition to their ordinary business. If the committee is influential enough, the offer will be accepted. In that case, the first performance will be the beginning of a classic repertory for the manager and his company which every subsequent performance will extend. The formation of the repertory will go hand in hand with the discovery and habituation of a regular audience for it; and it will eventually become profitable for the manager to multiply the number of performances at his own risk. It might even become worth his while to take a second theatre and establish the repertory permanently in it. In the event of any of his classic productions proving a fashionable success, he could transfer it to his fashionable house and make the most of it there. Such managership would carry a knighthood with it; and such a theatre would be the needed nucleus for municipal or national endowment. I make the suggestion quite disinterestedly; for as I am not an academic person, I should not be welcomed as an unacted classic by such a committee; and cases like mine would still leave forlorn hopes like The Independent Theatre its reason for existing. The committee plan, I may remind its critics, has been in operation in London for two hundred years in support of Italian opera.

Returning now to the actual state of things, it is clear that I have no grievance against our theatres. Knowing quite well what I was doing, I have heaped difficulties in the way of the performance of my plays by ignoring the majority of the manager's customers: nay, by positively making war on them. To the actor I have been more considerate, using all my cunning to enable him to make the most of his technical methods; but I have not hesitated on occasion to tax his intelligence very severely, making the stage effect depend not only on nuances of execution quite beyond the average skill produced by the routine of the English stage in its present condition, but on a perfectly sincere and straightforward conception of states of mind which still seem cynically perverse to most people, and on a goodhumoredly contemptuous or profoundly pitiful attitude towards ethical conventions which seem to them validly heroic or venerable. It is inevitable that actors should suffer more than most of us from the sophistication of their consciousness by romance; and my view of romance as the great heresy to be swept off from art and life—as the food of modern pessimism and the bane of modern self-respect, is far more puzzling to the performers than it is to the pit. It is hard for an actor whose point of honor it is to be a perfect gentleman, to sympathize with an author who regards gentility as a dishonest folly, and gallantry and chivalry as treasonable to women and stultifying to men.

The misunderstanding is complicated by the fact that actors, in their demonstrations of emotion, have made a second nature of stage custom, which is often very much out of date as a representation of contemporary life. Sometimes the stage custom is not only obsolete, but fundamentally wrong: for instance, in the simple case of laughter and tears, in which it deals too liberally, it is certainly not based on the fact, easily enough discoverable in real life, that we only cry now in the effort to bear happiness, whilst we laugh and exult in destruction, confusion, and ruin. When a comedy is performed, it is nothing to me that the spectators laugh: any fool can make an audience laugh. I want to see how many of them, laughing or grave, are in the melting mood. And this result cannot be achieved, even by actors who thoroughly understand my purpose, except through an artistic beauty of execution unattainable without long and arduous practice, and an intellectual effort which my plays probably do not seem serious enough to call forth.

Beyond the difficulties thus raised by the nature and quality of my work, I have none to complain of. I have come upon no ill will, no inaccessibility, on the part of the very few managers with whom I have discussed it. As a rule I find that the actor-manager is over-sanguine, because he has the artist's habit of underrating the force of circumstances and exaggerating the power of the talented individual to prevail against them; whilst I have acquired the politician's habit of regarding the individual, however talented, as having no choice but to make the most of his circumstances. I half suspect that those managers who have had most to do with me, if asked to name the main obstacle to the performance of my plays, would unhesitatingly and unanimously reply "The author." And I confess that though as a matter of business I wish my plays to be performed, as a matter of instinct I fight against the inevitable misrepresentation of them with all the subtlety needed to conceal my ill will from myself as well as from the manager.

The main difficulty, of course, is the incapacity for serious drama of thousands of playgoers of all classes whose shillings and half guineas will buy as much in the market as if they delighted in the highest art. But with them I must frankly take the superior position. I know that many managers are wholly dependent on them, and that no manager is wholly independent of them; but I can no more write what they want than [Joseph] Joachim [1831–1907, virtuoso violinist] can put aside his fiddle and oblige a happy company of beanfeasters [slang for merrymakers] with a marching tune on the German concertina [accordion-like instrument]. They must keep away from my plays: that is all.

There is no reason, however, why I should take this haughty attitude towards those representative critics whose complaint is that my talent, though not unentertaining, lacks elevation of sentiment and seriousness of purpose. They can find, under the surface-brilliancy for which they give me credit, no coherent thought or sympathy, and accuse me, in various terms and degrees, of an inhuman and freakish wantonness; of preoccupation with "the seamy side of life"; of paradox, cynicism, and eccentricity, reducible, as some contend, to a trite formula of treating bad as good and good as bad, important as trivial and trivial as important, serious as laughable and laughable as serious, and so forth. As to this formula I can only say that if any gentleman is simple enough to think that even a good comic opera can be produced by it, I invite him to try his hand, and see whether anything resembling one of my plays will reward him.

I could explain the matter easily enough if I chose; but the result would be that the people who misunderstand the plays would misunderstand the explanation ten times more. The particular exceptions taken are seldom more than symptoms of the underlying fundamental disagreement between the romantic morality of the critics and the natural morality of the plays. For example, I am quite aware that the much criticized Swiss officer in *Arms and the Man* is not a conventional stage soldier. He suffers from want of food and sleep; his nerves go to pieces after three days under fire, ending in the horrors of a rout and pursuit; he has found by experience that it is more important to have a few bits of chocolate to eat in the field than cartridges for his revolver. When many of my critics rejected these circumstances as fantastically improbable and cynically unnatural, it was not necessary to argue them into common sense: all I had to do was to brain them, so to speak, with the first half dozen military authorities at hand, beginning with the present Commander in Chief [Lord Wolseley; see page 88]. But when it proved that such unromantic (but all the more dramatic) facts implied to them a denial of the existence of courage, patriotism, faith, hope, and charity, I saw that it was not really mere matter of fact that was at issue between us. One strongly Liberal critic, the late [William] Moy Thomas [1828–1910], who had, in the teeth of a chorus of dissent, received my first play [*Widowers' Houses*] with the most generous encouragement, declared, when *Arms and the Man* was produced, that I had struck a wanton blow at the cause of liberty in the Balkan Peninsula by mentioning that it was not a matter of course for a Bulgarian in 1885 to wash his hands every day. He no doubt saw soon afterwards the squabble, reported all through Europe, between Stambouloff and an eminent lady of the Bulgarian court who took exception to his neglect of his fingernails. After that came the news of his ferocious assassination, with a description of the room prepared for the reception of visitors by his widow, who draped it with black, and decorated it with photographs of the mutilated body of her husband. Here was a sufficiently sensational confirmation of the accuracy of my sketch of the theatrical nature of the first apings of western civilization by spirited races just emerging from slavery. But it had no bearing on the real issue between my critic and myself, which was, whether the political and religious idealism which had inspired [William Ewart] Gladstone [1809–98, British Liberal politician and four-time Prime Minister] to call for the rescue of these Balkan principalities from the despotism of the Turk, and converted miserably enslaved provinces into hopeful and gallant little States, will survive the general onslaught on idealism which is implicit, and indeed explicit, in *Arms and the Man* and the naturalist plays of the modern school. For my part I hope not; for idealism, which is only a flattering name for romance in politics and morals, is as obnoxious to me as romance in ethics or religion. In spite of a Liberal Revolution or two, I can no longer be satisfied with fictitious morals and fictitious good conduct, shedding fictitious glory on robbery, starvation, disease, crime, drink, war, cruelty, cupidity, and all the other commonplaces of civilization which drive men to the theatre to make foolish pretences that such things are progress, science, morals, religion, patriotism, imperial supremacy, national greatness and all the other names the newspapers call them. On the other hand, I see plenty of good in the world working itself out as fast as the idealists will allow it; and if they would only let it alone and learn to respect reality, which would include the beneficial exercise of respecting themselves, and incidentally respecting me, we should all get along much better and faster. At all events, I do not see moral chaos and anarchy as the alternative to romantic convention; and I am not going to pretend I do merely to please the people who are convinced that the world is held together only by the force of unanimous, strenuous, eloquent, trumpet-tongued lying. To me the tragedy and comedy of life lie in the consequences, sometimes terrible, sometimes ludicrous, of our persistent attempts to found our institutions on the ideals suggested to our imaginations by our half-satisfied passions, instead of on a genuinely scientific natural history. And with that hint as to what I am driving at, I withdraw and ring up the curtain.

## 4. From the Preface to *Three Plays by Brieux*, 1913.

*[Eugène Brieux (1858–1932) was a French naturalist playwright, whose plays dealt frankly with social issues like syphilis and birth control.* Shaw's *wife, Charlotte Payne-Townshend (1857–1943)* translated Maternity *for this volume, St John Hankin (1869–1909)* translated The Three Daughters of M. Dupont, *(Sir Frederick) John Pollock (1878–1963) contributed translations of* Damaged Goods *and another version of* Maternity, *and Shaw provided the preface.]*

### From Molière to Brieux.

After the death of Ibsen, Brieux confronted Europe as the most important dramatist west of Russia. In that kind of comedy which is so true to life that we have to call it tragicomedy, and which is not only an entertainment but a history and a criticism of contemporary morals, he is incomparably the greatest writer France has produced since Molière. The French critics who take it for granted that no contemporary of theirs could possibly be greater than [Pierre-Augustin] Beaumarchais [1732–99, author of the Figaro plays] are really too modest. They have never read Beaumarchais, and therefore do not know how very little of him there is to read, and how, out of the two variations he wrote on his once famous theme, the second is only a petition in artistic and intellectual bankruptcy. Had the French theatre been capable of offering a field to [French realist novelist, Honoré de] Balzac [1799–1850], my proposition might have to be modified. But as it was no more able to do that than the English theatre was to enlist the genius of Dickens, I may say confidently that in that great comedy which Balzac called 'the comedy of humanity,' to be played for the amusement of the gods rather than for that of the French public, there is no summit in the barren plain that stretches from Mount Molière to our own times until we reach Brieux.

## How the XIX century found itself out.

It is reserved for some great critic to give us a study of the psychology of the XIX century. Those of us who as adults saw it face to face in that last moiety of its days when one fierce hand after another—[German economist philosopher Karl] Marx's [1818–83], [French naturalist writer Émile] Zola's [1840–1902], Ibsen's, Strindberg's, [Russian realist writer Ivan] Turgenief's [Turgenev, 1818–83], Tolstoy's—stripped its masks off and revealed it as, on the whole, perhaps the most villainous page of recorded human history, can also recall the strange confidence with which it regarded itself as the very summit of civilization, and talked of the past as a cruel gloom that had been dispelled for ever by the railway and the electric telegraph. But centuries, like men, begin to find themselves out in middle age....

In this new phase we see the bourgeoisie, after a century and a half of complacent vaunting of its own probity and modest happiness (begun by Daniel Defoe [1660–1731] in Robinson Crusoe's praises of 'the middle station of life'), suddenly turning bitterly on itself with accusations of hideous sexual and commercial corruption. Thackeray's campaign against snobbery and Dickens's against hypocrisy were directed against the vices of respectable men; but now even the respectability was passionately denied: the bourgeois was depicted as a thief, a tyrant, a sweater, a selfish voluptuary whose marriages were simple legalizations of unbridled licentiousness. Sexual irregularities began to be attributed to the sympathetic characters in fiction not as the blackest spots in their portraits, but positively as redeeming humanities in them. ...

## Zolaism as a Superstition.

It is, unfortunately, much easier to throw the forces of art into a reaction than to recall them when the reaction has gone far enough. ...The men who trained themselves as writers by dragging the unmentionable to light, presently found that they could do that so much better than anything else that they gave up dealing with the other subjects. Even their quite mentionable episodes had an unmentionable air. Their imitators assumed that unmentionability was an end in itself—that to be decent was to be out of the movement. Zola and Ibsen could not, of course, be confined to mere reaction against taboo. Ibsen was to the last fascinating and full of a strange moving beauty; and Zola often broke into sentimental romance. But neither Ibsen nor Zola, after they once took in hand the work of unmasking the idols of the bourgeoisie, ever again wrote a happy or pleasant play or novel....

## The Passing of the Tragic Catastrophe and the Happy Ending.

Not only is the tradition of the catastrophe unsuitable to modern studies of life: the tradition of an ending, happy or the reverse, is equally unworkable. The moment the dramatist gives up accidents and catastrophes, and takes 'slices of life' as his material, he finds himself committed to plays that have no endings. The curtain no longer comes down on a hero slain or married: it comes down when the audience has seen enough of the life presented to it to draw the moral, and must either leave the theatre or miss its last train.

The man who faced France with a drama fulfilling all these conditions was Brieux. He was as scientific, as conscientious, as unflinching as Zola without being in the least morbid. He was no more dependent on horrors than Molière, and as sane in his temper. He threw over the traditional forced catastrophe uncompromisingly. You do not go away from a Brieux play with the feeling that the affair is finished or the problem solved for you by the dramatist. Still less do you go away in 'that happy, easy, ironically indulgent frame of mind that is the true test of comedy', as Mr. Walkley put it in *The Times* of the 1st October 1909. You come away with a very disquieting sense that you are involved in the affair, and must find the way out of it for yourself and everybody else if civilization is to be tolerable to your sense of honor.

## The Difference between Brieux and Molière or Shakespear.

...The reason why Shakespear and Molière are always well spoken of and recommended to the young is that their quarrel is really a quarrel with God for not making men better. If they had quarrelled with a specified class of persons with incomes of four figures for not doing their work better, or for doing no work at all, they would be denounced as seditious, impious, and profligate corruptors of morality.

Brieux wastes neither ink nor indignation on Providence.... His fisticuffs are not aimed heavenward: they fall on human noses for the good of human souls. When he sees human nature in conflict with a political abuse he does not blame human nature, knowing that such blame is the favorite trick of those who wish to perpetuate the abuse without being able to defend it. He does not even blame the abuse: he exposes it, and then leaves human nature to tackle it with its eyes open. And his method of exposure is the dramatic method. He is a born dramatist... The conflict which inspires his dramatic genius must be a big one and a real one. To ask an audience to spend three hours hanging on the question of which particular man some particular woman shall mate with does not strike him as a reasonable proceeding; and if the audience does not agree with him, why, it can go to some fashionable dramatist of the boulevard who does agree with it....

## The Pedantry of Paris.

...Commercially, the classic play was supplanted by a nuisance which was not a failure: to wit, the 'well made play' of Scribe and his school. The manufacture of well made plays is not an art: it is an industry. It is not at all hard for a literary mechanic to acquire it: the only difficulty is to find a literary mechanic who is not by nature too much of an artist for the job; for nothing spoils a well made play more infallibly than the least alloy of high art or the least qualm of conscience on the part of the writer. 'Art for art's sake' is the formula of the well made play, meaning in practice 'Success for money's sake.' Now great art is never produced for its own sake. It is too difficult to be worth the effort. All the great artists enter into a terrible struggle with the public, often involving bitter poverty and personal humiliation, and always involving calumny and persecution, because they believe they are apostles doing what used to be called the Will of God, and is now called by many prosaic names, of which 'public work' is the least controversial. And when these artists have travailed and brought forth, and at last forced the public to associate keen pleasure and deep interest with their methods and morals, a crowd of smaller men—art confectioners, we may call them—hasten to make pretty entertainments out of scraps and crumbs from the masterpieces....

But the well made play was not confectionery: it had not even the derived virtue of being borrowed from the great playwrights. Its formula grew up in the days when the spread of elementary schooling produced a huge mass of playgoers sufficiently educated to want plays instead of dog-fights, but not educated enough to enjoy or understand the masterpieces of dramatic art. Besides, education or no education, one cannot live on masterpieces alone, not only because there are not enough of them, but because new plays as well as great plays are needed, and there are not enough Molières and Shakespears in the world to keep the demand for novelty satisfied. Hence it has always been necessary to have some formula by which men of mediocre talent and no conscience can turn out plays for the theatrical market. Such men have written melodramas since the theatre existed. It was in the XIX century that the demand for manufactured plays was extended to drawing room plays in which the Forest of Bondy and the Auberge des Adrets, the Red Barn and the Cave at Midnight [rural settings in popular melodramas], had to be replaced by Lord Blank's flat in Whitehall Court [upscale urban London location] and the Great Hall, Chevy Chace. Playgoers, being by that time mostly poor playgoers, wanted to see how the rich live; wanted to see them actually drinking champagne and wearing real fashionable dresses and trousers with a neatly ironed crease down the knee.

## How to Write a Popular Play.

The formula for the well made play is so easy that I give it for the benefit of any reader who feels tempted to try his hand at making the fortune that awaits all successful manufacturers in this line. First, you 'have an idea' for a dramatic situation. If it strikes you as a splendidly original idea whilst it is in fact as old as the hills, so much the better. For instance, the situation of an innocent person convicted by circumstances of a crime may always be depended on. If the person is a woman, she must be convicted of adultery. If a young officer, he must be convicted of selling information to the enemy, though it is really a fascinating female spy who has ensnared him and stolen the incriminating document. If the innocent wife, banished from her home, suffers agonies through her separation from her children, and, when one of them is dying (of any disease the dramatist chooses to inflict), disguises herself as a nurse and attends it through its dying convulsion until the doctor, who should be a serio-comic character, and if possible a faithful old admirer of the lady's, simultaneously announces the recovery of the child and the discovery of the wife's innocence, the success of the play may be regarded as assured if the writer has any sort of knack for his work. Comedy is more difficult, because it requires a sense of humor and a good deal of vivacity; but the process is essentially the same: it is the manufacture of a misunderstanding. Having manufactured it, you place its culmination at the end of the last act but one, which is the point at which the manufacture of the play begins. Then you make your first act out of the necessary introduction of the characters to the audience, after elaborate explanations, mostly conducted by servants, solicitors, and other low life personages (the principals must all be dukes and colonels and millionaires), of how the misunderstanding is going to come about. Your last act consists, of course, of clearing up the misunderstanding, and generally getting the audience out of the theatre as best you can.

Now please do not misunderstand me as pretending that this process is so mechanical that it offers no opportunity for the exercise of talent. On the contrary, it is so mechanical that without very conspicuous talent nobody can make much reputation by doing it, though some can and do make a living at it. And this often leads the cultivated classes to suppose that all plays are written by authors of talent. As a matter of fact the majority of those who in France and England make a living by writing plays are unknown and, as to education, all but illiterate. Their names are not worth putting on the playbill, because their audiences neither know nor care who the author is, and often believe that the actors improvise the whole piece, just as they in fact do sometimes improvise the dialogue. To rise out of this obscurity you must be a Scribe or a Sardou, doing essentially the same thing, it is true, but doing it wittily and ingeniously, at moments almost poetically, and giving the persons of the drama some touches of real observed character.

## Why the Critics are always Wrong.

Now it is these strokes of talent that set the critics wrong. For the talent, being all expended on the formula, at last consecrates the formula in the eyes of the critics. Nay, they become so accustomed to the formula that at last they cannot relish or understand a play that has grown naturally, just as they cannot admire the Venus of Milo [ancient Greek statue] because she has neither a corset nor high heeled shoes. They are like the peasants who are so accustomed to food reeking with garlic that when food is served to them without it they declare that it has no taste and is not food at all.

This is the explanation of the refusal of the critics of all nations to accept great original dramatists like Ibsen and Brieux as real dramatists, or their plays as real plays. No writer of the first order needs the formula any more than a sound man needs a crutch. In his simplest mood, when he is only seeking to amuse, he does not manufacture a plot: he tells a story. He finds no difficulty in setting people on the stage to talk and act in an amusing, exciting or touching way. His characters have adventures and ideas which are interesting in themselves, and need not be fitted into the Chinese puzzle of a plot.

## The Interpreter of Life.

But the great dramatist has something better to do than to amuse either himself or his audience. He has to interpret life. This sounds a mere pious phrase of literary criticism; but a moment's consideration will discover its meaning and its exactitude. Life as it appears to us in our daily experience is an unintelligible chaos of happenings. You pass Othello in the bazaar in Aleppo, Iago on the jetty in Cyprus, and Desdemona in the nave of St. Mark's in Venice without the slightest clue to their relations to one another. The man you see stepping into a chemist's shop to buy the means of committing murder or suicide, may, for all you know, want nothing but a liver pill or a toothbrush. The statesman who has no other object than to make you vote for his party at the next election may be starting you on an incline at the foot of which lies war, or revolution, or a smallpox epidemic, or five years off your lifetime. The horrible murder of a whole family by the father who finishes by killing himself, or the driving of a young girl on to the streets, may be the result of your discharging an employee in a fit of temper a month before. To attempt to understand life from merely looking on at it as it happens in the streets is as hopeless as trying to understand public questions by studying snapshots of public demonstrations.... Life as it occurs is senseless: a policeman may watch it and work in it for thirty years in the streets and courts of Paris without learning as much of it or from it as a child or a nun may learn from a single play by Brieux. For it is the business of Brieux to pick out the significant incidents from the chaos of daily happenings, and arrange them so that their relation to one another becomes significant, thus changing us from bewildered spectators of a monstrous confusion to men intelligently conscious of the world and its destinies. This is the highest function that man can perform—the greatest work he can set his hand to; and this is why the great dramatists of the world, from Euripides and Aristophanes to Shakespear and Molière, and from them to Ibsen and Brieux, take that majestic and pontifical rank which seems so strangely above all the reasonable pretensions of mere strolling actors and theatrical authors.

## How the Great Dramatists torture the Public.

Now if the critics are wrong in supposing that the formula of the well made play is not only an indispensable factor in playwriting, but is actually the essence of the play itself—if their delusion is rebuked and confuted by the practice of every great dramatist even when he is only amusing himself by story telling, what must happen to their poor formula when it impertinently offers its services to a playwright who has taken on his supreme function as the Interpreter of Life? Not only has he no use for it; but he must attack and destroy it; for one of the very first lessons he has to teach to a play-ridden public is that the romantic conventions on which the formula proceeds are all false, and are doing incalculable harm in these days when everybody reads romances and goes to the theatre. Just as the historian can teach no real history until he has cured his readers of the romantic delusion that the greatness of a queen consists in her being a pretty woman and having her head cut off; so the playwright of the first order can do nothing with his audiences until he has cured them of looking at the stage through the keyhole and sniffing round the theatre as prurient people sniff round the divorce court. The cure is not a popular one. The public suffers from it exactly as a drunkard or a snuff taker suffers from an attempt to conquer the habit....

## 5. From "The Quintessence of Ibsenism," 1922.

*[Shaw originally drafted this essay for a series of Fabian Society lectures in 1890. It was published in 1891, and updated for a second edition in 1913 to include the plays that Ibsen had not yet written in 1891. Shaw admires Ibsen's plays for the way they expose the cherished illusions of idealists and present a more realistic image of society and human nature instead. Shaw is also eager to defend Ibsen's use of discussion in his plays, which many critics found theatrically tedious, but which Shaw sees as the proper dramatic mode for these realist characters struggling to understand and come to terms with the complexity of their situations. Not coincidentally, Shaw's plays are also frequently accused of being "all talk."]*

The English newspaper which best represented the guilty conscience of the middle class was, when Ibsen's plays reached England, *The Daily Telegraph*.... The late Clement

Scott, at that time dramatic critic to *The Daily Telegraph*, was a sentimentally goodnatured gentleman, not then a pioneer, though he had in his time fought hard for the advance in British drama represented by the plays of [Thomas William] Robertson [1829–71, one of the first English naturalist playwrights]. He was also an emotional, impressionable, zealous, and sincere Roman Catholic. He accused Ibsen of dramatic impotence, ludicrous amateurishness, nastiness, vulgarity, egotism, coarseness, absurdity, uninteresting verbosity, and "suburbanity," declaring that he has taken ideas that would have inspired a great tragic poet, and vulgarized and debased them in dull, hateful, loathesome, horrible plays. This criticism, which occurs in a notice of the first performance of *Ghosts* in England, is to be found in *The Daily Telegraph* for the 14th March 1891, and is supplemented by a leading article which compares the play to an open drain, a loathsome sore unbandaged, a dirty act done publicly, or a lazar house with all its doors and windows open. Bestial, cynical, disgusting, poisonous, sickly, delirious, indecent, loathsome, fetid, literary carrion, crapulous stuff, clinical confessions: all these epithets are used in the article as descriptive of Ibsen's work. "Realism," said the writer, "is one thing; but the nostrils of the audience must not be visibly held before a play can be stamped as true to nature. It is difficult to expose in decorous words the gross and almost putrid indecorum of this play." As the performance of *Ghosts* took place on the evening of the 13th March, and the criticism appeared next morning, it is evident that Clement Scott must have gone straight from the theatre to the newspaper office, and there, in an almost hysterical condition, penned his share of this extraordinary protest. The literary workmanship bears marks of haste and disorder, which, however, only heighten the expression of the passionate horror produced in the writer by seeing *Ghosts* on the stage. He calls on the authorities to cancel the license of the theatre, and declares that he has been exhorted to laugh at honor, to disbelieve in love, to mock at virtue, to distrust friendship, and to deride fidelity.

If this document were at all singular, it would rank as one of the curiosities of criticism, exhibiting, as it does, the most seasoned playgoer in London thrown into convulsions by a performance which was witnessed with approval, and even with enthusiasm, by many persons of approved moral and artistic conscientiousness....

How then is it that Ibsen, a Norwegian playwright of European celebrity, attracted one section of the English people so strongly that they hailed him as the greatest living dramatic poet and moral teacher, whilst another section was so revolted by his works that they described him in terms which they themselves admitted to be, by the necessities of the case, all but obscene? This phenomenon, which has occurred throughout Europe whenever Ibsen's plays have been acted, as well as in America and Australia, must be exhaustively explained before the plays can be described without danger of reproducing the same confusion in the reader's own mind. Such an explanation, therefore, must be my first business.

Understand, at the outset, that the explanation will not be an explaining away. Clement Scott's judgment did not mislead him in the least as to Ibsen's meaning. Ibsen means all that most revolted his critic. For example, in *Ghosts*, the play in question, a clergyman and a married woman fall in love with one another. The woman proposes to abandon her husband and live with the clergyman. He recalls her to her duty, and makes her behave as a virtuous woman. She afterwards tells him that this was a crime on his part. Ibsen agrees with her, and has written the play to bring you round to his opinion. Clement Scott did not agree with her, and believed that when you are brought round to her opinion you have been morally corrupted. By this conviction he was impelled to denounce Ibsen as he did, Ibsen being equally impelled to propagate the convictions which provoked the attack. Which of the two is right cannot be decided until it is ascertained whether a society of persons holding Ibsen's opinions would be higher or lower than a society holding Clement Scott's.

There are many people who cannot conceive this as an open question. To them a denunciation of any recognized practices is an incitement to unsocial conduct; and every utterance in which an assumption of the eternal validity of these practices is not implicit is a paradox. Yet all progress involves the beating of them from that position.... The point to seize is that social progress takes effect through the replacement of old institutions by new ones; and since every institution involves the recognition of the duty of conforming to it, progress must involve the repudiation of an established duty at every step. If the Englishman had not repudiated the duty of absolute obedience to his king, his political progress would have been impossible. If women had not repudiated the duty of absolute submission to their husbands, and defied public opinion as to the limits set by modesty to their education, they would never have gained the protection of the Married Women's Property Act, the municipal vote, or the power to qualify themselves as medical practitioners....

[Shaw elaborates the argument that social progress depends on men and women repudiating mindless adherence to Duty, and especially, the idealistic illusions about love, self-fulfillment, and duty that are necessary to perpetuate marriage as an institution. Next, Shaw explains that women suffer particularly in idealistic societies because the ideal woman—the Womanly Woman—is expected to sacrifice herself entirely to the needs of others. He writes, "it is not surprising that our society, being directly dominated by men, comes to regard Woman, not as an end in herself like Man, but solely as a means of ministering to his appetite. The ideal wife is one who does everything that the ideal husband likes, and nothing else. Now to treat a person as a means instead of an end is to deny that person's right to live. And to be treated as a means to such an end as

*sexual intercourse with those who deny one's right to live is insuffer-*
*able to any human being. Woman, if she dares face the fact that she*
*is being so treated, must either loathe herself or else rebel." He then*
*proceeds to discuss each of Ibsen's plays individually, and how their*
*genius derives from the way they expose and dismantle the idealistic*
*misconceptions that society is founded on.]*

...We are now prepared to learn without misgiving that a typical Ibsen play is one in which the leading lady is an unwom-
anly woman, and the villain an idealist. It follows that the
leading lady is not a heroine of the Drury Lane type; nor does
the villain forge or assassinate, since he is a villain by virtue of
his determination to do nothing wrong. Therefore readers of
Ibsen—not playgoers—have sometimes so far misconceived
him as to suppose that his villains are examples rather than
warnings, and that the mischief and ruin which attend their
actions are but the tribulations from which the soul comes
out purified as gold from the furnace....

In following this sketch of the plays written by Ibsen to il-
lustrate his thesis that the real slavery of today is slavery to
ideals of goodness, it may be that readers who have conned
Ibsen through idealist spectacles have wondered that I could
so pervert the utterances of a great poet. Indeed I know already that many of those who are most fascinated by the
poetry of the plays will plead for any explanation of them
rather than that given by Ibsen himself in the plainest terms
through the mouths of Mrs Alving [character from *Ghosts*],
Relling [character from *The Wild Duck*], and the rest. No great
writer uses his skill to conceal his meaning. ...He [Ibsen] is
so great a poet that the idealist finds himself in the dilemma
of being unable to conceive that such a genius should have
an ignoble meaning, and yet equally unable to conceive his
real meaning otherwise than as ignoble. Consequently he
misses the meaning altogether in spite of Ibsen's explicit and

circumstantial insistence on it, and proceeds to substitute a meaning congenial to his own ideal of nobility.

Ibsen's deep sympathy with his idealist figures seems to countenance this confusion. Since it is on the weaknesses of the higher types of character that idealism seizes, his most tragic examples of vanity, selfishness, folly, and failure are not vulgar villains, but men who in an ordinary novel or melodrama would be heroes....

The statement that Ibsen's plays have an immoral tendency, is, in the sense in which it is used, quite true. Immorality does not necessarily imply mischievous conduct: it implies conduct, mischievous or not, which does not conform to current ideals.... The plain working truth is that it is not only good for people to be shocked occasionally, but absolutely necessary to the progress of society that they should be shocked pretty often. But it is not good for people to be garotted occasionally, or at all. That is why it is a mistake to treat an atheist as you treat a garotter, or to put 'bad taste' on the footing of theft and murder. The need for freedom of evolution is the sole basis of toleration, the sole valid argument against Inquisitions and Censorships, the sole reason for not burning heretics and sending every eccentric person to the madhouse.

In short, our ideals, like the gods of old, are constantly demanding human sacrifices. Let none of them, says Ibsen, be placed above the obligation to prove itself worth the sacrifices it demands; and let everyone religiously refuse to sacrifice himself and others from the moment he loses his faith in the validity of the ideal.... There can be no question as to the effect likely to be produced on an individual by his conversion from the ordinary acceptance of current ideals as safe standards of conduct, to the vigilant openmindedness of Ibsen. It must at once greatly deepen the sense of moral responsibility.... What Ibsen insists on is that there is no golden rule; that conduct must justify itself by its effect upon life and not by its conformity to any rule or ideal. And since life consists in the fulfilment of the will, which is constantly growing, and cannot be fulfilled today under the conditions which secured its fulfilment yesterday, he claims afresh the old Protestant right of private judgment in questions of conduct as against all institutions, the so-called Protestant Churches themselves included.

Here I must leave the matter, merely reminding those who may think that I have forgotten to reduce Ibsenism to a formula for them, that its quintessence is that there is no formula.

## The Technical Novelty in Ibsen's Plays

It is a striking and melancholy example of the preoccupation of critics with phrases and formulas to which they have given life by taking them into the tissue of their own living minds, and which therefore seem and feel vital and important to them whilst they are to everybody else the deadest and dreariest rubbish (this is the great secret of academic dryasdust), that to this day they remain blind to a new technical factor in the art of popular stage-play making which every considerable playwright has been thrusting under their noses night after night for a whole generation. This technical factor in the play is the discussion. Formerly you had in what was called a well made play an exposition in the first act, a situation in the second, and unravelling in the third. Now you have exposition, situation, and discussion; and the discussion is the test of the playwright. The critics protest in vain. They declare that discussions are not dramatic, and that art should not be didactic. Neither the playwrights nor the public take the smallest notice of them. The discussion conquered Europe in Ibsen's *Doll's House*; and now the serious playwright recognizes in the discussion not only the main test of his highest powers, but also the real centre of his play's interest....

Now when a play is only a story of how a villain tries to separate an honest young pair of betrothed lovers; to gain the hand of the woman by calumny; and to ruin the man by forgery, murder, false witness, and other commonplaces of the *Newgate Calendar* [popular publications detailing crimes, criminals, and executions, issued by London's Newgate Prison] the introduction of a discussion would clearly be ridiculous. There is nothing for sane people to discuss.... But this sort of drama is soon exhausted by people who go often to the theatre. In twenty visits one can see every possible change rung on all the available plots and incidents out of which plays of this kind can be manufactured. The illusion of reality is soon lost: in fact it may be doubted whether any adult ever entertains it: it is only to very young children that the fairy queen is anything but an actress.... In the long run nothing can retain the interest of the playgoer after the theatre has lost its illusion for his childhood, and its glamor for his adolescence, but a constant supply of interesting plays; and this is specially true in London, where the expense and trouble of theatregoing have been raised to a point at which it is surprising that sensible people of middle age go to the theatre at all. As a matter of fact, they mostly stay at home. Now an interesting play cannot in the nature of things mean anything but a play in which problems of conduct and character of personal importance to the audience are raised and suggestively discussed.

People have a thrifty sense of taking away something from such plays: they not only have had something for their money, but they retain that something as a permanent possession. Consequently none of the commonplaces of the box office hold good of such plays. In vain does the experienced acting manager declare that people want to be amused and not preached at in the theatre; that they will not stand long speeches; that a play must not contain more than 18,000 words; that it must not begin before nine nor last beyond eleven; that there must be no politics and no religion in it; that breach of these golden rules will drive people to the variety theatres; that there must be a woman of bad character, played by a very attractive actress, in the piece; and so on and so forth. All these counsels are valid for plays in which there is nothing to discuss. They may be disregarded by the playwright who is a moralist and a debater as well as a dramatist. From him, within the inevitable limits set by the clock and by the physical endurance of the human frame, people will stand anything as soon as they are matured enough and cultivated enough to be susceptible to the appeal of his particular form of art. The difficulty at present is that mature and cultivated people do not go to the theatre, just as they do not read penny novelets; and when an attempt is made to cater for them they do not respond to it in time, partly because they have not the habit of playgoing, and partly because it takes too long for them to find out that the new theatre is not like all the other theatres. But when they do at last find their way there, the attraction is not the firing of blank cartridges at one another by actors, nor the pretence of falling down dead that ends the stage combat, nor the simulation of erotic thrills by a pair of stage lovers, nor any of the other tomfooleries called action, but the exhibition and discussion of the character and conduct of stage figures who are made to appear real by the art of the playwright and the performers....

Accordingly, we now have plays, including some of my own, which begin with discussion and end with action, and others in which the discussion interpenetrates the action from beginning to end. When Ibsen invaded England discussion had vanished from the stage; and women could not write plays. Within twenty years women were writing better plays than men; and these plays were passionate arguments from beginning to end. The action of such plays consists of a case to be argued. If the case is uninteresting or stale or badly conducted or obviously trumped up, the play is a bad one. If it is important and novel and convincing, or at least disturbing, the play is a good one. But anyhow the play in which there is no argument and no case no longer counts as serious drama. It may still please the child in us as Punch and Judy does; but nobody nowadays pretends to regard the well made play as anything more than a commercial product which is not in question when modern schools of serious drama are under discussion. Indeed within ten years of the production of *A Doll's House* in London, audiences had become so derisive of the more obvious and hackneyed features of the methods of Sardou that it became dangerous to resort to them; and playwrights who persisted in 'constructing' plays in the old French manner lost ground not for lack of ideas, but because their technique was unbearably out of fashion.

In the new plays, the drama arises through a conflict of unsettled ideals rather than through vulgar attachments, rapacities, generosities, resentments, ambitions, misunderstandings, oddities and so forth as to which no moral question is raised. The conflict is not between clear right and wrong: the villain is as conscientious as the hero, if not more so: in fact, the question which makes the play interesting (when it is interesting) is which is the villain and which the hero. Or, to put it another way, there are no villains and no heroes. This strikes the critics mainly as a departure from dramatic art; but it is really the inevitable return to nature which ends all the merely technical fashions. Now the natural is mainly the everyday; and its climaxes must be, if not everyday, at least everylife, if they are to have any importance for the spectator.

...

Hence a cry has arisen that the post-Ibsen play is not a play, and that its technique, not being the technique described by Aristotle, is not a technique at all.... But... the new technique is new only on the modern stage. It has been used by preachers and orators ever since speech was invented. It is the technique of playing upon the human conscience; and it has been practised by the playwright whenever the playwright has been capable of it. Rhetoric, irony, argument, paradox, epigram, parable, the rearrangement of haphazard facts into orderly and intelligent situations: these are both the oldest and the newest arts of the drama; and your plot construction and art of preparation are only the tricks of theatrical talent and the shifts of moral sterility, not the weapons of dramatic genius. In the theatre of Ibsen we are not flattered spectators killing an idle hour with an ingenious and amusing entertainment: we are 'guilty creatures sitting at a play'; and the technique of pastime is no more applicable than at a murder trial.

The technical novelties of the Ibsen and post-Ibsen plays are, then: first, the introduction of the discussion and its development until it so overspreads and interpenetrates the action that it finally assimilates it, making play and discussion practically identical; and, second, as a consequence of making the spectators themselves the persons of the drama, and the incidents of their own lives its incidents, the disuse of the old stage tricks by which audiences had to be induced to take an interest in unreal people and improbable circumstances, and the substitution of a forensic technique of recrimination, disillusion, and penetration through ideals to the truth, with a free use of all the rhetorical and lyrical arts of the orator, the preacher, the pleader, and the rhapsodist.

## Needed: An Ibsen Theatre

It must now be plain to my readers that the doctrine taught by Ibsen can never be driven home from the stage whilst his plays are presented to us in haphazard order at the commercial theatres. Indeed our commercial theatres are so well aware of this that they have from the first regarded Ibsen as hopelessly uncommercial: he might as well never have lived as far as they are concerned. Even the new advanced theatres which now deal freely with what I have called post-Ibsenist plays hardly meddle with him. Had it not been for the great national service disinterestedly rendered by Mr William Archer in giving us a complete translation of Ibsen's plays (a virtually unremunerated public service which I hope the State will recognize fitly), Ibsen would be less known in England than [Swedish mystical theologican and philosopher Emanuel] Swedenborg [1688–1772, whose writings influenced many important writers and cultural figures]. By losing his vital contribution to modern thought we are losing ground relatively to the countries which, like Germany, have made his works familiar to their playgoers....

But I think Ibsen has proved the right of the drama to take scriptural rank, and his own right to canonical rank as one of the major prophets of the modern Bible. The sooner we recognize that rank and give up the idea of trying to make a fashionable entertainment of his plays the better. It ends in our not performing them at all, and remaining in barbarous and dangerous ignorance of the case against idealism. We want a frankly doctrinal theatre. There is no more reason for making a doctrinal theatre inartistic than for putting a cathedral organ out of tune: indeed all experience shews that doctrine alone nerves us to the effort called for by the greatest art. I therefore suggest that even the sciolists [those with only superficial knowledge] and voluptuaries who care for nothing in art but its luxuries and its executive feats are as strongly interested in the establishment of such a theatre as those for whom the What is always more important than the How, if only because the How cannot become really magical until such magic is indispensable to the revelation of an all-important What....

For this sort of enterprise an endowment is necessary, because commercial capital is not content in a theatre with reasonable interest: it demands great gains even at the cost of great hazards. Besides, nobody will endow mere pleasure, whereas doctrine can always command endowment. It is the foolish disclaiming of doctrine that keeps dramatic art unendowed. When we ask for an endowed theatre we always take the greatest pains to assure everybody that we do not mean anything unpleasantly serious, and that our endowed theatre will be as bright and cheery (meaning as low and common) as the commercial theatres. As a result of which we get no endowment. When we have the sense to profit by this lesson and promise that our endowed theatre will be an important place, and that it will make people of low tastes and tribal or commercial ideas horribly uncomfortable by its efforts to bring conviction of sin to them, we shall get endowment as easily as the religious people who are not foolishly ashamed to ask for what they want.

## 6. From "The Need for Expert Opinion in Sexual Reform," 1929. [*Platform and Pulpit*, pp. 200–7]

*[Shaw delivered this address before the third International Congress of the World League for Sexual Reform, held in London. The World League for Sexual Reform was founded by German activist physician Magnus Hirschfield (1868–1935) and flourished in the 1920s before being crushed by Nazis in the early 1930s.]*

...There are two effects to be considered in any definite measure of sexual reform. There is the psychological effect, and there is the political effect. Now, it is on the psychological side that I wish to speak tonight, because I am speaking as an expert. [*Laughter.*] [*The audience's response is included in Shaw's original.*] I do not in the least know why that remark of mine has elicited laughter; but as a matter of fact I am an expert in sex appeal. What I mean is that I am a playwright. I am connected with the theatre. The theatre is continually occupied with sex appeal. It has to deal in sex appeal exactly as a costermonger has to deal in turnips; and a costermonger's opinion on turnips is worth having. He is an expert. In the same way the opinion of playwrights and other theatre people is worth having because they know how the thing is done through having to do it as part of their daily work.

One very important function of the theatre in society is to educate the audience in matters of sex. Besides the people who take that duty seriously there are those who only exploit sex appeal commercially. But no matter, they all have to know how to do it, because if their sex appeal fails, they lose money; and you can hardly call any man a real expert unless he loses money if his practice happens to be wrong.

And yet when sex appeal has to be discussed scientifically nobody ever calls in the playwright, and he himself does not come forward without an invitation. But the priest always rushes in and demands to be accepted as an authority on sex. Well, if he went behind the scenes of a theatre and made such a claim, we should say: "Mind your own business. This evidently is the one subject about which you as a celibate can know nothing. If you attempt to meddle with it you will make literally an unholy mess of it!"

However, there is always a certain tendency to go to the man who knows nothing about it, because we are always a little afraid that if we consult a genuine expert his opinion will go against us.

The Pope represents the priest in this matter. The Pope is the Chief Priest of Europe, and he speaks very strongly on the subject of sex appeal. I, of course, should never dream of appealing in that matter to the Chief Priest of Europe, but if there were such a person as the Chief Prostitute of Europe I should call her in immediately. I should say: "Here, clearly, is a person who deals professionally in sex appeal, and will lose her livelihood if her method is wrong. She can speak to us with authority."

Unfortunately, or fortunately, just as you choose to look at it, there is no such person as the Chief Prostitute of Europe to balance the Chief Priest, which is perhaps the reason that the priest's opinion gets heard whilst the prostitute's opinion is not heard. Therefore it is that I proffer myself as being the next best authority to the prostitute, that is to say, the playwright.

I find myself up against two sets of amateurs. One set seeks to minimize sex appeal by a maximum of clothing. The other seeks to maximize sex appeal by a minimum of clothing. I come in as an expert and tell them that they are both hopelessly and completely wrong. If you want sex appeal raised to the utmost point, there is only one way of doing it, and that is by clothes. In hot climates the purpose of clothing must have been sex appeal and not protection from the inclemency of the weather, because in such places the weather tempts people to take off their clothes instead of to put them on.

...Being a born artist I have always been specially impressionable by sex. My first impressions were derived from the Victorian women. The Victorian woman was a masterpiece of sex appeal. She was sex appeal from the top of her head to the sole of her feet. She was clothed, of course, from head to foot: all clothes! Everything about her except her cheeks and her nose was a guilty secret, a thing you had to guess at. All young men and boys then thrilled with the magic and mystery of the invisible world under those clothes. In the Christmas pantomime the call-boy [stagehand] always played the Old Woman in the harlequinade, and the one unfailing joke was when the old woman, in scrambling over a wall, shewed one leg with its white stocking visible up to the knee. Then the whole house shrieked and rocked and roared with laughter. A modern London audience, which sees a hundred thousand stockings every day, would hardly see the joke.

When you turned from the ridiculous call-boy dressed as a woman to the real lady, the way she was dressed was like the temptation of St Anthony. They did not dress her: they upholstered her. That is the only word. Every contour, all her

contours, all four of them, may I say, were voluptuously em-
phasized. When the lady herself could not emphasize them
sufficiently by her own person, artificial aids were introduced.
She fitted on her breasts little wire-cages which were called
palpitators. She had, of course, the bustle which gave the
Hottentot [archaic term now offensive, referring to Saartje
Baartman, the Khoikhoi woman with large buttocks who was
displayed as "the Hottentot Venus"] outline. I really think if
I could exhibit here one of the ordinary portraits of the fashionable woman of that day, you would be shocked. But if you
stopped to think "What is the woman like?" you would see
that the idea was to conceal the fact that she was a human
being and make her like a very attractive and luxurious sofa.
It was done by clothing, and could not have been done by
any other means. And every woman knew that. Every actress
knew that. Those actresses of the French stage who made a
speciality of sex appeal never undressed themselves in public. I do not know how many petticoats they wore; but at any
rate, instead of exposing their persons, they just gave you a
little glimpse of what looked like a dozen frilled pink petticoats round the ankles, and the effect was tremendous.

The result was that the Victorian age was an exceedingly
immoral age: an age in which there arose the reaction which
modern psychiatrists call exhibitionism. The upholstered
ladies felt that they must do something dreadful: shew their
ankles, for instance. Hardly the most desperate or abandoned
of them ever dreamed of shewing anything more. Thus you
had on the one hand this intense sex appeal produced by
clothes, and on the other hand the tendency to defy it or exploit it by making a naughty little revelation of some kind.

Alexandre Dumas *père* [1802–70; French author of *The
Count of Monte Cristo* and *The Three Musketeers*], in describing
the great French actress Mademoiselle Mars [Anne Françoise
Hyppolyte Boutet Salvetat, 1779–1847], who used to receive
people in her dressing room when she was changing, said that

she was a wonderful woman because she could change from head to foot and never let you see more than a thumbnail. That gives you the measure of sex appeal in the nineteenth century....

## 7. The Play of Ideas, 1950. [*Shaw on Theatre,* 289–94]

[*Shaw wrote this article in August, in response to an article of the same title by playwright Terence Rattigan (1911–77).*]

I read Mr Rattigan's article on this subject... let me say a word in his defence.

He is, of course, vulnerable as a reasoner; but he is not a reasoner, nor does he profess to be one. The difference between his practice and mine is that I reason out every sentence I write to the utmost of my capacity before I commit it to print, whereas he slams down everything that comes into his head without reasoning about it at all. This of course leads him into all sorts of Jack o' Lantern contradictions, dead ends, and even delusions; but as his head is a bright one and the things that come into it, reasonable or not, are all entertaining, and often penetrating and true, his practice is pleasing, whilst my reasoned-out syllogisms amuse my readers by seeming the first things that would come into a fool's head and only my fun, provoking hasty contradictions and reactions instead of stimulating thought and conviction.

Now there are ideas at the back of my plays; and Mr Rattigan does not like my plays because they are not exactly like his own, and no doubt bore him; so he instantly declares that plays that have any ideas in them are bad plays, and indeed not plays at all, but platform speeches, pamphlets, and leading articles. This is an old story! It used to take the form of complaints that my plays are all talk. Now it is quite true that my plays are all talk, just as Raphael's pictures are all paint,

Michael Angelo's statues all marble, Beethoven's symphonies all noise. Mr Rattigan, not being a born fool, does not complain of this, but, being an irrational genius, does let himself in for the more absurd complaint that, though plays must be all talk, the talk should have no ideas behind it, though he knows as well as I do when, if ever, he thinks for a moment, that without a stock of ideas, mind cannot operate and plays cannot exist. The quality of a play is the quality of its ideas.

What, then, is the function of the playwright? If he only "holds a mirror up to nature" his vision of life will be that of a policeman on point duty. Crowds of people pass him; but why they pass him, who they are, whither they are going and why, what they will do when they pass on and what they have done before they came into his field of vision, whether they are married or single or engaged, which of them is a criminal and which a philanthropist, he cannot tell, though he knows that there are all sorts in every thousand of them....

*[Continuing the theme of differentiating individuals from the crowd, Shaw notes that some individuals have exceptional talents for "pretending," that is, acting in both tragic and comic modes.]*

Now, as tragedians and clowns alike must have fictitious stories and plots invented for them, another specialization produces a class of professional liars who make no pretence that their tales are true. Here is where your playwright comes in.

But here also the differences in mental capacity come in. One playwright is capable of nothing deeper than short-lived fictitious police and divorce court cases of murder and adultery. Another can rise to the masterpieces of Aeschylus, Euripides, and Aristophanes [ancient Greek playwrights], to *Hamlet, Faust* [1604, by Christopher Marlowe], *Peer Gynt,* and—well, no matter: all these having to be not only entertaining but intensely didactic (what Mr Rattigan calls plays with ideas), and long-lived enough to be hyperbolically called immortal. And there are many gradations between these extremes: tragedy and melodrama, high and low comedy, farce and filth.

Why this occurs I do not know. If I did, I should be the supreme god among all biologists, philosophers, and dramatists. I should have solved the riddle of the universe, as every criticaster complains I have never done. Of course not. Nobody knows. Only Simple Simons ask.

Theatre technique begins with the circus clown and ringmaster and the Greek tribune, which is a glorified development of the pitch from which the poet of the market place declaims his verses, and, like Dickens's Sloppy [a character in *Our Mutual Friend* who used varied voices when reading newspaper stories] or a modern playwright reading his play to the players, reads all the parts "in different voices." On any fine Sunday in Ceylon the street poet may still be seen declaiming his works and taking round his hat: I have seen him do it.

But you need not go so far as Ceylon to see this primitive performance. Wherever there is a queue waiting for the doors of a theatre to open you may see some vagabond artist trying to entertain it in one way or another; and that vagabond may be an incipient Shakespear or Garrick. Nor need you go to the doors of a theatre to witness this parturition of pavement art. In Hyde Park I have seen an elderly man, dressed in black (his best, but old and seedy), step aside to the grass and address the empty air with the exordium "Ah, fahst EEbrews is very campfitn." ["Ah, first Hebrews is very comforting."] Presently people stopped to listen to him; and he had a congregation. I myself have done the same on Clapham Common, and collected sixteen shillings in my hat at the end for the Socialist cause. I have stopped on the Thames Embankment; set my back to the river wall; and had a crowd listening to me in no time. A friend of mine who happened to pass described the scene to Henry James, who could not believe that such a thing was possible for a man of letters. He asked me at our next meeting was the tale true? I said it was. In his most impressive manner (he was always impressive) he said: "I could not do that. I could not." And from that day his affectionate regard for me was tinged with wonder and even veneration.

Now I, the roofless pavement orator, ended in the largest halls in the country with overcrowds that filled two streets. I harangued an audience of millionaires in the Metropolitan Opera House in New York. I was specially proud of a speech in the Usher Hall in Edinburgh, where 8,640 pennies were collected at the end. Why do I tell this tale? Because it illustrates the development of the theatre from the pavement to the tribune and the cathedral, and the promotion of its outcasts to palaces, parliaments, and peerages. On the tribune there was no changeable picture scenery; but there were structures to represent houses, temple gates, or the like. When the tribune developed into a stage for the religious Mystery and Passion plays of the Middle Ages, these structures were multiplied until Pilate's pretorium, Herod's palace, the mouth of hell, the Blessed Virgin's throne in heaven, the Mount of Olives, the Hill of Calvary, and the court of Caiaphas were on the stage all through the play as now at Oberammergau, the players moving from one to the other as the action required.

Then came the Elizabethan stage (Shakespear's), with neither structures nor scenery but with a balcony above, an inner stage made with curtains called traverses, an apron stage projecting into the auditorium (relic of the innyard), and placards describing where the action was supposed to be taking place. The traverses distinguished indoor scenes from outdoor. The balcony distinguished castle ramparts from the plain below. But still there was no movable changeable scenery. Suddenly Italian Opera came along and was tolerated and encouraged by Cromwell, who ranked the theatre as the gate of hell, but loved music. With it came changeable pictorial scenery, side wings, flats, and perspective. Still more sensational, women came on the stage as sopranos, mezzo-sopranos, and contraltos, replacing epicene boys, and founding the tradition that every actress is, or must pretend to be, sexually immoral. Opera taught me to shape my plays into recitatives, arias, duets, trios, ensemble finales, and bravura pieces to display the technical accomplishments of the executants, with the quaint result that all the critics, friendly and hostile, took my plays to be so new, so extraordinary, so revolutionary, that the *Times* critic declared they were not plays at all as plays had been defined for all time by Aristotle. The truth was that I was going back atavistically to Aristotle, to the tribune stage, to the circus, to the didactic Mysteries, to the word music of Shakespear, to the forms of my idol Mozart, and to the stage business of the great players whom I had actually seen acting, from Barry Sullivan [1821–91], Salvini, and Ristori to Coquelin and Chaliapin [1873–1938, opera singer known for his naturalistic acting]. I was, and still am, the most old-fashioned playwright outside China and Japan. But I know my business both historically and by practice as playwright and producer; and I am writing all this to show that without knowing it historically and studying critically the survivals of it that are still in practice—for instance the Westminster School performances of the ancient Latin drama, where the women's parts are played by boys as Shakespear's women's parts were, and are so effective that Shakespear must have been as strongly against having them played by women as any Holy Willie—no playwright can be fully qualified, nor any theatre critic know what he is pontificating about.

And so I close, I hope, this series of essays started by Mr Rattigan, all of them entertaining in their way, but containing no convincing evidence that the writers have ever seen, written or produced a play.

# Part IV: Censorship

*Even before Shaw became a playwright, he was an outspoken critic of the legal requirement to obtain a license from the Lord Chamberlain for any play before it could be publicly performed, a practice that amounted to a de facto censorship by discouraging playwrights from tackling highly controversial social, political, or religious issues if they wanted to see their plays produced commercially, or forcing them into the "alternate" production system of private stage societies where they could not hope to earn a living. Private stage societies got around the licensing requirement because they didn't sell tickets to the public: they sold individuals subscriptions or memberships to the society, and mounted private, "members-only" productions. In addition to philosophical objections to state censorship of the theatre, Shaw railed against the practical flaw of a system that vested absolute authority over theatrical production in a low-level functionary of the royal household who was not required to have any education or expertise in dramatic literature or theatre. The selections in this section span a period of thirty years, and demonstrate Shaw's consistent—and persistent—objections to the licensing system that would remain essentially unchanged throughout his lifetime (it was finally repealed in 1968).*

# 1. The Censorship of the Stage in England, 1899.
## [*The North American Review* Vol. 169, No. 513, pp. 251–262]

*[Shaw wrote this article shortly after his play Mrs Warren's Profession had been denied a license for production in 1898—the first in several direct battles he fought with the various Examiners of Plays. Here, he focuses on the ridiculous shortcomings of the system, the practical and financial benefits it confers on the Examiner of Plays, and the hardships that it imposes on playwrights and theatre managers in both England and America.]*

In England, no play may be publicly performed until a certificate has been procured from the Lord Chamberlain that it "does not in its general tendency contain anything immoral or otherwise improper for the stage." The Lord Chamberlain, who must be distinguished from the hereditary Great Chamberlains of England [a largely ceremonial office in the royal household], is not a democratic official. He has nothing to do with the great offices by which the British Empire is administered—such as the Home Office, the Colonial Office, the India Office, staffed by bureaucrats elected by competitive examination to posts which they hold irremovably, through all changes of government, under the command of the Secretary of State for their department, a cabinet minister resigning whenever his party, defeated in the House of Commons, goes out of office. He is only a member of the Queen's household retinue—the Malvolio [fool character in Shakespeare's *Twelfth Night*] of St James' Palace [the reigning monarch's official residence]—responsible to nobody but the Queen [Victoria, who reigned 1837–1901], and therefore really not responsible at all, because the Queen's interference with the fantastic agglomeration of little dignities and functions which serve as excuses for the perquisites of her retinue, does not spread far beyond her presence and her residence (which is not St James' Palace) [the Queen preferred to live in other royal palaces], and is politically and conventionally limited even there.

The Lord Chamberlain does not condescend to read plays himself; and the Examiner of Plays, who does it for him, is perhaps the obscurest unit in the imposing procession of Pages of the Back Stairs, Pages of the Chambers, Pages of the Presence, Masters of the Music, Keepers of the Jewels, Keepers of the Swans, Gentleman Usher Daily Waiters, Gentlemen Usher Quarterly Waiters, Bargemasters, Grooms of the Privy Chamber, Gentlemen Ushers of Privy Chamber, and all the other breath-bereaving retainers of whom only one, the Poet Laureate, has succeeded in imposing the fact of his existence on the consciousness of the British public. The Lord Chamberlain himself, with all this pageantry to superintend, has no time to keep any check on his subordinate, even if he could pretend to know anything more than he about dramatic criticism and the foundations of morality. The result is that the Examiner of Plays, humble, untitled, "middle-class" though he be, is yet the most powerful man in England or America. Other people may make England's laws; he makes and unmakes its drama, and therefore also the drama of America; for no American dramatic author can afford to defy a despot who can, by a nod, cut him off from an English stageright worth possibly $20,000 in London alone. The monarchy is limited; the Cabinet, with tears of rage, cannot assert itself even against Anti-Vaccinators; the House of Lords, nominally omnipotent, puts down its foot only to emphasize the humiliation of having to take it up again; but the Examiner of Plays, greater than all these, does what he likes, caring not a dump for nations or constitutions, English or American. The President of the United States himself practically cannot see a new play with first getting the Examiner's leave.

It will be inferred that no pains are spared to secure the services of a very highly qualified and distinguished person to wield this astonishing power—say the holder of a University chair of Literature or Dramaturgy. The inference is erroneous. You are not allowed to sell stamps in an English post office without previously passing an examination; but you may become Examiner of Plays without necessarily knowing how to read or write. The post is held at present by one George Alexander Redford [he held the office from 1895–1911], said to have been a bank clerk, but not ascertained to have been anything except lucky enough to obtain a place at court with a salary of some fifteen hundred or two thousand dollars a year, and powers to exact from every author or manager producing a new play five dollars and a quarter for each one-act piece, and ten dollars and a half for each piece of two or more acts.

The resultant income must not be estimated merely by the number of English plays whose fame reaches the United States. In England the law of dramatic copyright, or stageright, is mere madness and confusion. Not long ago a popular novelist announced for performance a stage version of one of his books. He was promptly warned that his version was an infringement of the stageright of a version already made by a sharp country solicitor, and duly licensed by the Examiner of Plays and performed. The author had actually to buy back the stageright of his own story from the pirate who had stolen a march on him. In such a state of affairs, every prudent novelist whose book contains valuable dramatic material takes the precaution to put together some sort of stage version, no matter how brief or inept, and to have it furtively performed at a suburban hall with a theatrical license, the actors being a few friends who read their parts anyhow, and the audience a single confederate who complies with the law by paying for his seat. The price of admission is prohibitive to the casual student of the bill on the door—usually about five dollars and a quarter.

Further, the English stageright in a play is forfeited if the play is performed first in America. Consequently, the first thing a dramatic author has to do, when his play is not written for immediate production in England, is to give a copyrighting performance of the kind described above. The dramatic authors and the novelists between them thus keep up a series of theatrical performances of which the public knows nothing, but upon every one of which the Examiner of Plays levies his ten dollars and a half. What is more, these freaks of the law of copyright greatly increase his power, since not only the performance of the play in England, but the acquisition of valuable property rights elsewhere, is made dependent on his pleasure.

There is another way in which the Examiner can increase his emoluments. Formerly, if a play was susceptible of amendment, the Examiner specified the lines to which he objected, suggesting additions to alter the complexion of the moral situation in the play, and even altering expressions which were against his rules: for example, changing "as drunk as a Lord" to "as drunk as a Heaven," in pursuance of a rule, now fallen into disuse, that Heaven should always be substituted for the name of any of the Persons of the Trinity. Mr. Redford's immediate predecessor [E.F.S. Pigott, 1824–95], refusing to license a translation of a French play, on the ground that the heroine, a married woman, had been guilty of an indiscretion in early life, was visited by the actress cast for the part, who naturally used all her powers of persuasion to induce him to revoke his decision. Finally he consented, on condition that the words "I sinned but in intention" were introduced into her part. Accordingly, every night, during the burst of welcome which hailed her first entrance in the piece, the actress remarked confidentially to the conductor of the band, "I sinned but in intention," and thereby rescued her country from demoralization by French levity. A little later, a gifted American actress wrote a painfully powerful piece in which a mother, to save her child from growing up a helpless cripple, kills it. To this the Examiner had no objection; but, unfortunately, the mother baptized the child before killing it, a proceeding incompatible with his rules. He refused the necessary license. The American lady, unaccustomed to be so suppressed, swooped down on the Examiner as he sat at breakfast, and demanded an explanation. He soon weakened so far as to ask what, exactly, the lady proposed to do with the infant. She thereupon made a rag baby of his napkin, and, with the help of the hot water from his tea-tray, rehearsed the scene. He admitted its propriety; and she went off in triumph with her license. The very form in which the license is issued provides for these contingencies by excepting such passages as may be endorsed on the back of the certificate.

But Mr. Redford is a sharper man of business than his predecessor. On his refusal to license a certain play of mine, I asked the usual questions as to the particular passages objected to. Mr. Redford replied impressively that, if a new play were submitted to him, he would endeavor to forget having read the former one. This meant that if I would guess the obnoxious passages, and send him another ten dollars and a half, he would tell me whether my guess was right. He thus extracted double fees from me; and if I had required the license for an ordinary production of the play, instead of for a mere copyrighting formality, it might very well have taken half a dozen minimum guesses at ten dollars and a half apiece to ascertain the exact line drawn by his moral opinions without needlessly going beyond it. As it was, I simply deprived the play of the passages which explained its meaning (the residue being sufficient for my purpose), and so secured my license without further expenditure. This procedure on the part of the Examiner is unquestionably both logical and businesslike. It must increase his fees and economize his work very considerably. No wonder his post, with its fees, its powers, its unassailable permanence, and its unimpeachable gentility as a post in Her Majesty's household, is much sought after.

The statutory penalty for defying the Censor is a fine of fifty pounds, which can, theoretically, be levied on any person connected with a forbidden performance, call-boy, checktaker, carpenter, bandsman, actor, author, manager, stage-doorkeeper, and who not? No attempt has been made in recent cases to recover this penalty, ostensibly because the department has no funds with which to institute prosecutions, but really, one suspects, because the cases would have to be tried by jury, and the average British juryman, though usually a worm under the foot of the judge, can turn if he likes. Even judges have flashes of the constitutional spirit at odd moments. Here we have the weak place in the Examiner's powers which led to the famous evasion of him on the centenary of Shelley's birth. It was proposed to celebrate that occasion by a performance of "The Cenci." The Examiner would not hear of it; but the performance was given for all that in the Grand Theatre, Islington (a northern suburb of London), before an audience of poets, headed by Browning, and a crowd of their disciples. Technically, this performance was not a public representation of the play: it was only a meeting of the Shelley Society. The spectators did not pay at the doors: they had all joined the Shelley Society for the season, and were attending this particular "private" meeting of it in the exercise of their ordinary right as members. For the moment the defeat of the Censor was complete. But the performance had taken place in a London theatre; and London theatres are subject to the Lord Chamberlain, who licenses them from year to year. The unfortunate lessee, having let his house to the Shelley Society (without any knowledge of the plot in hand), found himself at the mercy of the outraged Chamberlain when the time came for renewing his license. What passed between them is not known; but there is now a clause in the lease of that theatre stipulating that no performances of un-licensed plays shall be given in it. When the Shelley Society proposed to repeat "The Cenci" some years later, the Lord Chamberlain was master of the situation. With a single revolutionary exception, no manager dared lend or let his theatre for the purpose. The terror was so complete that a manager who, not realising his risk, had discussed quite favorably the possibility of placing his house at the disposal of the Society, was compelled to write to the press vehemently denying that he had ever contemplated such an enormity, although his letters were in the hands of the very persons he was publicly contradicting.

Since then, the blockade has been run only by the Independent Theatre, which succeeded in producing Ibsen's "Ghosts" on three occasions without a license. In this case, no license was applied for, its refusal being practically certain; and the first performance, which was technically "private," like that of the Shelley Society, was over before the lessee of the theatre knew that anything exceptional was happening. After this, the theatres were thoroughly on their guard; but, later on, the founder of the Independent Theatre, Mr. Grein, invited his friends (including all the subscribers) to an "At Home," hiring for the purpose one of the numerous halls which are let in London for dances, minor political meetings, lectures and the like. Here he entertained his guests with a second performance of "Ghosts." A third was accomplished some years later, virtually in the same way. No attempt was made by the Lord Chamberlain, on any of these occasions, to enforce the statutory fine, restrain the projectors by injunction, or otherwise assert any right of interference with performances which are not opened to the public by taking money at the doors for admission. But it is evident, from the fact that nothing will now persuade any manager or proprietor of a licensed theatre to allow such a performance to take place in his house, that the power of closing theatres which the Lord Chamberlain wields as the licensing authority, makes him effectively the Tzar of the drama.

To Americans, who, as I have pointed out, are as much concerned in the Censorship as the English are, the drama being practically international, this state of things may seem so Russianly subversive of fundamental western rights as to stand condemned by the mere statement of it. In England, the only question that arises is: How does the institution work? The fact that it violates these Rights of Man which are expressly constitutional in America is to the English mind all in its favor. No doubt the Englishman is earnestly jealous for his religious liberty, and at least excitable about his political liberty. An attempt to force the Salvation Army to have their hymns licensed by the Archbishop of Canterbury, or the daily papers to have their political leaders licensed by the Queen's Lectrice [official who read books to the Queen for pleasure], would produce an overwhelming agitation at once; though there is rather more to be said for either measure than for the censorship of the English dramatists by Mr. Redford. But beyond this the Englishman does not go. Far from believing that either he himself or anybody else can be safely trusted with further liberties, he lives absolutely convinced that only by a strenuous maintenance of restrictive laws and customs, supported on every public occasion by the most reverent professions of faith and loyalty, feigned or sincere, can society be withheld from casting all moral considerations to the winds and committing suicide in a general Saturnalia [wild reverie] of reckless debauchery. I do not pretend that this will be accepted in England as a sane statement of fact; for, if England were conscious of its own absurdity, it would cease to be absurd. Still less do I mean to suggest that it is a delusion at all peculiar to England or unknown in America. But I am concerned here only with an application of it which *is* peculiar to England. Nobody will deny that the normal assumption in England is that without a Censor the stage would instantly plunge to the lowest practicable extreme of degradation—an assumption quite undisturbed by the fact that Literature, without a Censor, behaves far more decently than Drama with one. For myself, as a dramatic author, I can say that few things would surprise me more than to meet a representative Englishman who regarded my desire to abolish the Censor otherwise than he would regard the desire of a pickpocket to abolish the police. To such an Englishman, it seems the most obvious piece of common sense that some respectable person should be made responsible for the propriety of the plays to which his daughters go; so that he may be guaranteed against the natural propensity of the theatre towards licentiousness. Accepting the court standard of decorousness as absolute, he considers that if a lord who is a member of Her Majesty's household cannot be trusted to decide questions of propriety, nobody can. No competitive examination, no professorship of Dramatic Literature, no control by an elected representative body, could give him any greater sense of security than the position of the Lord Chamberlain. And, I may add, they could give the dramatists no greater sense of security either. Let us, then, embrace this apparently common-sensible view of the institution, and inquire simply how it fulfils, not its original purpose (it was instituted [in 1737] by [Sir Robert] Walpole [1676–1745, considered Britain's first prime minister, 1721–42] to prevent [satirist Henry] Fielding [1707–54] from exposing parliamentary corruption on the stage), but the purpose for which it survives. What sort of plays does it license; and what sort of plays does it suppress? A very conclusive answer to this question would be a description of the most unpleasant play licensed within my experience by Mr. Redford's predecessor, who refused to license "The Cenci," and of the most unpleasant play licensed by Mr. Redford himself. But, fastidious reader, suffice it to say that, were such an answer attempted, the guaranteed morality of the Censor-protected stage would appear as an outrage in the columns of the free Press.

Since the Censorship does not protect the playgoer's daughter from improper plays, it is evident that it either does not protect her at all, or else protects her only from further extremities. But further extremities would be dealt with by the police. The Censor does not prevent either the sexual sensationalists or the mere blackguards from doing their worst on the stage; he only protects them by his certificates.

This is not the fault of the Censor. A moment's consideration will show it to be so inevitable, that if you or I, punctilious reader, were Examiner of Plays, it would not be altered in the least. Let us examine the position. You take a commonplace official; confront him with a play by a man probably cleverer than himself, possibly a genius destined to be remembered for many centuries; and ask him to decide whether the net effect of a performance of that play on the destiny of the human race will be helpful or harmful. The Delphic oracle itself would not have the impudence to pretend that it could answer such a question. Even the Roman Catholic Church does not profess to exercise its censorship without supernatural guidance; and the Roman Catholic Church, which is at least not less qualified for the task than Mr. Redford, has admittedly made serious mistakes both through the Inquisition and in the compilation of its *Index Expurgatorius*; failing to add anything to the natural check of public opinion upon really licentious literature, whilst restricting popular access to the Bible, and missing its mark in the suppression of books so frequently that the placing of a work in the *Index* almost raises a European and American presumption in its favor. But, pray, do not be so unjust as to conclude, because the British citizen thoughtlessly expects Mr. Redford to succeed where a great Church has failed, that Mr. Redford himself puts forward any such pretension. When Mr. Redford refuses to license Tolstoï's "Dominion of Darkness," for example, he does not refuse on the ground that he, Redford, is a more highminded man, or a philosopher with a greater power of distinguishing the conventions of propriety from the realities of moral evil, or a more disinterested and public-spirited citizen of the world, a deeper seer into the future, a keener observer of the present, a wiser critic of life than Tolstoï. If he took that ground, a shout of laughter from the whole civilized world would be the answer. What Mr. Redford and every such censor does say to Tolstoï (if he has sense enough to understand his own position) is: "You are a much cleverer and, no doubt, a better fellow than I am; and I cannot pretend to criticise you. But I must administer the rules of my office as a judge administers the laws; and your play is against my rules. It may be a very good play; and certainly lots of the plays that are inside my rules are shockingly bad ones; but I can't help that: if I were to discriminate outside my rules I should be setting myself up as a sort of Platonic philosopher-king, which I'm not, and which no official is at all likely to be. I do my best to march with the times, stretching the rules as much as possible, or even dropping one out when it becomes too ridiculous; but I must point out to you that there is one rule that never varies, and never can vary; and that rule is that a play must not be made the vehicle of new opinions on important subjects, because new opinions are always questionable opinions, and I cannot make Her Majesty the Queen responsible for questionable opinions by licensing them. The other rules are simple enough. You mustn't dramatize any of the stories in the Bible. You mustn't make fun of ambassadors, cabinet ministers, or any living persons who have influence in fashionable society, though no notice will be taken of a gag at the expense of General Booth, or a Socialist or Labor member of the County Council, or people of that sort. You mustn't have any love affairs within the tables of Consanguinity in the Prayer Book. If you introduce a male libertine in a serious play, you had better 'redeem' him in the end by marrying him to an innocent young lady. If a female libertine, it will not matter if she dies at the end, and takes some opportunity to burst into tears on touching the hand of a respectable girl. There are lots of little ways in which a play can disclaim any unusual views as to the relations of the sexes, even when it stretches our rules as to conduct. In farcical comedy and musical farce, you cannot come into conflict with us, because all the fun in them depends on the conventional view of bad conduct. The observance of these rules of ours constitutes a sort of technique which is easily picked up, which is in harmony with the common usages of gentlemen, and which is never objected to by anybody but the people who would be disqualified anyhow by having new views—the cranks, in short. That's how our place works. You owe me two guineas, please, for refusing to allow you to produce your play. Thank you. Good morning."

The rules here spoken of are not printed for the guidance of dramatists. They are traditional and probably unwritten. They are not the invention of any individual Censor: they simply codify the present and most of the past prejudices of the class he represents. To write a play which complies with them in form whilst grossly violating their purpose is as easy as lying: it is the trade of the adapter of French farces. To write a play which holds their purpose as sacred as any Examiner can, whilst violating their form in every scene, is as difficult as the achievement of greatness: it is the fate of the man of genius, necessarily always defending humanity against plutocracy and reality against hypocrisy. Each successive Censor makes the best of these rules when he is young and elastic, and the worst of them when he is old and ossified; but, in the main, they bind him as tightly as they bind the public.... Mr. Redford cannot help himself: a Censorship cannot work in any other way, until a Censor can be found greater than the greatest dramatists. That being impossible, he is doomed still to put his hall-mark on profligate farces and thinly sentimentalized tom-cat love tales, and to shut the stage door against the great dramatic poets. ...

And so, in the end, the public gets neither the dramatist's view of life, nor the Examiner's view of life, nor its own view of life, nor in fact any real view of life at all. It does not get a clean stage, simple as that seemed: there is always one theatre, at least, in London where the fun consists of mere blackguardism under a royal certificate of propriety. It does not even get the laws against the exhibition on the stage of very young children enforced: reproachful-eyed babies are still tossed about from hand to hand in lewd farces; and infamous ballets are danced at eleven o'clock at night by tiny children kept awake only by unhealthy excitement. This at least the Censorship might stop; but it never does. No serious steps to make London theatres safe were taken, until the responsibility was transferred to the County Council. Desiring to give a judicial air to this article, I have racked my brains and searched my pretty exhaustive experience as a critic of the theatres to find a single item to the credit of the Censorship's account in the books of the Recording Angel. I find none. Shame, folly, ridicule, and mischief are the fruits of it, and the sole possible ones, as, I repeat, they would equally be if I or Tolstoï himself were Censor. Nobody profits by it except the Examiner, who lives by it, and the Lord Chamberlain, who is occasionally presented by the managers with silver plate, which he publicly accepts as naïvely as those Stuart Masters of the Revels (the original Censors), who entered in their journals the presents made to their wives by the actor-managers of the day.

What, then, is to be done with the Censorship? Nothing can be simpler. Abolish it, root and branch, throwing the whole legal responsibility for plays on the author and manager, precisely as the legal responsibility for a book is thrown on the author, the printer, and the publisher. The managers will not like this: their present slavery is safer and easier;

but it will be good for them, and good for the Drama. And transfer the authority to license theatres from year to year from the Lord Chamberlain to the London County Council, which already deals with music halls, and is jealously criticised by the Press and the electorate. Alas! when we pass from the What to the How, the simplicity of the problem vanishes. Some years ago, when the London Playgoer's Club invited my opinion as to how the Censor could be got rid of, I had to reply that, as far as I could see, nothing short of abolishing the monarchy could touch him. But we are not going to burn down our house to roast our pig in that fashion. Besides, nobody, except Mr. William Archer and a few dramatists whose plays have been suppressed, seems to object to the Censorship. There are no complaints in Parliament, none in the Press, no petitions from the Society of Authors or from the managers. A forgotten Royal Commission on the subject came to the unimpeachable conclusion that a perfect censorship is a desirable thing; and the consensus among the manager-witnesses as to the superhuman personal qualities of their master, the then Examiner, quite outweighed the display of petulant shallowness made by that gentleman when he was invited to shine on the Commission in person. The public is either satisfied or indifferent, because the class in England which feels social matters deeply does not go to the theatre, and the class which does go wants to be amused there, and not edified or conscience-stricken. There is no money in the question, no vote-catching power, no popular interest in or knowledge or comprehension of it, and consequently no political capital to be made out of it. The censorship will probably outlive the House of Lords and the supremacy of the Established Church, as quietly as it has outlived the Metropolitan Board of Works and the Irish Church. In England this article will be entirely wasted: no English editor has ever dreamt of asking me to deal with the subject. In America, it may be useful, in view of the likelihood of attempts to set up State Censorships in that country. In which case, O my friends across the sea, remember how the censorship works in England, and DON'T.

## 2. From the Preface to *The Shewing-up of Blanco Posnet*, 1909. [*The Bodley Head Bernard Shaw: Collected Plays with their Prefaces*, vol. 3, pp. 673–762]

[*As a well-known critic of theatrical censorship, Shaw was called to testify in front of the Joint Select Committee investigating the issue. Shaw was an experienced politician as well as a playwright, and prepared a written statement to read, distributing copies to the committee ahead of time so they could prepare questions. Instead, it became obvious that the committee members hadn't read the statement, and tried to recover from their embarrassment by improperly refusing to accept it, a mistake that Shaw exploited to its satirical fullest. When the Examiner of Plays refused to license* The Shewing-up of Blanco Posnet *the following year and Shaw published the play instead, he used the opportunity to describe the committee proceedings and publish the complete text of his rejected statement. As a result, the published preface to the play is more than double the length of the play itself. In exhaustively explaining the effects of censorship on all theatrical stakeholders, Shaw demonstrates his propensity—often admittedly justified—to correct other people's arguments.*]

## The Censorship

This little play is really a religious tract in dramatic form. If our silly censorship would permit its performance, it might possibly help to set right-side-up the perverted conscience and re-invigorate the starved self-respect of our considerable class of loose-lived playgoers whose point of honor is to deride all official and conventional sermons. As it is, it only gives me an opportunity of telling the story of the Select

Committee of both Houses of Parliament which sat last year
to inquire into the working of the censorship, against which
it was alleged by myself and others that as its imbecility and
mischievousness could not be fully illustrated within the limits of decorum imposed on the press, it could only be dealt
with by a parliamentary body subject to no such limits.

*[Shaw lists the names of many famous theatrical and political per-
sons whose witness testimony is recorded in the parliamentary blue
book, claiming that "Few books of the year 1909 can have been
cheaper and more entertaining than the report of this Committee....
The publication of a book by so many famous contributors would be
beyond the means of any commercial publishing firm. His Majesty's
Stationery Office sells it to all comers by weight at the very reasonable price of three-and-threepence a copy."]*

## How Not To Do It

It was pointed out by Charles Dickens in *Little Dorrit*,
which remains the most accurate and penetrating study of
the genteel littleness of our class governments in the English
language, that whenever an abuse becomes oppressive
enough to persuade our party parliamentarians that something must be done, they immediately set to work to face the
situation and discover How Not To Do It. Since Dickens's
day the exposures effected by the Socialists have so shat-
tered the self-satisfaction of modern commercial civilization
that it is no longer difficult to convince our governments that
something must be done, even to the extent of attempts at a
reconstruction of civilization on a thoroughly uncommercial
basis. Consequently, the first part of the process described by
Dickens: that in which the reformers were snubbed by front
bench demonstrations that the administrative departments
were consuming miles of red tape in the correctest forms of
activity, and that everything was for the best in the best of
all possible worlds, is out of fashion; and we are in that other

phase, familiarized by the history of the French Revolution, in which the primary assumption is that the country is in danger, and that the first duty of all parties, politicians, and governments is to save it. But as the effect of this is to give governments a great many more things to do, it also gives a powerful stimulus to the art of How Not To Do Them: that is to say, the art of contriving methods of reform which will leave matters exactly as they are.

The report of the Joint Select Committee is a capital illustration of this tendency. The case against the censorship was overwhelming; and the defence was more damaging to it than no defence at all could have been. Even had this not been so, the mere caprice of opinion had turned against the institution; and a reform was expected, evidence or no evidence. Therefore the Committee was unanimous as to the necessity of reforming the censorship; only unfortunately, the majority attached to this unanimity the usual condition that nothing should be done to disturb the existing state of things. How this was effected may be gathered from the recommendations finally agreed on, which are as follows.

1. The drama is to be set entirely free by the abolition of the existing obligation to procure a licence from the Censor before performing a play; but every theatre lease is in future to be construed as if it contained a clause giving the landlord power to break it and evict the lessee if he produces a play without first obtaining the usual licence from the Lord Chamberlain.

2. Some of the plays licensed by the Lord Chamberlain are so vicious that their present practical immunity from prosecution must be put an end to; but no manager who procures the Lord Chamberlain's licence for a play can be punished in any way for producing it, though a special tribunal may order him to discontinue the performance; and even this order must not be recorded to his disadvantage on the licence of his

theatre, nor may it be given as a judicial reason for cancelling that licence.

3. Authors and managers producing plays without first obtaining the usual licence from the Lord Chamberlain shall be perfectly free to do so, and shall be at no disadvantage compared to those who follow the existing practice, except that they may be punished, have the licences of their theatres endorsed and cancelled, and have the performance stopped pending the proceedings without compensation in the event of the proceedings ending in their acquittal.

4. Authors are to be rescued from their present subjection to an irresponsible secret tribunal which can condemn their plays without giving reasons, by the substitution for that tribunal of a Committee of the Privy Council, which is to be the final authority on the fitness of a play for representation; and this Committee is to sit in camera if and when it pleases.

5. The power to impose a veto on the production of plays is to be abolished because it may hinder the growth of a great national drama; but the Office of Examiner of Plays shall be continued; and the Lord Chamberlain shall retain his present powers to license plays, but shall be made responsible to Parliament to the extent of making it possible to ask questions there concerning his proceedings, especially now that members have discovered a method of doing this indirectly.

And so on, and so forth. The thing is to be done; and it is not to be done. Everything is to be changed and nothing is to be changed. The problem is to be faced and the solution to be shirked. And the word of Dickens is to be justified....

## Why The Managers Love The Censorship

The only one of these influences which seems to be generally misunderstood is that of the managers. It has been assumed repeatedly that managers and authors are affected in the same way by the censorship. When a prominent author protests against the censorship, his opinion is supposed to be balanced by that of some prominent manager who declares that the censorship is the mainstay of the theatre, and his relations with the Lord Chamberlain and the Examiner of Plays a cherished privilege and an inexhaustible joy. The error was not removed by the evidence given before the Joint Select Committee. The managers did not make their case clear there, partly because they did not understand it, and partly because their most eminent witnesses were not personally affected by it, and would not condescend to plead it, feeling themselves, on the contrary, compelled by their self-respect to admit and even emphasize the fact that the Lord Chamberlain in the exercise of his duties as licenser had done those things which he ought not to have done, and left undone those things which he ought to have done. Mr Forbes Robertson and Sir Herbert Tree, for instance, had never felt the real disadvantage of which managers have to complain. This disadvantage was not put directly to the Committee; and though the managers are against me on the question of the censorship, I will now put their case for them as they should have put it themselves, and as it can be read between the lines of their evidence when once the reader has the clue.

The manager of a theatre is a man of business. He is not an expert in politics, religion, art, literature, philosophy, or law. He calls in a playwright just as he calls in a doctor, or consults a lawyer, or engages an architect, depending on the playwright's reputation and past achievements for a satisfactory result. A play by an unknown man may attract him sufficiently to induce him to give that unknown man a trial; but this does not occur often enough to be taken into account: his normal course is to resort to a well-known author and take (mostly with misgiving) what he gets from him. Now this does not cause any anxiety to Mr Forbes Robertson and Sir Herbert Tree, because they are only incidentally managers and men of business: primarily they are highly cultivated artists, quite capable of judging for themselves anything that the most abstruse playwright is likely to put before them. But the plain-sailing tradesman who must be taken as the typical manager (for the west end of London is not the whole theatrical world) is by no means equally qualified to judge whether a play is safe from prosecution or not. He may not understand it, may not like it, may not know what the author is driving at, may have no knowledge of the ethical, political, and sectarian controversies which may form the intellectual fabric of the play, and may honestly see nothing but an ordinary "character part" in a stage figure which may be a libellous and unmistakable caricature of some eminent living person of whom he has never heard. Yet if he produces the play he is legally responsible just as if he had written it himself. Without protection he may find himself in the dock answering a charge of blasphemous libel, seditious libel, obscene libel, or all three together, not to mention the possibility of a private action for defamatory libel. His sole refuge is the opinion of the Examiner of Plays, his sole protection the licence of the Lord Chamberlain. A refusal to license does not hurt him, because he can produce another play: it is the author who suffers. The granting of the licence practically places him above the law; for though it may be legally possible to prosecute a licensed play, nobody ever dreams of doing it. The really responsible person, the Lord Chamberlain, could not be put into the dock; and the manager could not decently be convicted when he could produce in his defence a certificate from the chief officer of the King's Household that the play was a proper one.

## A Two Guinea Insurance Policy

The censorship, then, provides the manager, at the negligible premium of two guineas per play, with an effective insurance against the author getting him into trouble, and a complete relief from all conscientious responsibility for the character of the entertainment at his theatre. Under such circumstances, managers would be more than human if they did not regard the censorship as their most valuable privilege. This is the simple explanation of the rally of the managers and their Associations to the defence of the censorship....

## The Committee's Attitude Towards The Theatre

In England, thanks chiefly to the censorship, the theatre is not respected. It is indulged and despised as a department of what is politely called gaiety. It is therefore not surprising that the majority of the Committee began by taking its work uppishly and carelessly. When it discovered that the contemporary drama, licensed by the Lord Chamberlain, included plays which could be described only behind closed doors, and in the discomfort which attends discussions of very nasty subjects between men of widely different ages, it calmly put its own convenience before its public duty by ruling that there should be no discussion of particular plays, much as if a committee on temperance were to rule that drunkenness was not a proper subject of conversation among gentlemen.

## A Bad Beginning

This was a bad beginning. Everybody knew that in England the censorship would not be crushed by the weight of the constitutional argument against it, heavy as that was, unless it were also brought home to the Committee and to the public that it had sanctioned and protected the very worst practicable examples of the kind of play it professed to extirpate. For it must be remembered that the other half of the practical side of the case, dealing with the merits of the play it had suppressed, could never secure a unanimous assent. If the Censor had suppressed *Hamlet*, as he most certainly would have done had it been submitted to him as a new play, he would have been supported by a large body of people to whom incest is a tabooed subject which must not be mentioned on the stage or anywhere else outside a criminal court.... The Censor may prohibit all such plays with complete certainty that there will be a chorus of "Quite right too" sufficient to drown the protests of the few who know better. The Achilles heel of the censorship is therefore not the fine plays it has suppressed, but the abominable plays it has licensed: plays which the Committee itself had to turn the public out of the room and close the doors before it could discuss, and which I myself have found it impossible to expose in the press because no editor of a paper or magazine intended for general family reading could admit into his columns the baldest narration of the stories which the Censor has not only tolerated but expressly [sic] certified as fitting for presentation on the stage. When the Committee ruled out this part of the case it shook the confidence of the authors in its impartiality and its seriousness....

*[Shaw describes, in great and witty detail, the "comic interlude" of the controversy surrounding his appearance before the Committee and his public shaming of the members over their inappropriate handling of his prepared statement.]*

In spite of the fun of the scene on the surface, my public sense was, and still is, very deeply offended by it. It made an end for me of the claim of the majority to be taken seriously. When the Government comes to deal with the question, as it presumably will before long, I invite it to be guided by the Chairman, the minority, and by the witnesses according to their weight, and to pay no attention whatever to those recommendations which were obviously inserted solely to conciliate the majority and get the report through and the Committee done with.

My evidence will be found in the Bluebook, pp. 46–53. And here is the terrible statement which the Committee went through so much to suppress.

# The Rejected Statement—Part I

*THE WITNESS'S QUALIFICATIONS*

I am by profession a playwright. I have been in practice since 1892. I am a member of the Managing Sub-Committee of the Society of Authors and of the Dramatic Sub-Committee of that body. I have written nineteen plays, some of which have been translated and performed in all European countries except Turkey, Greece, and Portugal. They have been performed extensively in America. Three of them have been refused licences by the Lord Chamberlain. In one case a licence has since been granted. The other two are still unlicensed. I have suffered both in pocket and reputation by the action of the Lord Chamberlain. In other countries I have not come into conflict with the censorship except in Austria, where the production of a comedy of mine was postponed for a year because it alluded to the part taken by Austria in the Servo-Bulgarian war. This comedy was not one of the plays suppressed in England by the Lord Chamberlain. One of the plays so suppressed was prosecuted in America by the police in consequence of an immense crowd of disorderly persons having been attracted to the first performance by the Lord Chamberlain's condemnation of it; but on appeal to a higher court it was decided that the representation was lawful and the intention innocent, since when it has been repeatedly performed.

I am not an ordinary playwright in general practice. I am a specialist in immoral and heretical plays. My reputation has been gained by my persistent struggle to force the public to reconsider its morals. In particular, I regard much current morality as to economic and sexual relations as disastrously wrong; and I regard certain doctrines of the Christian religion as understood in England today with abhorrence. I write plays with the deliberate object of converting the nation to my opinions in these matters. I have no other effectual incentive to write plays, as I am not dependent on the theatre for my livelihood. If I were prevented from producing immoral and heretical plays, I should cease to write for the theatre, and propagate my views from the platform and through books. I mention these facts to shew that I have a special interest in the achievement by my profession of those rights of liberty of speech and conscience which are matters of course in other professions. I object to censorship not merely because the existing form of it grievously injures and hinders me individually, but on public grounds.

## THE DEFINITION OF IMMORALITY

In dealing with the question of the censorship, everything depends on the correct use of the word immorality, and a careful discrimination between the powers of a magistrate or judge to administer a code, and those of a censor to please himself.

Whatever is contrary to established manners and customs is immoral. An immoral act or doctrine is not necessarily a sinful one: on the contrary, every advance in thought and conduct is by definition immoral until it has converted the majority. For this reason it is of the most enormous importance that immorality should be protected jealously against the attacks of those who have no standard except the standard of custom, and who regard any attack on custom—that is, on morals—as an attack on society, on religion, and on virtue.

A censor is never intentionally a protector of immorality. He always aims at the protection of morality. Now morality is extremely valuable to society. It imposes conventional conduct on the great mass of persons who are incapable of original ethical judgment, and who would be quite lost if they were not in leading-strings devised by lawgivers, philosophers, prophets, and poets for their guidance. But morality is not dependent on censorship for protection. It is already powerfully fortified by the magistracy and the whole body of law. Blasphemy, indecency, libel, treason, sedition, obscenity, profanity, and all the other evils which a censorship is supposed to avert, are punishable by the civil magistrate with all the severity of vehement prejudice. Morality has not only every engine that lawgivers can devise in full operation for its protection, but also that enormous weight of public opinion enforced by social ostracism which is stronger than all the statutes. A censor pretending to protect morality is like a child pushing the cushions of a railway carriage to give itself the sensation of making the train travel at sixty miles an hour. It is immorality, not morality, that needs protection: it is morality, not immorality, that needs restraint; for morality, with all the dead weight of human inertia and superstition to hang on the back of the pioneer, and all the malice of vulgarity and prejudice to threaten him, is responsible for many persecutions and many martyrdoms.

Persecutions and martyrdoms, however, are trifles compared to the mischief done by censorships in delaying the general march of enlightenment. This can be brought home to us by imagining what would have been the effect of applying to all literature the censorship we still apply to the stage. The works of Linnaeus and the evolutionists of 1790–1830, of Darwin, Wallace, Huxley, Helmholtz, Tyndall, Spencer, Carlyle, Ruskin, and Samuel Butler, would not have been published, as they were all immoral and heretical in the very highest degree, and gave pain to many worthy and pious people... the still more startling blasphemy of Jesus when He declared God to be the son of man and Himself to be the son of God, are all examples of shocking immoralities (every immorality shocks somebody), the suppression and extinction of which would have been more disastrous than the utmost mischief that can be conceived as ensuing from the toleration of vice.

These facts, glaring as they are, are disguised by the promotion of immoralities into moralities which is constantly going on.... The respectable Englishman... has never willingly tolerated immorality. He did not adopt any innovation until it had become moral; and then he adopted it, not on its merits, but solely because it had become moral. In doing so he never realized that it had ever been immoral: consequently its early struggles taught him no lesson; and he has opposed the next step in human progress as indignantly as if neither manners, customs, nor thought had ever changed since the beginning of the world. Toleration must be imposed on him as a mystic and painful duty by his spiritual and political leaders, or he will condemn the world to stagnation, which is the penalty of an inflexible morality....

## THE LIMITS TO TOLERATION

But the large toleration these considerations dictate has limits. For example, though we tolerate, and rightly tolerate, the propaganda of Anarchism as a political theory which embraces all that is valuable in the doctrine of Laisser-Faire and the method of Free Trade as well as all that is shocking in the views of [Mikhail Alexandrovich] Bakounine [1814–76, Russian revolutionary anarchist], we clearly cannot, or at all events will not, tolerate assassination of rulers on the ground that it is "propaganda by deed" or sociological experiment. A play inciting to such an assassination cannot claim the privileges of heresy or immorality, because no case can be made out in support of assassination as an indispensable instrument of progress.... Assassination is the extreme form of censorship; and it seems hard to justify an incitement to it on anti-censorial principles. The very people who would have scouted the notion of prohibiting the performances of *Julius Caesar* at His Majesty's Theatre in London last year, might now entertain very seriously a proposal to exclude Indians from them, and to suppress the play completely in Calcutta and Dublin; for if the assassin of Caesar was a hero, why not the assassins of Lord Frederick Cavendish [1836–82, who was assassinated hours after he arrived in Dublin to take up his post as Chief Secretary for Ireland], Presidents Lincoln and McKinley, and Sir Curzon Wyllie [official of the British Indian government, assassinated by an Indian revolutionary]? Here is a strong case for some constitutional means of preventing the performance of a play. True, it is an equally strong case for preventing the circulation of the Bible, which was always in the hands of our regicides; but as the Roman Catholic Church does not hesitate to accept the consequence of the censorial principle, it does not invalidate the argument.

Take another case. A modern comedy, *Arms and the Man*, though not a comedy of politics, is nevertheless so far historical that it reveals the unacknowledged fact that as the Servo-Bulgarian War of 1885 was much more than a struggle between the Servians and Bulgarians, the troops engaged were officered by two European Powers of the first magnitude. In consequence, the performance of the play was for some time forbidden in Vienna, and more recently it gave offence in Rome at a moment when popular feeling was excited as to the relations of Austria with the Balkan States. Now if a comedy so remote from political passion as *Arms and the Man* can, merely because it refers to political facts, become so inconvenient and inopportune that Foreign Offices take the trouble to have its production postponed, what may not be the effect of what is called a patriotic drama produced at a moment when the balance is quivering between peace and war? Is there not something to be said for a political censorship, if not for a moral one? May not these continental governments who leave the stage practically free in every other respect, but muzzle it politically, be justified by the practical exigencies of the situation?

## THE DIFFERENCE BETWEEN LAW AND CENSORSHIP

The answer is that a pamphlet, a newspaper article, or a resolution moved at a political meeting can do all the mischief that a play can, and often more; yet we do not set up a permanent censorship of the press or of political meetings. Any journalist may publish an article, any demagogue may deliver a speech without giving notice to the government or obtaining its licence. The risk of such freedom is great; but as it is the price of our political liberty, we think it worth paying. We may abrogate it in emergencies by a Coercion Act, a suspension of the Habeas Corpus Act, or a proclamation of martial law, just as we stop the traffic in a street during a fire, or shoot thieves at sight if they loot after an earthquake. But when the emergency is past, liberty is restored everywhere except in the theatre. The [Theatres] Act of 1843 is a permanent Coercion Act for the theatre, a permanent suspension of the Habeas Corpus Act as far as plays are concerned, a permanent proclamation of martial law with a single official substituted for a court martial. It is, in fact, assumed that actors, playwrights, and theatre managers are dangerous and dissolute characters whose existence creates a chronic state of emergency, and who must be treated as earthquake looters are treated....

The abolition of the censorship does not involve the abolition of the magistrate and of the whole civil and criminal code. On the contrary, it would make the theatre more effectually subject to them than it is at present; for once a play now runs the gauntlet of the censorship, it is practically placed above the law. It is almost humiliating to have to demonstrate the essential difference between a censor and a magistrate or a sanitary inspector; but it is impossible to ignore the carelessness with which even distinguished critics of the theatre assume that all the arguments proper to the support of a magistracy and body of jurisprudence apply equally to a censorship.

A magistrate has laws to administer: a censor has nothing but his own opinion. A judge leaves the question of guilt to the jury: the Censor is jury and judge as well as lawgiver.... The law may be only the intolerance of the community; but it is a defined and limited intolerance.... [*Shaw provides some specific examples of the limits to a magistrate's powers.*] But a playwright's livelihood, his reputation, and his inspiration and mission are at the personal mercy of the Censor....

## THE DIPLOMATIC OBJECTION TO THE LORD CHAMBERLAIN

There is another reason, quite unconnected with the susceptibilities of authors, which makes it undesirable that a member of the King's Household should be responsible for the character and tendency of plays. The drama, dealing with all departments of human life, is necessarily political. Recent events have shewn—what indeed needed no demonstration—that it is impossible to prevent inferences being made, both at home and abroad, from the action of the Lord Chamberlain. The most talked-about play of the present year (1909), *An Englishman's Home* [by Guy du Maurier], has for its main interest an invasion of England by a fictitious power which is understood, as it is meant to be understood, to represent Germany. The lesson taught by the play is the danger of invasion and the need for every English citizen to be a soldier. The Lord Chamberlain licensed this play, but refused to license a parody of it. Shortly afterwards he refused to license another play in which the fear of a German invasion was ridiculed. The German press drew the inevitable inference that the Lord Chamberlain was an anti-German alarmist, and that his opinions were a reflection of those prevailing in St. James's Palace. Immediately after this, the Lord Chamberlain licensed the play. Whether the inference, as far as the Lord Chamberlain was concerned, was justified, is of no consequence. What is important is that it was sure to be made, justly or unjustly, and extended from the Lord Chamberlain to the Throne.

*THE OBJECTION OF COURT ETIQUET*

There is another objection to the Lord Chamberlain's censorship which affects the author's choice of subject. Formerly very little heed was given in England to the susceptibilities of foreign courts. For instance, the notion that the Mikado of Japan should be as sacred to the English playwright as he is to the Japanese Lord Chamberlain would have seemed grotesque a generation ago. Now that the maintenance of *entente cordiale* between nations is one of the most prominent and most useful functions of the crown, the freedom of authors to deal with political subjects, even historically, is seriously threatened by the way in which the censorship makes the King responsible for the contents of every play. One author—the writer of these lines, in fact—has long desired to dramatize the life of Mahomet. But the possibility of a protest from the Turkish Ambassador—or the fear of it—causing the Lord Chamberlain to refuse to license such a play has prevented the play from being written. Now, if the censorship were abolished, nobody but the author could be held responsible for the play....

*WHY NOT AN ENLIGHTENED CENSORSHIP?*

In the above cases the general question of censorship is separable from the question of the present form of it. Everyone who condemns the principle of Censorship must also condemn the Lord Chamberlain's control of the drama; but those who approve of the principle do not necessarily approve of the Lord Chamberlain being the Censor *ex officio*. They may, however, be entirely opposed to popular liberties, and may conclude from what has been said, not that the stage should be made as free as the church, press, or platform, but that these institutions should be censored as strictly as the stage. It will seem obvious to them that nothing is needed to remove all objections to a censorship except the placing of its powers in better hands.

Now though the transfer of the censorship to, say, the Lord Chancellor, or the Primate, or a Cabinet Minister, would be much less humiliating to the persons immediately concerned, the inherent vices of the institution would not be appreciably less disastrous. They would even be aggravated, for reasons which do not appear on the surface, and therefore need to be followed with some attention.

It is often said that the public is the real censor. That this is to some extent true is proved by the fact that plays which are licensed and produced in London have to be expurgated for the provinces. This does not mean that the provinces are more strait-laced, but simply that in many provincial towns there is only one theatre for all classes and all tastes, whereas in London there are separate theatres for separate sections of playgoers: so that, for example, Sir Herbert Beerbohm Tree can conduct His Majesty's Theatre without the slightest regard to the tastes of the frequenters of the Gaiety Theatre; and Mr George Edwardes [1855–1915] can conduct the Gaiety Theatre without catering in any way for lovers of Shakespear. Thus the farcical comedy which has scandalized the critics in London by the libertinage of its jests is played to the respectable dress circle of Northampton with these same jests slurred over so as to be imperceptible by even the most prurient spectator. The public, in short, takes care that nobody shall outrage it.

But the public also takes care that nobody shall starve it, or regulate its dramatic diet as a school-mistress regulates the reading of her pupils. Even when it wishes to be debauched, no censor can—or at least no censor does—stand out against it. If a play is irresistibly amusing, it gets licensed no matter what its moral aspect may be. A brilliant instance is the *Divorçons* [1880] of the late Victorien Sardou, which may not have been the naughtiest play of the 19th century, but was certainly the very naughtiest that any English manager in his senses would have ventured to produce. Nevertheless, being a very amusing play, it passed the licenser with the exception of a reference to impotence as a ground for divorce which no English actress would have ventured on in any case. Within the last few months a very amusing comedy with a strongly polygamous moral was found irresistible by the Lord Chamberlain. Plenty of fun and a happy ending will get anything licensed, because the public will have it so, and the Examiner of Plays, as the holder of the office testified before the Commission of 1892 (Report, page 330), feels with the public, and knows that his office could not survive a widespread unpopularity. In short, the support of the mob—that is, of the unreasoning, unorganized, uninstructed mass of popular sentiment—is indispensable to the censorship as it exists today in England. This is the explanation of the toleration by the Lord Chamberlain of coarse and vicious plays. It is not long since a judge before whom a licensed play came in the course of a lawsuit expressed his scandalized astonishment at the licensing of such a work. Eminent churchmen have made similar protests. In some plays the simulation of criminal assaults on the stage has been carried to a point at which a step further would have involved the interference of the police. Provided the treatment of the theme is gaily or hypocritically popular, and the ending happy, the indulgence of the Lord Chamberlain can be counted on. On the other hand, anything unpleasing and unpopular is rigorously censored. Adultery and prostitution are tolerated and even encouraged to such an extent that plays which do not deal with them are commonly said not to be plays at all. But if any of the unpleasing consequences of adultery and prostitution—for instance, an unsuccessful illegal operation (successful ones are tolerated) or venereal disease—are mentioned, the play is prohibited. This principle of shielding the playgoer from unpleasant reflections is carried so far that when a play was submitted for licence in which the relations of a prostitute with all the male characters in the piece was described as "immoral," the Examiner of Plays objected to that passage, though he made no objection to the relations themselves. The Lord Chamberlain dare not, in short, attempt to exclude from the stage the tragedies of murder and lust, or the farces of mendacity, adultery, and dissolute gaiety in which vulgar people delight. But when these same vulgar people are threatened with an unpopular play in which dissoluteness is shewn to be no laughing matter, it is prohibited at once amid the vulgar applause, the net result being that vice is made delightful and virtue banned by the very institution which is supported on the understanding that it produces exactly the opposite result.

## THE WEAKNESS OF THE LORD CHAMBERLAIN'S DEPARTMENT

Now comes the question, Why is our censorship, armed as it is with apparently autocratic powers, so scandalously timid in the face of the mob? Why is it not as autocratic in dealing with playwrights below the average as with those above it? The answer is that its position is really a very weak one. It has no direct coercive forces, no funds to institute prosecutions and recover the legal penalties of defying it, no powers of arrest or imprisonment, in short, none of the guarantees of autocracy. What it can do is to refuse to renew the licence of a theatre at which its orders are disobeyed. When it happens that a theatre is about to be demolished, as was the case recently with the Imperial Theatre after it had passed into the hands of the Wesleyan Methodists, unlicensed plays can be performed, technically in private, but really in full publicity, without risk. The prohibited plays of Brieux and Ibsen have been performed in London in this way with complete impunity. But the impunity is not confined to condemned theatres. Not long ago a West End manager allowed a prohibited play to be performed at his theatre, taking his chance of losing his licence in consequence. The event proved that the manager was justified in regarding the risk as negligible; for the Lord Chamberlain's remedy—the closing of a popular and well-conducted theatre—was far too extreme to be practicable. Unless the play had so outraged public opinion as to make the manager odious and provoke a clamor for his exemplary punishment, the Lord Chamberlain could only have had his revenge at the risk of having his powers abolished as unsupportably tyrannical.... The institution is at once absurdly despotic and abjectly weak.

*[Shaw argues that trying to create a more "enlightened censorship" would be still worse than the current system. He explains that some serious social dramas currently get licensed because the censor simply doesn't understand their implications, so a more astute censor who would be better at recognizing "dangerously heretical" ideas in plays would actually be compelled to censor more of them. See point 5, page 215.]*

### THE PRACTICAL IMPOSSIBILITIES OF CENSORSHIP

There is, besides, a crushing material difficulty in the way of an enlightened censorship. It is not too much to say that the work involved would drive a man of any intellectual rank mad. Consider, for example, the Christmas pantomimes. Imagine a judge of the High Court, or an archbishop, or a Cabinet Minister, or an eminent man of letters, earning his living by reading through the mass of trivial doggerel represented by all the pantomimes which are put into rehearsal simultaneously at the end of every year. The proposal to put such mind-destroying drudgery upon an official of the class implied by the demand for an enlightened censorship falls through the moment we realize what it implies in practice.

Another material difficulty is that no play can be judged by merely reading the dialogue. To be fully effective a censor should witness the performance. The *mise-en-scène* of a play is as much a part of it as the words spoken on the stage. No censor could possibly object to such a speech as "Might I speak to you for a moment, miss?" yet that apparently innocent phrase has often been made offensively improper on the stage by popular low comedians, with the effect of changing the whole character and meaning of the play as understood by the official Examiner. In one of the plays of the present season, the dialogue was that of a crude melodrama dealing in the most conventionally correct manner with the fortunes of a good-hearted and virtuous girl. Its morality was that of the Sunday school. But the principal actress, between two speeches which contained no reference to her action, changed her underclothing on the stage! It is true that in this case the actress was so much better than her part that she succeeded in turning what was meant as an impropriety into an inoffensive stroke of realism; yet it is none the less clear that stage business of this character, on which there can be no check except the actual presence of a censor in the theatre, might convert any dialogue, however innocent, into just the sort of entertainment against which the Censor is supposed to protect the public.

It was this practical impossibility that prevented the London County Council from attempting to apply a censorship of the Lord Chamberlain's pattern to the London music halls. A proposal to examine all entertainments before permitting their performance was actually made; and it was abandoned, not in the least as contrary to the liberty of the stage, but because the executive problem of how to do it at once reduced the proposal to absurdity....

*THE ARBITRATION PROPOSAL*

On the occasion of a recent deputation of playwrights to the Prime Minister it was suggested that if a censorship be inevitable, provision should be made for an appeal from the Lord Chamberlain in cases of refusal of licence. The authors of this suggestion propose that the Lord Chamberlain shall choose one umpire and the author another. The two umpires shall then elect a referee, whose decision shall be final.

This proposal is not likely to be entertained by constitutional lawyers. It is a naive offer to accept the method of arbitration in what is essentially a matter, not between one private individual or body and another, but between a public offender and the State. It will presumably be ruled out as a proposal to refer a case of manslaughter to arbitration would be ruled out. But even if it were constitutionally sound, it bears all the marks of that practical inexperience which leads men to believe that arbitration either costs nothing or is at least cheaper than law. Who is to pay for the time of the three arbitrators, presumably men of high professional standing? The author may not be able: the manager may not be willing: neither of them should be called upon to pay for a public service otherwise than by their contributions to the revenue. Clearly the State should pay. But even so, the difficulties are only beginning. A licence is seldom refused except on grounds which are controversial. The two arbitrators selected by the opposed parties to the controversy are to agree to leave the decision to a third party unanimously chosen by themselves. That is very far from being a simple solution. An attempt to shorten and simplify the passing of the Finance Bill by referring it to an arbitrator chosen unanimously by Mr [Herbert Henry] Asquith [Liberal Prime Minister of the UK, 1908–16] and Mr [Arthur James] Balfour [leader of the Conservative opposition, 1905–11] might not improbably cost more and last longer than a civil war. And why should the chosen referee—if he ever succeeded in getting chosen—be assumed to be a safer authority than the Examiner of Plays? He would certainly be a less responsible one: in fact, being (however eminent) a casual person called in to settle a single case, he would be virtually irresponsible. Worse still, he would take all responsibility away from the Lord Chamberlain, who is at least an official of the King's Household and a nominee of the Government. The Lord Chamberlain, with all his shortcomings, thinks twice before he refuses a licence, knowing that his refusal is final and may promptly be made public. But if he could transfer his responsibility to an arbitrator, he would naturally do so whenever he felt the slightest misgiving, or whenever, for diplomatic reasons, the licence would come more gracefully from an authority unconnected with the court. These considerations, added to the general objection to the principle of censorship, seem sufficient to put the arbitration expedient quite out of the question.

*END OF THE FIRST PART OF THE REJECTED STATEMENT*

*[In the second part of the statement, Shaw examines the case for and against licensing theatres as an alternative to licensing plays. See the summary beginning at point 8, page 216]*

*SUMMARY OF THE REJECTED STATEMENT*

The general case against censorship as a principle, and the particular case against the existing English censorship and against its replacement by a more enlightened one, is now complete. The following is a recapitulation of the propositions and conclusions contended for.

1. The question of censorship or no censorship is a question of high political principle and not of petty policy.

2. The toleration of heresy and shocks to morality on the stage, and even their protection against the prejudices and superstitions which necessarily enter largely into morality and public opinion, are essential to the welfare of the nation.

3. The existing censorship of the Lord Chamberlain does not only intentionally suppress heresy and challenges to morality in their serious and avowed forms, but unintentionally gives the special protection of its official licence to the most extreme impropriety that the lowest section of London playgoers will tolerate in theatres especially devoted to their entertainment, licensing everything that is popular and forbidding any attempt to change public opinion or morals.

4. The Lord Chamberlain's censorship is open to the special objection that its application to political plays is taken to indicate the attitude of the Crown on questions of domestic and foreign policy and that it imposes the limits of etiquet on the historical drama.

5. A censorship of a more enlightened and independent kind, exercised by the most eminent available authorities, would prove in practice more disastrous than the censorship of the Lord Chamberlain, because the more eminent its members were the less possible would it be for them to accept the responsibility for heresy or immorality by licensing them, and because the many heretical and immoral plays which now pass the Lord Chamberlain because he does not understand them, would be understood and suppressed by a more highly enlightened censorship.

6. A reconstructed and enlightened censorship would be armed with summary and effective powers which would stop the evasions by which heretical and immoral plays are now performed in spite of the Lord Chamberlain; and such powers would constitute a tyranny which would ruin the theatre spiritually by driving all independent thinkers from the drama into the uncensored forms of art.

7. The work of critically examining all stage plays in their written form, and of witnessing their performance in order to see that the sense is not altered by the stage business, would, even if it were divided among so many officials as to be phys-

ically possible, be mentally impossible to persons of taste and enlightenment.

8. Regulation of theatres is an entirely different matter from censorship, inasmuch as a theatre, being not only a stage, but a place licensed for the sale of spirits, and a public resort capable of being put to disorderly use, and needing special provision for the safety of audiences in cases of fire, etc., cannot be abandoned wholly to private control, and may therefore reasonably be made subject to an annual licence like those now required before allowing premises to be used publicly for music and dancing.

9. In order to prevent the powers of the licensing authority being abused so as to constitute a virtual censorship, any Act transferring the theatres to the control of a licensing author-ity should be made also a charter of the rights of dramatic authors and managers by the following provisions:

A. The public prosecutor (the Attorney-General) alone should have the right to set the law in operation against the manager of a theatre or the author of a play in respect of the character of the play or entertainment.

B. No disclosure of the particulars of a theatrical entertain-ment shall be required before performance.

C. Licences shall not be withheld on the ground that the existence of theatres is dangerous to religion and morals, or on the ground that any entertainment given or contemplated is heretical or immoral.

D. The licensing area shall be no less than that of a County Council or City Corporation, which shall not delegate its licensing powers to any minor local authority or to any offi-cial or committee; it shall decide all questions affecting the existence of a theatrical licence by vote of the entire body; managers, lessees, and proprietors of theatres shall have the right to plead, in person or by counsel, against a proposal to withhold a licence; and the licence shall not be withheld except for stated reasons, the validity of which shall be subject to the judgment of the high courts.

E. The annual licence, once granted, shall not be cancelled or suspended unless the manager has been convicted by public prosecution of an offence against the ordinary laws against disorderly housekeeping, indecency, blasphemy, etc., except in cases where some structural or sanitary defect in the building necessitates immediate action for the protection of the public against physical injury.

F. No licence shall be refused on the ground that the proximity of the theatre to a church, mission hall, school, or other place of worship, edification, instruction, or entertainment (including another theatre) would draw the public away from such places into its own doors....

## Preface Resumed

*MR GEORGE ALEXANDER'S PROTEST*

On the facts mentioned in the foregoing statement, and in my evidence before the Joint Select Committee, no controversy arose except on one point. Mr [later Sir] George Alexander [1858–1918] protested vigorously and indignantly against my admission that theatres, like public-houses, need special control on the ground that they can profit by disorder, and are sometimes conducted with that end in view. Now, Mr Alexander is a famous actor-manager; and it is very difficult to persuade the public that the more famous an actor-manager is the less he is likely to know about any theatre except his own. When the [Select] Committee [on theatre censorship] of 1892 reported, I was considered guilty of a perverse paradox when I said that the witness who knew least about the theatre was Henry Irving. Yet a moment's consideration would have shewn that the paradox was a platitude. For about quarter of a century Irving was confined night after night to his own theatre and his own dressing-room, never seeing a play even there because he was himself part of the play; producing the works of long departed authors; and, to the extent to which his talent was extraordinary, necessarily making his theatre unlike any other theatre. When he went to the provinces or to America, the theatres to which he went were swept and garnished for him, and their staffs replaced—as far as he came in contact with them—by his own lieutenants. In the end, there was hardly a first-nighter in his gallery who did not know more about the London theatres and the progress of dramatic art than he; and as to the provinces, if any chief constable had told him the real history and character of many provincial theatres, he would have denounced that chief constable as an ignorant libeller of a noble profession. But the constable would have been right for all that. Now if this was true of Sir Henry Irving, who did not become a London manager until he had roughed it for years in the provinces, how much more true must it be of, say, Mr George Alexander, whose successful march through his profession has passed as far from the purlieus of our theatrical world as the king's naval career from the Isle of Dogs [a peninsula in London's East end formed by a meander in the River Thames]? The moment we come to that necessary part of the censorship question which deals with the control of theatres from the point of view of those who know how much money can be made out of them by managers who seek to make the auditorium attractive rather than the stage, you find the managers divided into two sections. The first section consists of honorable and successful managers like Mr Alexander, who know nothing of such abuses, and deny, with perfect sincerity and indignant vehemence, that they exist except, perhaps, in certain notorious variety theatres. The other is the silent section which knows better, but is very well content to be publicly defended and privately amused by Mr Alexander's innocence. To accept a West End manager as an expert in theatres because he is an actor is much as if we were to accept the organist of St Paul's Cathedral as an expert on music halls because he is a musician. The real experts are all in the conspiracy to keep the police out of the theatre. And they are so successful that even the police do not know as much as they should.

The police should have been examined by the Committee, and the whole question of the extent to which theatres are disorderly houses in disguise sifted to the bottom. For it is on this point that we discover behind the phantoms of the corrupt dramatists who are restrained by the censorship from debauching the stage, the reality of the corrupt managers and theatre proprietors who actually do debauch it without let or hindrance from the censorship. The whole case for giving control over theatres to local authorities rests on this reality.

*ELIZA AND HER BATH*

The persistent notion that a theatre is an Alsatia [section of London designated as legal sanctuary, populated by criminals who were virtually untouchable there] where the king's writ does not run, and where any wickedness is possible in the absence of a special tribunal and a special police, was brought out by an innocent remark made by Sir William Gilbert, who, when giving evidence before the Committee, was asked by Colonel Lockwood whether a law sufficient to restrain impropriety in books would also restrain impropriety in plays. Sir William replied: "I should say there is a very wide distinction between what is read and what is seen. In a novel one may read that 'Eliza stripped off her dressing-gown and stepped into her bath' without any harm; but I think if that were presented on the stage it would be shocking." All the stupid and inconsiderate people seized eagerly on this illustration as if it were a successful attempt to prove that without a censorship we should be unable to prevent actresses from appearing naked on the stage. As a matter of fact, if an actress could be persuaded to do such a thing (and it would be about as easy to persuade a bishop's wife to appear in church in the same condition) the police would simply arrest her on a charge of indecent exposure. The extent to which this obvious safeguard was overlooked may be taken as a measure of the thoughtlessness and frivolity of the excuses made for the censorship. It should be added that the artistic representation of a bath, with every suggestion of nakedness that the law as to decency allows, is one of the most familiar subjects of scenic art....

*[Shaw continues his summary of testimonies to the Joint Committee hearings and consideration of various alternatives to the current censorship system.]*

## Conclusion

I must conclude by recommending the Government to take my advice wherever it conflicts with that of the Joint Select Committee. It is, I think, obviously more deeply considered and better informed, though I say it that should not. At all events, I have given my reasons; and at that I must leave it. As the tradition which makes Malvolio not only Master of the Revels but Master of the Mind of England, and which has come down to us from Henry VIII, is manifestly doomed to the dustbin, the sooner it goes there the better; for the democratic control which naturally succeeds it can easily be limited so as to prevent it becoming either a censorship or a tyranny. The Examiner of Plays should receive a generous pension, and be set free to practise privately as an expert adviser of theatrical managers. There is no reason why they should be deprived of the counsel they so highly value.

It only remains to say that public performances of *The Shewing-up of Blanco Posnet* are still prohibited in Great Britain by the Lord Chamberlain. An attempt was made to prevent even its performance in Ireland by some indiscreet Castle officials in the absence of the Lord Lieutenant. This attempt gave extraordinary publicity to the production of the play; and every possible effort was made to persuade the Irish public that the performance would be an outrage to their religion, and to provoke a repetition of the rioting that attended the first performances of Synge's *Playboy of the Western World* [in 1907] before the most sensitive and, on provocation, the most turbulent audience in the kingdom. The directors of the Irish National Theatre, Lady [Augusta] Gregory [1852–1932] and Mr William Butler Yeats [1865–1939], rose to the occasion with inspiring courage. I am a conciliatory person, and was willing, as I always am, to make every concession in return for having my own way. But Lady Gregory and Mr Yeats not only would not yield an inch, but insisted, within the due limits of gallant warfare, on taking the field with every circumstance of defiance, and winning the battle with every trophy of victory. Their triumph was as complete as they could have desired. The performance exhausted the possibilities of success, and provoked no murmur, though it inspired several approving sermons. Later on, Lady Gregory and Mr Yeats brought the play to London and performed it under the Lord Chamberlain's nose, through the instrumentality of the Stage Society.

After this, the play was again submitted to the Lord Chamberlain. But, though beaten, he, too, understands the art of How Not To Do It. He licensed the play, but endorsed on his licence the condition that all the passages which implicated God in the history of Blanco Posnet must be omitted in representation. All the coarseness, the profligacy, the prostitution, the violence, the drinking-bar humor into which the light shines in the play are licensed, but the light itself is extinguished. I need hardly say that I have not availed myself of this licence, and do not intend to. There is enough licensed darkness in our theatres today without my adding to it.

POSTSCRIPT.—Since the above was written the Lord Chamberlain has made an attempt to evade his responsibility and perhaps to postpone his doom by appointing an advisory committee, unknown to the law, on which he will presumably throw any odium that may attach to refusals of licences in the future. This strange and lawless body will hardly reassure our moralists, who object much more to the plays he licenses than to those he suppresses, and are therefore unmoved by his plea that his refusals are few and far between. It consists of two eminent actors (one retired), an Oxford professor of literature, and two eminent barristers. As their assembly is neither created by statute nor sanctioned by custom, it is difficult to know what to call it until it advises the Lord Chamberlain to deprive some author of his means of livelihood, when it will, I presume, become a conspiracy, and be indictable accordingly; unless, indeed, it can persuade the Courts to recognize it as a new Estate of the Realm, created by the Lord Chamberlain. This constitutional position is so questionable that I strongly advise the members to resign promptly before the Lord Chamberlain gets them into trouble.

## 3. From "Censorship as a Police Duty," 1928.
### [*Platform and Pulpit*, pp. 183–200]

[*Shaw delivered this address at the Special General Conference of the Chief Constables' Association on 8 June. He opens the speech with a lengthy apparent digression about the evolution of policing in his lifetime in terms of the duties and functions that police forces are expected to discharge, eventually working towards cautioning police about the difficulty of enforcing laws that require them to interpret society's threshold of morality.*]

...You may wonder why I, who undertook to address you on the question of censorship of plays, have not yet said a word about it. But it has been necessary, before I could get you to see the difficulties of the position, to bring you to this point. Because, of all the impossible opinionative duties that could be put on you, the censorship of plays is the most impossible, and the most odious.

And I am going to advise you to resist the imposition of that duty on you with all your might and main. It will give you a lot of trouble. It will give you no credit, and from time to time will bring upon you discredit and ridicule, as it has many times brought on the Lord Chamberlain. Plays, like political speeches and books, bring you up against those constitutional liberties which you are supposed to preserve. Our main liberties are freedom of speech, freedom of the press, freedom of conscience—that is, freedom to worship in any church in any way we like—and the freedom of the stage, which comes in with the freedom of speech and the freedom of the newspapers.

These freedoms, as we call them, are a curious and entirely illogical exception to the laws which are made for the regulation of our other activities. When an author, for instance, says, "I am claiming my freedom to write as I please," he is making a very strong claim. He is not making a claim to write a book which everyone will recognize as being a decent and proper book. That does not require freedom at all. The author is asserting a right to write something which may horrify you.

Experience has led us to concede that curious claim to a great extent, because the history of the world shews that if you refuse to allow a man to express unusual and even shocking ideas there will never be any progress made. Ideas would never change, and a world where ideas never change means stagnation, decline, and decay. That is why this curious exception is made.

When a Chief Constable reads the newspapers he must occasionally wonder whether the freedom of the press is really a good thing or not, because no one knows better the amount of mischief which they occasionally do by the exercise of their freedom. And, in spite of the freedoms, he has to carry out a law which makes blasphemy an offence, sedition an offence, and obscenity an offence. How is he to judge of what is blasphemous and what is freedom of speech?

[Shaw offers examples of religious, political, and social issues to ask at what point ideas and practices become intolerable.]

Take the question of venereal disease. Everyone in this room can remember when this was an unmentionable subject. For instance, there is a very well-known play by a noted French author [Eugène Brieux's Damaged Goods] which dealt with the question, and, at first, the Censor would not allow it to be produced. Yet the time came during the war when the authorities were very glad to have that play performed from one end of the country to the other. Now you have venereal disease discussed by assemblies of ladies and gentlemen all over the country. What was unmentionable yesterday is a common topic of polite conversation today. ...

If there is a subject on earth on which you might think there could be no two opinions among decent people it is the subject of incest. But incest is only marriage within the tables of consanguinity; and those tables differ from time to time, from nation to nation, and from religion to religion.

Take, for instance, the play Hamlet, which many people think the greatest of Shakespear's plays. In it Hamlet reproaches his mother for committing incest in such horrible terms that if the actors make it real I always feel very uncomfortable while it is being performed. But what Chief Constables dare prosecute Sir Johnston Forbes-Robertson for playing Hamlet? ...

*[Shaw describes the incestuous plot elements in* Hamlet, *Wagner's* Die Walküre, *and Shelley's* The Cenci, *all by this time licensed for performance and considered "classics." He then introduces the futility of censoring a play based on a printed text.]*

You can read the play, but you cannot control the gesture made, and do not know what the play will be like when it comes to the performance.

Again, you may come to a passage which appears to be revoltingly blasphemous. That occurred in a play of mine. I wrote a play which, if it had not been put in dramatic form, might have been a religious tract, *The Shewing-up of Blanco Posnet.* The Lord Chamberlain handed it to his reader, Mr Redford. He was a little puzzled by the play. It had a passage in it, "He is a mean one; he is a sly one." Mr Redford could not make out to whom the speaker was referring. I presume he asked someone in the office who was meant by the "mean one; the sly one." The reply must have been, "I am afraid he is alluding to God Almighty, because immediately afterwards, when someone asks who it is, he points upwards."

What could Mr Redford do? He could not allow God Almighty to be described on the stage as "a mean one; a sly one." He issued a license conditionally on all references to God Almighty being cut out. The result was curious. I could not allow the play to be performed with these lines cut out, because without them it became a senseless, rowdy, blasphemous, coarse play—a horrible play, a thing I could not have my name connected with.

But you can imagine Mr Redford's astonishment when, on the first Sunday after the play was published, no less than three sermons were preached on the subject of the play. The clergy were delighted with it, and it has been the subject of several sermons since. When Lord Sandhurst became Lord Chamberlain [1912–21] he withdrew the ban, and the play is now licensed. Yet, if you had been in the position of Mr Red-

THE CRITICAL SHAW: ON THEATER

ford you would have found it very hard, on coming to that passage, to see that the dramatic effect was no more blasphemous than the reproaches addressed by Job to his Maker in the Bible are blasphemous. The truth is, Mr Redford and the Lord Chamberlain were confronted with a task which, in itself, was impossible. You cannot tell whether or not a play will do harm until you have seen it performed.

All the argument for stopping the play to prevent the evil is equivalent to the argument for handcuffing me before I get back to my hotel, on the ground that if you do not I might punch someone's head on the way. You have got to allow the dog his first bite. The moment they come to you and talk about reading plays and prohibiting them, you should say, "No, let them perform it first, and if there is an offence we can deal with it then. We cannot come in beforehand. The thing has been tried out and it is of no use. Not only have the most scandalous plays got through, but edifying plays like Mr Shaw's *The Shewing-up of Blanco Posnet* have been stopped." And think of the number of people who might have been turned to salvation by that religious tract of mine during all these years during which I was branded as a blasphemer!

Let me give one illustration as to the things that get through. I was once asked by a leading American magazine to write an article on the subject of the censorship (see page 178). I replied that it was quite impossible for me to describe the most scandalous of the plays passed by the censorship and performed under the Lord Chamberlain's license in a magazine intended for family reading.

They said they were interested in this question, and they went so far as to count the words in my article and to give me a pledge that every single word would be published. But when it came to the point they had to cut it drastically in spite of their solemn pledge, and I did not wonder at it. It really was not fit for publication, and yet all that stuff had been licensed by the Lord Chamberlain, and if you had been the Lord Chamberlain you would have licensed it.

The political situation is a quaint one. Every one of the plays that come along to the provinces has been licensed by the Lord Chamberlain; and the Lord Chamberlain is the chief officer of the King's household. Well, if you prosecute a play that has been licensed in that way, it appears to me you are committing an act verging on high treason.

You go into court to prosecute a play on the ground that it is blasphemous, obscene, or seditious, and the manager immediately protests that the Lord Chamberlain has licensed it from St James's Palace, and certified that it is fit and proper for presentation. And he has had two guineas for doing it and you have had nothing for your opinion. What are you to do under these circumstances? Your conduct cannot be challenged in Parliament, because any member of Parliament can move the reduction of the Police vote by £100 in order to draw attention to the conduct of a Chief Constable. Not so the Lord Chamberlain. His salary does not come up in the House of Commons; he is part of the King's household. Years and years ago it was asked how are we to get rid of the censorship of the Lord Chamberlain, and I said, "You will have to abolish the Monarchy first."

My advice to you is to resist any attempt to put on you the duty of the Lord Chamberlain. For my own part, I do not want to abolish the Lord Chamberlain only to expose myself to the attacks of the common informer—to the secretary of the vigilance society which looks after public morals. I should be in a much worse case than I was before. I should be at the mercy, too, of every Chief Constable. Now, the Chief Constable would have nothing to fear from me. I am only an author. But he would be up against big money in this matter. A play often represents a very large investment of money. There is not only the production of the play in London, but the carefully-planned tour round the country. If a

Chief Constable suddenly butts in in the middle of a tour, and throws the touring company idle for a week or a fortnight, he is knocking big business on the head to that extent; and immediately he has the whole power of the big business men against him.

That is an antagonism which no prudent Chief Constable will lightly take on. You would have all the managers up against you, because they are strenuous supporters of the Lord Chamberlain. For the two guineas which they give him they receive what is practically an insurance policy against being prosecuted for the production of the play. If you prosecute, you are breaking that bargain.

I call attention especially to this point because some of you might imagine that, because the managers support the Lord Chamberlain so strongly, they would also support you strongly. Not a bit of it. The reason for which they support the Lord Chamberlain will make them oppose you furiously.

Is the theatre, then, to be left unregulated? That is a thing which virtually cannot be done. There are still theatres in this country which are little more than disorderly houses. You may have a theatre where tickets of admission are given away wholesale in order to induce people to visit them. When they get there the attraction is the drinking bar and a promenade full of prostitutes, and the money is made out of them in that way. Of course, numbers of theatrical managers, especially in London, will be horrified at this statement. Such things do not go on while they are there, but what goes on at other times may make it necessary for the police to keep an eye on the theatre, and to make it possible for them to get it closed.

I suggest that the proper way to deal with the theatre questions is to have the theatre licensed by the local authority from year to year. In London, the establishment of this control by the London County Council over the London music halls made a most beneficent transformation. From being places to which respectable people did not go, they have been turned into variety theatres in which you find the most distinguished audience. Sometimes half the House of Lords is there with its wives and daughters; and all that change has been made by municipal control.

People will say, "Is the London County Council, or the Birmingham Corporation, for instance, going to read all the plays?" There is nothing of that kind proposed. If the theatres were licensed, the police in the first place would have access to them and would have the power to oppose the renewal of the license. They could bring forward what evidence they liked as regards the way the place was conducted, and they could call attention to the character of the entertainment.

I do not suggest that local authorities should be empowered to refuse licenses for other than judicial reasons. Justices must not refuse to renew licenses of public houses because they individually may happen to think that there should be no public houses in the world. In the same way, I should not allow a Puritan member of a local authority to oppose the renewal of a license merely because he thought that the theatre was the gate to Hell and that there should be no such things as theatres. The judicial reason is a perfectly well understood and established feature of licensing practice.

Unless a theatre was really badly conducted, and was an undesirable and disreputable place, you could never get a majority of our large councils or city corporations to vote for the closing of the house. But the power to close it would keep the managers in good order for all practical purposes.

Then there is the question of the prosecution of a play. That should not be done locally, but by the Public Prosecutor. No common informer should have the power to institute a prosecution. Chief Constables should not have the power to do it. It would be very undesirable and troublesome to themselves. It is one of the things of which you have a right to say, "This is not a proper function for us. If a play is improper for one town, it is improper for all towns; and it should be prosecuted by a central authority representing the whole country."

To sum up, I advise you to press for the licensing of theatres by local authorities as a substitute for the censorship. I have taken up an unconscionable amount of time, but I thought it better to do the thing thoroughly while I was about it.

# Part V: The Business of Theater

Shaw's commitment to the quasi-religious significance of theatre was rooted in a very realistic recognition of theatre, even non-commercial theatre, as a business venture. He was acutely aware of the cost of producing theatre, and well knew that how much money was available had a real impact on what kind of theatre could be produced. When his own plays began making money, he made sure that his royalties were being properly negotiated and collected, not necessarily because he needed them—his marriage to Irish heiress Charlotte Payne-Townshend liberated him from money concerns early in his career—but from a belief that he was helping to hold theatre to a standard of professional ethics that would benefit everyone working in it. Shaw's interest in The Business of Theater went far beyond just money, however: he also took an active interest in placing, casting and directing his plays. Shaw knew which managers or theatre venues could likely muster the right audiences for his plays, and kept track of which actors and actresses were best suited for the parts. He took an active role in rehearsals for London productions until the volume of the work became unmanageable, becoming a pioneer in the emerging field of directing.

# 1. Preface to *The Theatrical "World" of 1894*, by William Archer, 1895.

*[William Archer published several collections of the theatre criticism he wrote for* The World, *each including a preface by a well-known playwright.* Shaw had been The World's *music critic in 1894, resigning just prior to the publication of this volume. He had not yet fully established his own reputation as a theatre critic, but had already attracted some attention in dramatic circles as a playwright. In this essay, Shaw describes the financial and business aspects of theatre that create the conditions of production for London theatre and can significantly affect the reception of a work, but are rarely acknowledged in reviews.]*

My qualification for introducing this annual record is, as I have vainly urged upon my friend the author, the worst qualification possible. For years past those readers of *The World* whose interest in art gave them an appetite for criticism, turned every Tuesday from a page on the drama by W. A. to a page on music by G. B. S. Last year the death of Edmund Yates [1831–94, founder and chief editor of *The World*] closed a chapter in the history of the paper; and G. B. S., having exhausted his message on the subject of contemporary music, took the occasion to write Finis at the end of his musical articles. But the old association was so characteristic, and is still so recent, that we have resolved to try whether the reader will not, just this once more, turn over the page and pass from G. B. S. to W. A., by mere force of habit, without noticing the glaring fact that the musical duties of G. B. S., by cutting him off almost entirely from the theatre, have left him, as aforesaid, quite the most unsuitable person to meddle in a book about the theatre and nothing else.

However, one can learn something about the theatre even at the opera: for instance, that there are certain permanent conditions which deeply affect every artistic performance in

London. No journalist, without intolerable injustice to artists and managers whose livelihood is at stake, can pass judgment without taking these conditions into account; and yet he may not mention them, because their restatement in every notice would be unbearable. The journalist is therefore forced to give his reader credit for knowing the difficulties under which plays are produced in this country, just as the writer of the leading article is forced to assume that his reader is acquainted with the British constitution and the practical exigencies of our system of party government. And it is because the reader hardly ever does know these things that newspapers so often do more harm than good.

Obviously Mr Archer, in reprinting his weekly articles exactly as they appeared, and thereby preserving all their vividness and actuality, preserves also this dependence of the journalist on the public for a considerate and well-informed reading of his verdicts. I need hardly add that he will not get it, because his readers, though interested in the art of the theatre, neither know nor care anything about the business of the theatre; and yet the art of the theatre is as dependent on its business as a poet's genius is on his bread and butter. Theatrical management in this country is one of the most desperate commercial forms of gambling. No one can foresee the fate of a play: the most experienced managers carefully select failure after failure for production; and the most feather-headed beginners blunder on successes. At the London West End theatres, where all modern English dramas are born, the minimum expense of running a play is about £400 a week, the maximum anything you please to spend on it. And all but the merest fraction of it may be, and very frequently is, entirely lost. On the other hand, success may mean a fortune of fifty thousand pounds accumulated within a single year. Very few forms of gambling are as hazardous as this. At roulette you can back red or black instead of yellow. On the turf you can take the low odds against the favorite instead of the high odds against the outsider. At both games you can stake as much or as little as you choose. But in the theatre you must play a desperate game for high stakes, or not play at all. And the risk falls altogether on the management. Everybody, from the author to the charwoman, must be paid before the management appropriates a farthing.

The scientific student of gambling will see at once that these are not the conditions which permanently attract the gambler. They are too extreme, too inelastic; besides, the game requires far too much knowledge. Consequently, the gambler pure and simple never meddles with the theatre: he has ready to his hand dozens of games that suit him better. And what is too risky for the gambler is out of the question for the man of business. Thus, from the purely economic point of view, the theatre is impossible. Neither as investment nor speculation, enterprise nor game, earnest nor jest, can it attract a single sovereign of capital. You must disturb a man's reason before he will even listen to a proposal to run a playhouse. It will now be asked why, under these circumstances, have we a couple of dozen West End theatres open in London. Are they being run by people whose reason is disturbed? The answer is, emphatically, Yes. They are the result of the sweeping away of all reasonable economic prudence by the immense force of an artistic instinct which drives the actor at all hazards for the exercise of his art, and which makes the theatre irresistibly fascinating to many rich people who can afford to keep theatres just as they can afford to keep racehorses, yachts, or newspapers. The actor who is successful enough to obtain tolerably continuous employment as "leading man" in London at a salary of from twenty to forty pounds a week, can in a few years save enough to try the experiment of taking a theatre for a few months and producing a play on his own account. The same qualities which have enabled him to interest the public as an actor will help him, as actor-manager, to interest the rich theatre fanciers, and to persuade them to act as his "backers." If the enterprise thus started be watered now and then by the huge profits of a successful play, it will take a great deal to kill it. With the help of these profits and occasional subsidies, runs of ill luck are weathered with every appearance of brilliant prosperity, and are suspected only by experienced acting-managers, and by shrewd observers who have noticed the extreme scepticism of these gentlemen as to the reality of any apparently large success.

The system of actor-manager and backer is practically supreme in London. The drama is in the hands of Mr Irving, Mr Alexander, Mr Beerbohm Tree, Mr Lewis Waller [1860–1916], Mrs John Wood, Mr Hare, Mr [Edward] Terry [1844–1912, brother to Ellen Terry], Mr Wyndham, Mr Penley, and Mr [John Lawrence] Toole [1830–1906]. Nearly all the theatres other than theirs are either devoted, like the Adelphi and Drury Lane, to the routine of those comparatively childish forms of melodrama which have no more part in the development of the theatre as one of the higher forms of art than Madame Tussaud's [wax sculptor who founded the wax museums] or the Christy Minstrels, or else they are opera-houses.

We all know by this time that the effect of the actor-manager system is to impose on every dramatic author who wishes to have his work produced in a first-rate style, the condition that there shall be a good part for the actor-manager in it. This is not in the least due to the vanity and jealousy of the actor-manager: it is due to his popularity. The strongest fascination at a theatre is the fascination of the actor or actress, not of the author. More people go to the Lyceum Theatre to see Mr Irving and Miss Ellen Terry than to see Shakespear's plays; at all events, it is certain that if Mr Irving were to present himself in as mutilated a condition as he presented *King Lear*, a shriek of horror would go up from all London. If Mr Irving were to produce a tragedy, or Mr Wyndham a comedy, in which they were cast for subordinate parts, the public would stay away; and the author would have reason to curse the self-denial of the actor-manager. Mr Hare's personally modest managerial policy is anything but encouraging to authors and critics who wish that all actor-managers were even as he. The absence of a strong personal interest on his part in the plays submitted to him takes all the edge off his judgment as to their merits; and except when he is falling back on old favorites like *Caste* [by T.W. Robertson, 1867] and *Diplomacy* [by C.W. Scott and B.C. Stephenson, 1878], or holding on to *A Pair of Spectacles* [by Sydney Grundy, 1890], which is as much a one-part actor-manager's play as *Hamlet* is, he is too often selecting all the failures of the modern drama, and leaving the successes to the actor-managers whose selective instincts are sharpened by good parts in them. We thus see that matters are made worse instead of mended by the elimination of personal motives from actor-management; whilst the economic conditions are so extremely unfavorable to anyone but an actor venturing upon the management of any but a purely routine theatre, that in order to bring up the list of real exceptions to the London rule of actor-management to three, we have to count Mr [Augustin] Daly and Mr [J.T.] Grein [1852–1935, Dutch-born founder] of the Independent Theatre along with Mr [Joseph W.] Comyns Carr [1849–1916]. Mr Grein, though his forlorn hopes have done good to the drama out of all apparent proportion to the show they have been able to make, tells us that he has lost more by his efforts than anybody but a fanatic would sacrifice; whilst Mr Daly, as the manager and proprietor of a London theatre (New York is his centre of operations), has had little success except in the Shakespearean revivals which have enabled him to exploit Miss Ada Rehan's [1860–1916, Irish comedienne and Daly's leading lady] unrivalled charm of poetic speech.

Taking actor-management, then, as inevitable, for the moment, and dismissing as untenable the notion that the actor-manager can afford to be magnanimous any more than he can afford to be lazy, why is it that, on the whole, the effect of the system is to keep the theatre lagging far behind the drama? The answer is, that the theatre depends on a very large public, and the drama on a very small one. A great dramatic poet will produce plays for a bare livelihood, if he can get nothing more. Even if a London theatre would perform them on the same terms, the sum that will keep a poet for a year—or five years at a pinch—will not keep the theatre open for more than a week. Ibsen, the greatest living dramatic poet, produces a play in two years. If he could sell twenty thousand copies of it at five shillings apiece within the following two years, he would no doubt consider himself, for a poet, a most fortunate man in his commercial relations. But unless a London manager sees some probability of from 50,000 to 75,000 people paying him an average five shillings apiece within three months, he will hardly be persuaded to venture.... This is how the theatre lags behind its own published literature. And the evil tends to perpetuate itself in two ways: first, by helping to prevent the formation of a habit of playgoing among the cultivated section of the London community; and second, by diverting the best of our literary talent from the theatre to ordinary fiction and journalism, in which it becomes technically useless for stage purposes.

The matter is further complicated by the conditions on which the public are invited to visit the theatre. These conditions, in my opinion, are sufficient by themselves to make most reasonable people regard a visit to the theatre rather as a troublesome and costly luxury to be indulged in three or four times a year under family pressure, than as the ordinary way of passing an unoccupied evening. The theatrical managers will not recognize that they have to compete with the British fireside, the slippers, the easy chair, the circulating library, and the illustrated press. They persist in expecting a man and his wife to leave their home after dinner, and, after worrying their way to the theatre by relays of train and cab or omnibus, pay seven-and-sixpence or half a guinea apiece for comfortable seats. In the United States, where prices are higher in other things, the accommodation can be had for five and six shillings. The cheaper parts of the London theatres are below the standard of comfort now expected by third-class travellers on our northern railway lines. The result is, not that people refuse to go to the theatre at all, but that they go very seldom, and then only to some house of great repute, like Mr Irving's, or to see some play which has created the sort of mania indicated by the term "catching on." No doubt, when this mania sets in, the profits are, as we have seen, enormous. But when it does not—and this is the more frequent case—the acting-manager is at his wit's end to find people who will sit in his half-guinea stalls and seven-and-sixpenny balcony seats for nothing, in order to persuade the provincial playgoer, when his turn comes to see the piece "on tour" from an excellent seat costing only a few shillings, that he is witnessing a "great London success." In the long run this system will succumb to the action of competition, and to the growing discrepancy between the distribution of prices in the theatre; but the reader who wishes to intelligently understand the failures and successes recorded in this book, must take account of the fact that, with the exception of the shilling gallery, every seat in a West End London theatre is at present charged for at a rate which makes it impossible for theatrical enterprise to settle down from a feverish speculation into a steady industry.

Among other effects of this state of things is an extreme precariousness of employment for actors, who are compelled to demand unreasonably high salaries in order that they may earn in the course of the year discouragingly small incomes. As we have seen, the few who have sufficient adaptable ability and popularity to be constantly employed, save rapidly enough to become actor-managers and even to build theatres for themselves. The result is that it becomes more and more difficult to obtain a fine cast for a play. The "star system," which is supposed to have disappeared in London, is really rampant there as far as acting is concerned. Compare, for example, the Opera, where the actor-manager is unknown, with the Lyceum Theatre. Sir Augustus Harris can present an opera with a whole constellation of stars in it.... Now try to imagine Mr Irving attempting to do for a masterpiece of Shakespear's what Sir Augustus Harris does for *Lohengrin*. All the other stars are like Mr Irving: they have theatres of their own, and are competing with him as men of business, instead of co-operating with him as artists.... One expects every month to hear that Mr [Herbert] Waring [1857–1932], Mr Fred Terry [1863–1933, brother to Ellen Terry], Mr Yorke Stephens [1860–1937], Mr Forbes-Robertson, Mr Brandon Thomas [1848–1914, playwright of *Charley's Aunt*], and Mr Hawtrey are about to follow Mr Alexander and Mr [Lewis] Waller [1860–1915] into actor-management. We should then have sixteen actor-managers competing with one another in sixteen different theatres, in a metropolis hardly containing good actors enough to cast three good plays simultaneously, even with the sixteen actor-managers counted in. No doubt such an increased demand for actors and plays as six additional managers would set up might produce an increased and improved supply if the demand of the public for theatrical amusements kept pace with the ambition of actors to become actor-managers; but is there, under existing conditions as to growth of population and distribution of income, the slightest likelihood of such an upward bound of public demand without a marked reduction of prices?

There is yet another momentous prospect to be taken into consideration. We have at present nine actor-managers and only one actress-manageress—Mrs John Wood. So far, our chief actresses have been content to depend on the position of "leading lady" to some actor-manager. This was sufficient for all ordinary ambitions ten years ago; but since then the progress of a revolution in public opinion on what is called the Woman Question has begun to agitate the stage.... The change is so patent, that one of the plays criticized by Mr Archer in the pages which follow is called *The New Woman* [1894, by Sydney Grundy]. Now it is not possible to put the new woman seriously on the stage in her relation to modern society, without stirring up, both on the stage and in the auditorium, the struggle to keep her in her old place. The play with which Ibsen conquered the world, *A Doll's House*, allots to the "leading man" the part of a most respectable bank manager, exactly the sort of person on whose quiet but irresistible moral superiority to women Tom Taylor [1817–1880, playwright and *Punch* editor] insisted with the fullest public applause in his *Still Waters Run Deep* [1855]. Yet the play ends with the most humiliating exposure of the vanity, folly, and amorous beglamorment of this complacent person in his attitude towards his wife, the exposure being made by the wife herself. His is not the sort of part that an actor-manager likes to play. Mr Wyndham has revived *Still Waters Run Deep*; he will not touch *A Doll's House*. The one part that no actor as yet plays willingly is the part of a hero whose heroism is neither admirable nor laughable. A villain if you like, a hunchback, a murderer, a kicked, cuffed, duped pantaloon by all means; but a hero *manqué*, never. Man clings to the old pose, the old cheap heroism; and the actor in particular, whose life aspiration it has been to embody that pose, feels, with inexpressible misgiving, the earth crumbling beneath his feet as the enthusiasm his heroism once excited turns to pity and ridicule. But this misgiving is the very material on which the modern dramatist of the Ibsen school seizes for his tragicomedy. It is the material upon which I myself have seized in a play of my own criticized in this book, to which I only allude here to gratify my friend the author, who has begged me to say something about *Arms and the Man*. I comply by confessing that the result was a misunderstanding so complete, that but for the pleasure given by the acting, and for the happy circumstance that there was sufficient fun in the purely comic aspect of the piece to enable it to filch a certain vogue as a novel sort of extravaganza, its failure would have been as evident to the public as it was to me when I bowed my acknowledgments before the curtain to a salvo of entirely mistaken congratulations (see page 78) on my imaginary success as a conventionally cynical and paradoxical castigator of "the seamy side of human nature." The whole difficulty was created by the fact that my Bulgarian hero, quite as much as Helmer in *A Doll's House*, was a hero shown from the modern woman's point of view. I complicated the psychology by making him catch glimpse after glimpse of his own aspect and conduct from this point of view himself, as all men are beginning to do more or less now, the result, of course, being the most horrible dubiety on his part as to whether he was really a brave and chivalrous gentleman, or a humbug and a moral coward. His actions, equally of course, were hopelessly irreconcilable with either theory. Need I add that if the straightforward Helmer, a very honest and ordinary middle-class man misled by false ideals of womanhood, bewildered the public, and was finally set down as a selfish cad by all the Helmers in the audience, *a fortiori* [Latin term for "even more certainly"] my introspective Bulgarian hero never had a chance, and was dismissed, with but moderately spontaneous laughter, as a swaggering impostor of the species for which contemporary slang has invented the term "bounder"?

But what bearing have the peculiarities of Helmer and my misunderstood Bulgarian on the question of the actress-manageress? Very clearly this, that it is just such peculiarities that make characteristically modern plays as repugnant to the actor as they are attractive to the actress, and that, consequently, the actress who is content to remain attached to an actor-manager as "leading lady," forfeits all chance of creating any of the fascinating women's parts which come at intervals of two years from the Ibsen mint. Among the newest parts open to the leading lady, Paula Tanqueray [title character from *The Second Mrs Tanqueray* by A.W. Pinero, 1893] counts as "advanced," although she would be perfectly in her place in a novel by Thackeray or [Anthony] Trollope [1815–85], to either of whom Nora Helmer would have been an inconceivable person. A glance at our theatres will show that the higher artistic career is practically closed to the leading lady. Miss Ellen Terry's position at the Lyceum Theatre may appear an enviable one; but when I recall the parts to which she has been condemned by her task of "supporting" Mr Irving, I have to admit that Miss Janet Achurch [1864–1916], for instance, who made for herself the opportunity of "creating" Nora Helmer in England by placing herself in the position virtually of actress-manageress, is far more to be envied. Again, if we compare Miss Elizabeth Robins [1862–1952], the creator of Hedda Gabler and Hilda Wangel, with Miss Kate Rorke at the Garrick Theatre, or the records of Miss Florence Farr and Miss Marion Lea [1861–1944] with that of Miss Mary Moore [1862–1931] at the Criterion, we cannot but see that the time is ripe for the advent of the actress-manageress, and that we are on the verge of something like a struggle between the sexes for the dominion of the London theatres, a struggle which, failing an honorable treaty, or the break-up of the actor-manager system by the competition of new forms of theatrical enterprise, must in the long run end disastrously for the side which is furthest behind the times. And that side is at present the men's side.

The reader will now be able to gratify his impatience, and pass on to Mr Archer's criticisms (if he has not done so long ago), with some idea of the allowances that must be made for circumstances in giving judgment on the curious pageant which passes before the dramatic critic as he sits in his stall night after night. He has had to praise or blame, advocate or oppose, always with a human and reasonable regard to what is possible under existing conditions. Most of his readers, preoccupied with pure ideals of the art of the theatre, know nothing of these conditions and perhaps imagine that all that lies beyond their ken is the working of the traps and the shifting of the scenery. Perhaps these few hints of mine may help them to understand that the real secrets of the theatre are not those of the stage mechanism, but of the box-office, the acting-manager's room, and the actor-manager's soul.

## 2. "On Nothing in Particular and the Theatre in General," 1896. [*Our Theatres in the Nineties*, vol. 2, pp. 67–73]

*[Shaw wrote this piece for his regular dramatic criticism column. As a critic, he didn't confine himself to just reviewing plays, but used the column as a platform for educating the public on all aspects of theatrical production, and exhorting them to become more critically engaged audiences.]*

Being at a loss for something to write about, I look through the tickets in my drawer, hoping to find by chance some forgotten first night to help me out of my difficulty. Among others I turn up an odd-looking green ticket with no less than four counter-foils, for a performance that is to last four nights—or rather four summer afternoons and evenings in July next. On the first evening the play will begin at five o'clock; and the performance will not be divided into acts. On the second and third evenings, the first act is timed for four o'clock, the second for six, the third for eight. On the fourth evening, the first act will begin at four, but the second and third not until half-past six and half-past eight. My seat each evening will cost me a pound; and, being an economical person, I shall perhaps keep the cost of my cabs, trains, and so forth, down to fifteen or sixteen pounds; so that I shall get safely out of this piece of playgoing for a twenty-pound note. Need I say that I cannot afford it? And yet what am I to do? The theatre is the best and most famous in the world—no, it is not Drury Lane: it is called the Stage Festival Playhouse of Bayreuth [Germany, designed for an annual opera festival dedicated to Richard Wagner]. It is the only theatre where you can wander from a pine forest into your stall, and wander out at the end of the act into the terebinthine air again, leaving the theatre to renew its freshness so that you can see the play out without a headache. He who has not been there knows nothing about theatres, no matter how often he may have been stuffed into a fabulously ground-rented cockpit in the Strand, and regaled with the delights of the British drama.

Now the aggravating thing about this is that the Stage Festival Playhouse might just as well be in Middlesex or Surrey. We could build it for ourselves better and cheaper than the Bayreuthers built it for Wagner. Within a shilling railway ride from Charing Cross we have heaths, commons, hills and forests, as lovely as the Fichtelgebirge. Our orchestral and scenic resources far surpass those of the Bühnenfestspielhaus; our wealth is to Bayreuth's as Lombard Street's to a China orange; and even our restaurants are not altogether inferior. When once our enthusiasm is aroused—say by a race meeting or the Crystal Palace fireworks [annual free fireworks displays held on the grounds of the Crystal Palace exhibition hall from 1865–1936]—we go afield readily in pursuit of amusement and edification.... Why then must I, next July, face those two weary journeys of a night and a day, with half a day thrown in, by sea and land, to see what I might as well see here at my ease if only English theatrical enterprise could rouse itself from its dull routine of boom, bankruptcy, and boredom to give us something that we really want, whether we know it or not?

I see it stated that the new theatre which Mr Beerbohm Tree is building on the site of Her Majesty's [theatre in the prime Haymarket area of London] is to be modelled on the Bayreuth Wagner Theatre. There is something exasperating in the cool, bluff innocence which reports such things as if they were possible. The very first requirement for a theatre modelled on Wagner's is practically unlimited ground space. The Bayreuth Festival Playhouse pays no rent. The space occupied by its scene docks alone would bring in several thousands a year in the Haymarket. In it there are no galleries; and the stalls, much more commodious than those in some of our London theatres, number thirteen hundred odd, fifty-six to the row in the widest part. Imagine the ground-rent of floor-space enough to accommodate thirteen hundred people within a minute's walk of Piccadilly Circus, not to mention the row of boxes at the back for kings and people of that sort, and room enough on the stage for the scenery of *Der Ring* and the panorama in *Parsifal*, with dressing-rooms for principals, and hiding-places for choruses, courts, and armies when they are not on the stage! Even at Covent Garden, with its tiers upon tiers of boxes and galleries, a subsidy has to be subscribed to make both ends meet. The notion that we are going to have anything like the Bühnenfestspielhaus in the Haymarket is one which London may put out of its silly head (on some matters it *is* a silly head) once and for ever. No doubt some improvement will be made.... but to suppose that the Festspielhaus can be reproduced in the heart of the theatrical west end is about as sensible as to expect to get a villa with grounds and a conservatory on the river between Waterloo and Charing Cross for the same rent as on the Downs just outside Guildford.

Then, it may be asked, why not build your theatre somewhere else? Why not on Hampstead Heath, in Battersea Park, on Richmond Hill, in Epping Forest, on Blackheath, Wimbledon Common, Hackney Downs, or the like, obtaining the use of the land from the County Council, or Corporation, or whatever the authority may be, on conditions designed to secure an equivalent public benefit from the existence of the theatre? The answer is conclusive. The theatres of the metropolis must be strictly centralized for the convenience of two all-important classes: to wit, the critics, who never pay for their seats, and the plutocracy and aristocracy of the west end, who never go to the theatre at all, having more effectual methods of boring themselves in one another's houses, with the contingent advantage of the marriage market for their daughters thrown in. The rest of London either has as much, or more, trouble in getting to the centre than to any point in the circumference, or else would very willingly go farther and fare better in the way of lower prices and greater comfort.

It is clear to me that we shall never become a playgoing people until we discard our fixed idea that it is the business of the people to come to the theatre, and substitute for it the idea that it is the business of the theatre to come to the people. Let me whisper a question which must not be overheard by those who regard the theatre as a dissolute wayside house on the road to ruin. Suppose we had no churches or chapels in London except St James's, Westminster Abbey, St Margaret's, St Martin's, St Mary-le-Strand, St Clement Danes, the Temple Church, and St Paul's [churches in London's urban centre], how often would an average inhabitant of Hammersmith, Kilburn, Hampstead, Highgate, Holloway, Stoke Newington, Bow, Blackheath, Peckham, Dulwich, Brixton, Clapham, Wandsworth, Battersea, or Richmond [suburban boroughs around central London] go to church? Probably about as often as he now goes to the pantomime. And how many, after discovering experimentally how easy it is to stay at home, would ever go to church at all? We know the answer so well that we multiply churches and chapels all over the suburbs, and are demolishing them in the central districts instead of building fresh ones. If you move into a new house or flat in London, you have hardly done nailing up your pictures when the clergyman comes to book you (if I may be permitted the expression) for his church next Sunday, and, if necessary, to argue and exhort you into a lively sense of the benefits of going there regularly and the infamy of staying away. And how much cleaner, wholesomer, roomier, cheaper than theatres these churches and chapels are! ...I wish I could instil some true religion into the minds of the theatrical profession. Then, ceasing to regard the Church as an institution for which they have the greatest respect, and whose good opinion they are anxious above all things to conciliate (both respect and conciliation taking the practical form of carefully staying away from the services), they would begin to regard it seriously as their most formidable rival, not only in business, but in the attachment, the esteem, the veneration of the masses. I rejoice to see Mr Wilson Barrett [1846–1904] "tumbling to" this with prodigious commercial success [Barrett's most successful production was his historical tragedy *The Sign of the Cross*]. It is by identifying its religion with its art that Bayreuth draws people to its theatre as Mecca draws its pilgrims. Thousands travel from San Francisco or St Petersburg to Bayreuth to see *Parsifal* or *The Ring*. What sane person would go from Eaton Square to Camberwell to see *Gossip* [by C. Fitch and L. Dietrichstein, 1895]? Whenever the Church loses supporters, it is not in the least because *The Origin of Species* has superseded the book of Genesis, but solely because, from one cause or another—usually irreligion and incapacity in the priesthood—people find that they are neither temporarily happier nor permanently better for attending its services. And the reason the theatre does not gain supporters just now, but seems, on the contrary, to be losing the few that it had, is that people do not find themselves any happier or better for going to it: in fact, there are plenty of more profitable and less expensive ways of spending an evening, even without resorting to the Church, at local

Polytechnics, concerts, entertainments, and societies for the cultivation of hobbies of all kinds, not to mention the music-halls. Half a dozen visits in the year serve all the purposes of those respectable literate citizens who are as anxious to see whatever is good in the theatre as to subscribe to Mudie's [subscription-based lending libraries] or trudge round the Royal Academy and New Gallery every year, winter and summer. Let me turn to the index of Mr William Archer's *Theatrical World of 1895* (see page 232), and try to pick out fifty-two new plays that would have justified such a citizen in going once a week to the theatre, and so qualifying as a regular playgoer to the same extent as he is a regular churchgoer. With about twenty-five west end theatres in full action, giving between four and five thousand representations during the year, I can hardly pick out thirty which I can describe as making reasonably endurable pastime; whilst if you ask me how many of them were of sufficient artistic value to justify me in pretending that it matters a straw to any Londoner whether he saw them or not, I simply dare not answer you. All I will say is that from most of them the public had nothing to learn, and the performers less; so that we were not even improving the skill of our actors—quite the reverse, in fact. Some futile person will here interrupt me by asking whether I am such a fool as to suppose that the public goes to the theatre to learn. I crush that walker in darkness by a bald Yes. Playgoing is at bottom as utilitarian as washing; and it is precisely because the managers have persisted in catering for the voluptuary and the sluggard that the theatre is now so discredited. The voluptuary will no more support the theatre than the glutton will pay to be allowed to stare through the shop window of an eating-house; the sluggard finds easier and cheaper enjoyment in second-rate novels than in sixth-rate plays. The theatre is for active workers and alert spirits. If it were generally understood that fare as grimly serious as Ibsen's *Brand* could be depended on always at our west end houses, they would always be crammed; and the same people would come again and again....

## 3. "There's no ring," a letter to Reginald Golding Bright, 10 June 1896. [*Bernard Shaw: Collected Letters 1874–1897*, pp. 630–2]

*[The relative success—at least in terms of publicity—of* Arms and the Man *left theatre audiences expecting new Shaw plays and productions. When none appeared, many, including Reginald Golding Bright, hypothesized that old-fashioned theatre managers were organized into a "ring" that were deliberately determined to keep Shaw's innovative plays out of their theatres. Shaw refuses to play that easy blame game, and offers a clear-headed explanation of a situation that must have surely been frustrating to him personally as a playwright (see also page 137).]*

No: there's no ring: there never really is. Since "Arms & the Man" I have written three plays, one of them only a one-act historical piece about Napoleon [*The Man of Destiny*]. The first of these was "Candida"; and there are obvious reasons for its not being produced—my insistence on Miss Achurch for the heroine, the fact that the best man's part in it is too young for any of our actor managers (Esmond appears to be the only possible man for it), and the character of the play itself, which is fitter for a dozen select *matinées* than for the evening bill. The second—the Napoleon piece—has practically never been offered to anybody, because Ellen Terry took a fancy to it, and Irving proposed to produce it and play Napoleon. But I want this kept strictly private, as it may easily come to nothing, like other projects that get talked over and are afterwards crowded out by the march of events. The third play is only just finished. The only manager who has seen it (in rough draft) is Daniel Frohman [1851–1940; one of three American brothers who managed theatrical companies and tours], who is perfectly friendly & is as likely as not to produce it in New York if we come to terms, whilst there is no backwardness on the part of our managers in wanting to see it. Considering that my plays are difficult, that nobody believes there is much money in them, that even their commonplaces—what you and I would think their commonplaces—strike our managers as curiously novel and advanced, and that all managers like to be courted a little and are perhaps offended by the reticence which my position as critic imposes on me in this respect—not to mention the infuriating effect of my criticisms occasionally: taking all this into account, I have nothing to complain of; indeed the wonder is that they are so attentive and so interested in my attempts. The fact is, the business of a manager is too desperately difficult and hazardous to admit of any trifling with rings or the like. Whatever Wyndham may have said or advised about a play not his own, I have not the slightest doubt that if I brought him a play tomorrow with which he could see his way to even three months' good business, he would jump at it, though it was calculated to send all the inmates of Marlboro' House [residence of the Prince of Wales in the posh Pall Mall part of London] into convulsions. A manager is kept so desperately sharply to business by the terrible drain of from £500 to £1000 a week going remorselessly on all the time, and his knowledge (derived from bitter experience) of how easily the receipts may drop from £100 a week to practically nothing, that he is forced to consider only what the public wants from him; and if you find him giving them what they don't want, and withholding what they do want, you may always take the straightforward explanation that his judgment is at fault. It is true that in the theatrical profession people are always talking Machiavelli [metaphor to describe people who are deviously manipulative in order to preserve their own self-interest], so to speak, and devising imaginary diplomacies and boycotts and compacts and the deuce knows what not; but at the first whiff of a success in prospect, all that is flung to the winds. The opinion of the Prince of Wales [later Edward VII] had absolutely no effect on "Arms & the Man". Nothing affected it, not even the cab strike [general strike of cab drivers that lasted four weeks in May-June, 1894]. Every night some twenty or thirty pounds worth of people solemnly walked in and paid their money, the total receipts for the run being £1777 (I always remember it because of the sevens). The cost was probably five or six thousand. The astonishing thing, to an outsider, is that this result, of which no secret has been made, does not really impress managers as being particularly disastrous: theatrical business means making one success pay for half a dozen failures, and the half dozen failures seldom come off as well as "Arms & the Man" when allowance is made for the absence of a regular clientèle such as can always be depended on for a minimum at the Lyceum or Criterion. Wyndham, for instance (who has been very friendly to me), would probably look at it in this way. "If this fellow Shaw can pull in a couple of thousand pounds 'on his own,' and I can always pull in so much on my own, no matter what I play in, and the Criterion can always pull in so much on its own as a theatre with a reputation as a safe place to go to for a jolly evening with people who don't know one author or actor from another, then, next time I run short of safe plays and am forced to risk an experiment, I stand to lose £2000 less, in the worst event, than if I ventured with a quite untried man." But of course as long as he has plays at hand with which he feels quite safe, he will not produce mine, which seem to him to be quarter of a century ahead of the public. So you see there is no more a ring against me than there is against Ibsen or [Hermann] Sudermann [1857–1928, German novelist and naturalist playwright of social problem plays]. Twenty years ago Grundy complained fiercely that there was a ring, because no manager would touch his plays as long as there was one by Byron to be had, or else the inevitable adaptation from the French. Nowadays no manager will produce one of my plays as long as there is one by Grundy available—or [Henry Arthur] Jones, or Pinero, or Carton &c. Twenty years hence, if I prove a success as a dramatist, nobody will produce a play by a beginner of 1916 as long as there is a play by me on the market. There is no ring—there never is, never has been, never will be, although there always seems to be one to the younger generation battering at the door.

The news about "Mrs. Warren's Profession" is no longer true. There is no question of its immediate or remote production. The facts are rather funny, in a way. My first three plays, "Widowers' Houses," "The Philanderer," and "Mrs. Warren's Profession" were what people would call realistic. They were dramatic pictures of middle class society from the point of view of a Socialist who regards the basis of that society as thoroughly rotten economically and morally. In "Widowers' Houses" you had the rich suburban villa standing on the rents of the foul rookery. In "The Philanderer" you had the fashionable cult of Ibsenism and "New Womanism" on a real basis of clandestine sensuality. In "Mrs. Warren's Profession" you had the procuress, the organiser of prostitution, convicting society of her occupation. All three plays were criticisms of a special phase, the capitalist phase, of modern organization, and their purpose was to make people thoroughly uncomfortable whilst entertaining them artistically.

But my four subsequent plays, "Arms & the Man," "Candida," "The Man of Destiny" (the one-act Napoleon piece) and the unnamed four act comedy just finished [You Never Can Tell], are not "realistic" plays. They deal with life at large, with human nature as it presents itself through all economic & social phases. "Arms and the Man" is the comedy of youthful romance & disillusion, "Candida" is the poetry of the Wife & Mother—the Virgin Mother in the true sense, & so on & so forth. Now for the funny part of it. These later plays are of course infinitely more pleasing, more charming, more popular than the earlier three. And of course the I. T. now wants one of these pleasant plays to make a popular success with, instead of sticking to its own special business & venturing on the realistic ones. It refuses to produce "The Philanderer" (written specially for it) because it is vulgar and immoral and cynically disrespectful to ladies and gentlemen; and it wants "Candida" or one of the later plays, which I of course refuse to let it have unless it is prepared to put it up in a first rate style for a London run on ordinary business terms. Consequently there is no likelihood of any work by me being produced by the I. T., although "Mrs. Warren" is still talked of on both sides as eligible. You must understand however, that we are all on the friendliest terms, and that I am rather flattered than otherwise at the preference of my friends for those plays of mine which have no purpose except the purpose of all poets & dramatists as against those which are exposures of the bad side of our social system.

Excuse this long and hasty scrawl. I let you into these matters because the man who gossips best in print about them is the man who knows what is behind the gossip.

## 4. Mr Bancroft's Pilgrimage, 19 December 1896. [*Our Theatres in the Nineties*, vol. 2, pp. 278–85]

[*Part of Shaw's objection to charity productions was his insistence that private fundraising for public institutions effectively absolved the government from properly funding services that were "not public luxuries, but public necessities" (see page 267). Once Shaw had money, he could be generous about it—often providing the money to finance productions of his plays—but never sentimental. Sir Squire Bancroft (1841–1926) and his wife Marie (1839–1921) were a very successful actor-manager couple and pioneers of the "cup-and-saucer" drama.*]

Mr Bancroft has emerged from his retirement to start on an errand of mercy through this England of ours. To cool the fevered brow, to moisten the parched lip, to wile away the long sleepless nights of sick children with fairy gifts, to stimulate the demand for chromolithographs of the devoted nurse in her snowy bands, with spoon and bowl and angel eyes: this is the high mission on which Seth Bancroft has gone forth from his comfortable fireside, his method being to read Dickens's *Christmas Carol* in public and give the proceeds to the hospitals.

I have not seen a single notice of Mr Bancroft's enterprise that has not breathed sympathy, admiration, approval, from beginning to end. Now I dont sympathize; I dont admire; I dont approve. Mr Bancroft is an actor. An opportunity for exercising his art, a sympathetic character to appear in, a wide advertisement, and an outpouring of gratitude and popularity must needs be so highly agreeable to him, that it is quite useless to try to persuade me that they represent any sacrifice on his part. He will not be called on to provide any money for the hospitals: the public will provide that and pay his expenses into the bargain. In refraining from any attempt to make money for himself out of his recreation, Mr Bancroft is only following the ordinary custom of English sportsmen of independent means. As long as Mr Bancroft needed to make money by his public appearances, he did make it. Therefore, I have no hesitation in regarding the pilgrimage, apart from its object, as an act of pure self-indulgence on Mr Bancroft's part. Please understand that Mr Bancroft has not, as far as I am aware, put forward any pretension to the contrary, and that he may rightly regard it as one of the special privileges of his art that it enables him to combine beneficence to others with great enjoyment to himself. But the public does not take the matter in this way; and the critics all speak as if Mr Bancroft had unquestionably placed his country under an obligation. My point is that unless Mr Bancroft can justify, as publicly serviceable, his administration and expenditure of the funds, the obligation is all the other way.

Let me then proceed to look the gift horse carefully in the mouth. Is the reading of Dickens's *Christmas Carol* likely to have any educational effect on public taste? Clearly none whatever. Half a century ago the *Carol* had a huge success as an exploitation of pre-existent popular sentiment of the vulgar Christmas kind; and its revival today has no more classical pretension than the forthcoming revival of *Black-eyed Susan* [by Douglas Jerrold, 1829] at the Adelphi. Dickens was a man of genius; but that fact is perfectly well-known, except perhaps in literary circles, where it is difficult to make a merit of not being able to write like Dickens without disparaging him somewhat. Besides, it is not exactly on the *Christmas Carol* that Dickens's reputation rests. Let us then put the possibility of the pilgrimage being educational and edificational out of the question, and come to the real point—the application of the proceeds.

Now I am loth to shatter Mr Bancroft's kindly illusions; and yet I must tell him bluntly that he would do less harm with the money by spending it at Monte Carlo than in arbitrarily (and most ungratefully) enriching the ratepayers of the towns he visits at the expense of the people who pay for tickets to hear him read. For that, and nothing else, is just precisely what he is doing. Hospitals are not public luxuries, but public necessities: when the private contributor buttons up his pocket—as he invariably now does if he understands what he is about—the result is not that the sick poor are left to perish in their slums, but that a hospital rate is struck, and the hospitals happily rescued from the abuses of practically irresponsible private management (which the rich writers of conscience-money cheques never dream of attempting to control), with income uncertain; authority scrambled for by committee, doctors, chiefs of the nursing staff, and permanent officials; and the angel-eyed nurses, coarsely and carelessly fed, sweated and overworked beyond all endurance except by women to whom the opportunity of pursuing a universally respected occupation with a considerable chance of finally marrying a doctor is worth seizing at any cost. For this the overthrow of the begging, cadging, advertising, voluntary-contribution system means the substitution of the certain income, the vigilant audit, the expert official management, the standard wages and hours of work, the sensitiveness to public opinion, including that of the class to which the patients belong, the subjection to the fierce criticism of party newspapers keen for scandals to be used as local electioneering capital, all of which have been called into action by the immense development in local government under the Acts of the last ten years. Of course, as long as ignorant philanthropists, and people anxious to buy positions as public benefactors, maintain private hospitals by private subscription, the ratepayers and the local authorities will be only too glad to shirk their burdens and duties, just as they would if they could induce Mr Bancroft to light and pave the streets for them; but when the philanthropists learn that the only practical effect of their misplaced bounty on the poor is that the patient gets less accommodation and consideration, and the nurse less pay and no security in return for longer hours of labor, they will begin to understand how all the old objections to pauperizing individuals apply with tenfold force to pauperizing the public. In short, Mr Bancroft is meddling, with the best intentions, in a matter which he has not studied, with the result that every one of his readings may be regarded as so much mischief done to everybody but himself and those who have the pleasure of hearing him read.

This is the more aggravating because, had Mr Bancroft directed his attention to matters that he understands, he would have seen in his own art unlimited openings for his benevolence. As a musical critic I protested with all my might against the handing over, at the provincial festivals, of the money earned by Music from lovers of music to relieve the rates in the name of "charity." The one consoling feature about that scandal was that the cheque with which the operatic prima donna headed the subscription list was always handed to her for the purpose along with her salary. I protest now against the same spoliation of Art in the case of the Drama. Why should Mr Bancroft hand over the proceeds of his reading to the town hospital, which will be the worse for it, when he might just as well hand it over to the town theatre, which might be made the better for it? Mr Bancroft will say "How? On what conditions?" I reply that the conditions are not my business. I am not on the philanthropic platform just at present, and therefore cannot be called on to sit down and gratuitously put in the hard work of thinking out a scheme. But Mr Bancroft has mounted that platform. Very well: let him do something to prove his good faith. I have shown that reading the *Carol* to enthusiastic audiences, and dropping the money, addressed to some hospital treasurer or other, into the nearest pillar-box, is no more philanthropic work than cricket, yachting, or bicycling. But if Mr Bancroft would sit down and think out the problem of what a man could do for the drama in any given place if he had a fifty-pound note to spend on it, then I should admit that he was doing a public service. Even if he were merely to invite proposals and take the trouble of reading them through, he might get and spread some light on the subject. Suppose, for instance, a clergyman wrote up from some village and said, "If you will guarantee my expenses to such and such an amount, I will take the school children and the Christmas mummers in hand, and produce a Bible play with the local artizans and laborers in the principal parts, as they do in the Bavarian Alps." Or suppose some country Pioneer Club wanted to promote a first-rate performance of *A Doll's House*, but could not induce the local manager to venture upon it without a subsidy. Suppose the Independent Theatre offered to get up a verbatim performance of *Peer Gynt*, lasting two nights, on condition of being so far assisted that the exploit could ruin nobody but itself; or that Miss Robins were to undertake an [Spanish playwright José] Echegaray [1832–1916] cycle on the same conditions. What about that Wagner Theatre on Richmond Hill? What about an Academy or "Royal College" of the Drama [Shaw would later himself contribute greatly to the Royal Academy of Dramatic Art, see page 273], with scholarships, and a library scantily furnished with memoirs and reminiscences, and liberally furnished with technical works, including theatrical construction and stage mechanism? Why not offer Macmillans a subsidy towards a Dictionary of the Drama, uniform with Grove's *Dictionary of Music and Musicians*, or set on foot an inquiry, like that which supplied the material for Mr Charles Booth's *Life and Labor of the People* [1889, statistical study of poverty in London] into the life and labor of the actor, dealing also with salaries, agreements, sharing arrangements, backing, syndicating, papering, and bribing critics? The appendix, contributed by retired managers, might consist of balance-sheets and detailed accounts of their most famous productions, especially the "successes" by which they lost most money. A missionary fund for affirming the social importance of the drama, and claiming for municipal theatres as high a place in the collectivist program as municipal gas, water, and tramways, would be quite worth considering. Even a fund for persuading actors not to make foolish second-hand remarks about Ibsen in public would be better than nothing. Surely if all these resources occur to me on the spur of the moment, an actor and manager of Mr Bancroft's ability and experience, with unlimited leisure, could find something to do for his profession with the money which he is now using to keep down the character of our hospitals and—if he will take my word for the political economy of the business—to save our landlords from the final incidence of the hospitals rate.

There is also an artistic objection to this pseudo-charitable business. The curse of our stage at present is the shameless prostitution of the art of acting into the art of pleasing. The actor wants "sympathy": the actress wants affection. They make the theatre a place where the public comes to look at its pets and distribute lumps of sugar to them. Even the critics are debauched: there is no mistaking our disconcerted, pettish note whenever a really great artist—Duse, for example—whilst interpreting a drama for us with exquisite intelligence, and playing it with a skill almost inconceivable when measured by our English standards, absolutely declines to flatter us with any sort of solicitation for a more personal regard. Our reluctant, humiliated, rebuffed admissions of the success of actresses who pursue their profession with complete integrity contrast so shockingly with the officious, smirkingly enthusiastic congratulations we shower on those charming women who throw themselves, as such, on the personal admiration, indulgence, and good fellowship of the public, that the more an actress respects herself and loves her profession, the more she hates the existing relations between the stage and the public. Occasionally an actress's heart is so happily constituted that she can spoil the public as she would spoil a nursery of children, and yet work hard at her art; but the average actress, when the author demands anything "unsympathetic" from her, refuses to act on exactly the same grounds as she might refuse to let her lover see her in curl papers. And the actors are worse than the actresses. Why is it that, with the exception of *An Enemy of the People*, and (partly) *The Master Builder*, no play of Ibsen's has been performed on the initiative of an actor since Mr [W.H.] Vernon's [1834–1905] experiment years ago with *Pillars of Society?* Simply because Dr Stockman and Solness are the only Ibsen heroes who can depend on a little vulgar "sympathy." Allmers, Helmar, Hjalmar Ekdal, and even Rosmer may be very interesting, very lifelike; but they are not "sympathetic": they are even ridiculous occasionally: at best they are not readily comprehensible by the average actor fancier—for that is what the word playgoer has come to mean nowadays. A player who is still dependent on his profession for his daily bread may plead that "those who live to please must please to live," though I shall take leave to consider any actor who takes that position as being not only the rogue he confesses himself to be, but a fool into the bargain. But an actor in Mr Bancroft's circumstances, retired and independent, what on earth need has he any longer for a sympathetic part? Of what use is a halo of ready-made Hospital Sunday sentiment to him? Why not attempt to create some new sentiment—if it were only to knock into the heads of his benighted profession the elementary truth that it is the business of the dramatic artist, as of other public men and women, to strive incessantly with the public; to insist on earnest relations with it, and not merely voluptuous ones; to lead it, nerve it, withstand its constant tendency to relapse into carelessness and vulgar familiarity; in short, to attain to public esteem, authority, and needfulness to the national welfare (things undreamt of in the relations between the theatrical profession and the public today), instead of to the camp-follower's refuge of mere popularity?

I have hardly left myself room to commemorate the latest exploit of the Elizabethan Stage Society—its performance of *The Two Gentlemen of Verona* in a City Company's hall in Threadneedle Street. It seems to me that Mr [William] Poel [1852–1934] has now abandoned himself wholly to his fancy in dresses and equipments and stage business. I am no expert in these matters; but if Valentine's Turkish costume was not as purely an eighteenth-century convention as the big drum and cymbals in Mozart's *Serail* [*The Abduction from the Seraglio*, an opera in which the hero rescues his beloved from a Turkish harem], I am prepared to eat it. The fantastic outlaws, with their plumes and drum, belonged to the same period. The other costumes were mostly Elizabethan; but, except in the case of the Duke, they were surely bourgeois rather than noble. I am bound to say that the number of lines neither intelligently nor intelligibly delivered was greater than at any previous performance of the Society. This was only partly the fault of the hall, which made a magnificent setting for the performance, but also presented acoustic difficulties which only very practised speakers could have overcome. Valentine and Proteus were the most successful of the company, Proteus playing with plenty of address, and Valentine shewing some promise of talent as an actor. The ladies were not emphatic or distinct enough to make any effect. The gentleman who played Launce did not know the difference between a Shakespearean clown and a Zany [a stock comic character who clowned by ludicrously imitating other performers]: he acted worse than his dog—quite the wrong sort of dog, by the way, but very amusing.

## 5. Letters about Production Rights and Royalties, 1907–1925.

[Shaw advocated, through his membership in the Society of Authors, for a system that would protect authors from having their work and copyrights exploited. Even though he disagreed with the principle of "amateur" theatre companies, he could sometimes be generous in waiving his licensing fees (see page 289) if they were not expecting to raise any money with their productions. On the other hand, he was very protective of both the fees he was due and the commercial theatre managers who might find themselves competing against amateur productions. As the misunderstandings with the Irish Players Club and the authors of The Chocolate Soldiers indicate, Shaw sometimes understood the legal complexities of the business better than his agents did.]

To Reginald Golding Bright, 10 January 1907. [*Advice to a Young Critic*, pp. 176-7]

[Samuel] French [dramatic publisher] used to reduce the 5 guinea fee to 4 guineas when two performances were given; but on the whole I think I shall leave matters as they are. I have no sympathy at all with amateurs on the money question, because any money they make they give to some hospital or other, and thereby encourage the private charity system which I have been preaching against all my life. The money goes first into the pocket of the ratepayer, who is relieved from the duty of providing public hospitals, and it is then screwed out of him by the landlord as rent, the upshot of the whole transaction being that I lose two guineas and you lose your commission on it for the sake of the Duke of Westminster or the Duke of Bedford. ...

To A. Evelyn Ashley, Esq. of the Irish Players Club, 6 March 1907. [*Advice to a Young Critic*, pp. 182–3]

*[Reginald Golding Bright, acting as Shaw's agent, had authorized the Irish Players Club to present 7 performances of Arms and the Man at the Gaiety Theatre, a commercial venue, and Shaw felt these terms went beyond what could reasonably be considered amateur. He was ultimately legally obligated to honor the terms his agent authorized, but immediately realized the importance of establishing a clear distinction between amateur and professional theatre productions.]*

Dear Sir,

    The question at issue—which is of such importance to authors that I shall have to make a test case of it if you seriously claim that you can ask for permission to give an amateur performance and pay amateur fees, and then embark on a commercial theatrical speculation—is whether the week at the Gaiety Theatre is going to be a week of amateur theatricals or a week of ordinary theatrical business. What is the nature of your contract with the Gaiety? Are the terms sharing terms? And if there be a profit where will that profit go to?

Until I am informed on these points I can say nothing more than I have already said. The principle involved is a most important one. It concerns a privilege which is worth, say, twenty guineas in the commercial market and five in the amateur market. To buy the privilege at amateur rates and then exploit it commercially, is a proceeding of which a very strong view indeed would be taken if it were attempted by a regular theatrical manager. I do not suggest that this aspect of the matter occurred to you; but now that I put it plainly before you, you will, I think, see that I am not acting unreasonably. It is quite likely that the net profit on a week of ARMS AND THE MAN may at this moment reach and even considerably exceed £500 if you admit the public by payment at the doors and invite the press. You propose to obtain that profit by paying me a fee fixed on the assumption that there is to be no profit at all and that the enterprise is entirely disinterested as far as money is concerned. Naturally, I refuse to sanction this. If you are an amateur, you must confine yourself to amateur conditions. If you are a man of business, you must pay me business terms.

I hope I do not convey an impression of being unfriendly to your Club; but you will see that it has sprung something on me which was never contemplated when the amateur conditions were fixed.

To Siegfried Trebitsch, 11 April 1908. [*Bernard Shaw: Collected Letters 1898–1910*, pp. 768–70]

[*Siegfried Trebitsch (1869–1956) was Shaw's German translator. He sold the rights to his German translation of* Arms and the Man

*to Rudolf Bernauer (1880–1953) and Leopold Jacobson (1878–1943),
who adapted the play into an operetta called Der tapfere Soldat
(The Brave Soldier) with music composed by Oscar Straus
(1870–1954). This letter shows how well Shaw understood the legal
complexities of copyright law and how to protect his rights as an author, as well as his generosity in making sure Trebitsch didn't have to
pay for his own mistake.]*

My dear Trebitsch

I have read Mr Jacobsen's [sic] letter. The difficulty is that
he does not know the law and is not in possession of the
facts. The agreement should have been made with me, not
with you. I never saw it until quite lately; and then, as you
know, I at once protested against it. It was represented to me
that you had had an offer of 1000 crowns for permission to
use "the idea" of the first act of *Arms & the Man* for an operetta: that is an opera in one act. I was very doubtful about
it at the time, not being able to see what they were paying
for; but I did not like to deprive you of 500 crowns; so I let
the thing pass on the understanding that the bargain was
to be limited as above. My receipt, drawn by my secretary,
was a mere matter between you and me: it was not a receipt
to Mr [Josef] Slivinski [1865–1930, Polish classical pianist; he
must have been involved in early negotiations but his name is
not otherwise associated with the operetta], and cannot imply any contract with him.

However, it is no use wrangling as to the facts. The question is, how to get out of the difficulty we are in. The first
thing to do is to return the 1000 crowns. You obtained them
by going beyond your legal powers; and since I refuse to con-
firm the contract (to do so would be to violate my own con-
tracts in other quarters) you cannot honorably keep the
money. I enclose a cheque for the amount, as it is really my
fault—or rather the fault of the heavy pressure of business
which compels me to let so many matters pass without suf-

ficient attention—and there is no reason why you should suffer for my negligence. When the money is returned and the contract torn up, then the position will be as follows.

The opera, as performed, must not be called Helden [Heroes, the German title of Arms and the Man], nor announced as a musical setting of it. None of the names of my characters must be used. None of my dialogue must be used. There must be no possibility of a foreign manager attempting to stop performances of my play on the ground that they violate his rights in the opera. Further, there must be no possibility of an attempt to stop a performance of a real attempt to set Arms & the Man to music, if I should at any future time authorize a composer to do it. This is not likely to happen; but it is possible that if [Sir Edward] Elgar [1857–1934, British composer] or Richard Strauss [1864–1949, German composer] were to propose to set the play—not paraphrased into a string of waltzes, but just as it stands—I might not refuse. This would not interfere with the Oscar Straus-Jacobsen paraphrase. You will note that these conditions are just as important to Herr Straus as to me: more so, in fact, as he could not claim an infringement against me without admitting the identity of his libretto with my play. If the similarity went beyond the limits of a general similarity of subject, he would be liable to an appeal to the courts to stop the performance in every copyright country in Europe. In France, where my translator is a member of the powerful Société des Auteurs, which under its traité générale with the theatres, can stop a performance at will, a contract signed ultra vires [Latin term for actions beyond someone's legal power or authority] by a German in violation of a Frenchman's rights would not be of much use to him. I should have to publish the warning I have already sent privately to Herr Straus in all the countries; and immediately a cloud of difficulties would arise, costly and troublesome to Herr Straus, costly and troublesome to me, very unfavorable to Herr Slivinski's international reputation as a careful man of business, and profitable to nobody but the lawyers.

On the other hand, if the libretto complies with my conditions, or is altered so as to comply with them, Herr Jacobsen is quite welcome to any suggestions or ideas he has taken from our play. If he or Herr Oscar Straus had applied directly to me (as I applied directly to Herr Strauss) without relying on these men of business who are regarded as men of business only by artists and as artists by real men of business, there would have been no trouble: I should have pointed out at once the limits within which my work could be used. I have no right to be generous at your expense; but now that I return the 1000 crowns, Herr Jacobsen gets his borrowed ideas for nothing. It may be that the borrowing is so obvious that the critics will accuse him of plagiarism, especially if he has done nothing very brilliant before. In that case he can put a note in the program as follows:— "One of the scenes in this Operetta has been suggested by Herr Siegfried Trebitsch's translation of one of Bernard Shaw's best known plays." But it would be much better to say nothing, as it is hard to devise a formula that is legally unobjectionable. At all events, any such statement must be submitted to us and agreed upon before publication. It must not convey the impression that the operetta is an authorized musical version of *Helden* or that I have disposed of any rights.

The next step is to get from them a copy of their libretto. Until I see that, I can give no undertaking in the matter. Any suggestions I may have to make about it are far more likely to be in the nature of improvements than otherwise. I am probably as clever a dramatist as Herr Jacobsen; and I know a good deal about music, and of the situations that musicians can handle effectively.

I consider that Herren Straus & Jacobsen will now have no reason to suspect me of any intention to act unreasonably or to make money out of them. I shall get nothing whatever out of the business except the loss of a good deal of time in which I might have been earning money with my pen. I have made no attempt to make them the butt of my wit. The difficulty has not been of my making. It would have been obvious to anyone in the world except a theatrical agent that your powers did not extend beyond the German language, and that an agreement for international rights should be made with the author.

I write this letter with great difficulty, as I have had a severe attack of influenza—in fact, I am in the middle of it, and am unfit for any sort of business.

Please lose no time in returning the money & getting a copy of the libretto. Impress on Herr Jacobsen that the matter is of great importance, as even if he could make his case good against me in Germany, he would still have to deal with seven translators throughout Europe who have exclusive rights of unquestionable validity in the text of *Helden* in their respective languages.

To Reginald Golding Bright, 30 October 1908. [*Advice to a Young Critic*, p. 186]

The Woodford people may go ahead. If they wish me to decide what is to be done with the profits (if any) I strongly advise them either to keep them for the promotion of future performances or give them to any public art gallery of the like that may exist at Woodford. Failing that, let them get drunk on it rather than give it to any charity.

To Reginald Golding Bright, 2 January 1913. [*Advice to a Young Critic*, p. 192]

I have to give you notice that on the 25th March next I shall have to transfer the collection of my amateur fees to the Society of Authors.

I am not taking this step because I am dissatisfied with Miss [Elisabeth] Marbury's [1856–1933, American theatre and literary agent] services, or on any other ground of dissatisfaction. On the contrary, I think it highly probable that for a year of so at any rate, the arrangement will be to my disadvantage. But I am not a free agent in this matter. As you probably know, most dramatic authors are, as far as their amateur business is concerned, in the hands of a firm which insists on charging a commission of 20%. The Society of Authors, after several attempts to bring this firm to reason, at last resolved to organize a bureau and undertake the collection of fees for its members. As a member of the Committee of Management I took a leading part in this enterprise, having in the meantime done what I could to persuade other dramatic authors to transfer their business to Miss Marbury. Now that the bureau is organized and in action, it is, you will see, impossible for me to continue having my fees collected by an outside organization.

I have stipulated that I must be allowed to give you three months notice, which I accordingly do, without malice.

To Reginald Golding Bright, 7 October 1917. [*Advice to a Young Critic*, p. 196]

...The agency game is changing. I never employ an agent now: why should I, when the agent does absolutely nothing for me but intercept my fees and send them to me minus 10% for delaying them? If the manager likes to employ an agent, that is his own affair; so long as he pays the agent's commission and it is made clear that the agent is not acting for me, I indulge his imbecility, though I have to advise him, make the agreement, and generally do for him everything that his agent professes to do and doesnt. When I can no longer write plays I will take up agency and become one of the idle rich, instead of envying you with the bitterness of an overworked man.

In the remote past, your American office used to collect my fees. It was not until it became too lazy to do even that, and I had to collect them myself, that I woke up to the situation and discarded agents for ever.

To J.E. Vedrenne, 19 July 1910. [*Bernard Shaw: Collected Letters 1898–1910*, pp. 934–5]

[*Der tapfere Soldat was adapted into English as The Chocolate Soldier. It had already been a hit in the 1909 Broadway season before American manager Frederick C. Whitney (1855–1930) brought it to London, at which time he attempted to protect himself by requesting, via Vedrenne, that Shaw identify any parts of the libretto that he objected to as violating copyright.*]

This libretto infringes my copyright, and in several places violates the conditions on which I promised Mr. Jacobsohn [sic] to raise no obstacle to the performance of the original libretto in Germany. One of the names—Louka—is borrowed from my play; and several passages of dialogue are not merely burlesqued but lifted from my book verbatim.

If this is the libretto which was used in America, then my agent should have stopped the performances. It is not a translation of the German book: it is a rehash of it, made without the slightest regard to the understanding to which I was a party.

An even more important matter than the libretto is the description of the work in the program. If it be stated, or even remotely implied, that the work is a musical setting of *Arms and the Man* or that I am in any way a party to it, I shall at once take proceedings. [When] Mr. Jacobsohn pleaded that if he did not acknowledge some indebtedness to me, he would be denounced as a plagiarist, I made matters as easy for Mr. Jacobsohn and Mr. Oscar Strauss [sic] as I could by allowing them to sail very close to the wind in the dialogue, and countenancing some such phrase in the program as "Suggested by one of Mr. Bernard Shaw's comedies," or "with apologies to Mr. Bernard Shaw for an unauthorized parody"; and beyond this I shall not go. In this copy I have struck out all the dialogue to which I object as being simply quoted from my play. I have replaced it with a few phrases which preserve the sense and continuity of the scenes (such as they are). I have struck out the name Louka, which can be replaced by Katinka or any Bulgarian name not taken from my play. I stipulate that the title *Arms and the Man* shall not be used on the program or in any announcement or communication to the press, and that if any reference whatever is made to me, it shall be worded as above "with apologies to Mr. Bernard Shaw for an unauthorized parody."

Why did not Mr. Whitney approach me directly on this matter before he produced this work in America? Why does he not approach me directly now?

To Reginald Golding Bright, 17 October 1925. [*Advice to a Young Critic*, pp. 204–6]

Nobody but myself has any rights whatever in *Arms and the Man*.

The history of *The Chocolate Soldier*, as far as I am concerned in it, is this. I saw a press paragraph to the effect that Oscar Strauss was making a musical version of *Arms and the Man*. I wrote to him warning him not to infringe my rights. He did not reply; but soon afterwards I received an appeal ad misericordium [appeal to pity, a logical fallacy] from Herr Jacobson not to ruin him by forbidding the performance of *The Chocolate Soldier*, as he had written the libretto, of which he sent me a copy. I read it, and found that he had used certain scraps of my dialogue, the effect of which in the context of his stuff was so bad that I improved the piece considerably by cutting them all out. I then told him I would have nothing whatever to do with *The Chocolate Soldier*; but if none of my dialogue was used I did not think I could appeal to the courts successfully to stop the performance, because (a) parodies and travesties of standard serious works are privileged by custom, (b) I had clearly no rights in the Servo-Bulgarian war as a dramatic subject, and (c) the incident of a fugitive soldier taking refuge in a lady's bedroom was too common to be patented by me or anyone else. There were no other features in *The Chocolate Soldier* apart from the title which could be found in *Arms and the Man*. Jacobson's characters were all cads, cowards, *vieux marcheurs* [old womanizers], and prostitutes with names invented by himself. His libretto was not a play, but a putrid opéra bouffe in the worst taste of 1860. Under these circumstances I did not propose to take any steps provided my name was not connected with the thing in any way.

Even with this Herr Jacobson was not satisfied. He pleaded that he would be accused of plagiarism if he were not allowed to say that he had borrowed an incident from *Arms and the Man*; and I said that he might say what he liked provided he conveyed no suggestion that I was in any way responsible for his libretto, or that Oscar Strauss's score was a setting of *Arms and the Man*.

I never departed from this attitude. It was evident that they all believed that I could have stopped *The Chocolate Soldier*, because they all offered to pay me a royalty. Mr. Whitney, who produced the play in America, was very anxious about me, as it seemed unaccountable that I should refuse money when there was so much of it going. But it was just because there was so much money in it that I did not stop it. It gave a lot of employment to the artists and others, and plenty of enjoyment to the public. Then there was Strauss to be considered. He was not to blame, as he evidently knew nothing about the copyright question. So I let them alone; and they all flourished exceedingly.

I believe I told Miss Marbury to come down on them if they used any of my dialogue in the American version; but as she was not collecting any fees for me she had no interest in the matter, and took no action. I afterwards found that some of my dialogue had been used.

Now that the film question has arisen over the success of the Theatre Guild production of *Arms and the Man* I shall probably deal with it just as I did with *The Chocolate Soldier*. If they make a film of *The Chocolate Soldier* by Strauss, Jacobson & Co, I may not meddle with them. But if they bring my name into it, or connect it with *Arms and the Man* in any way, then I shall come down on them at once.

I cannot, however, answer for the attitude of the Theatre Guild. It may object to the release of a film called *The Chocolate Soldier* as an infringement of their interest in the play; and they might possibly get an injunction.

In any case Mr. [Murray] Rumsey [dates unknown, American composer] will not find it worth his while to interfere, as I will not be bought off by a royalty or anything of that sort, and there will therefore be nothing for him to collect. I shall instruct my American lawyer to warn Mr. Goldwin [Samuel Goldwyn, 1879–1974, Hollywood film producer] and also put the Theatre Guild on its guard.

By the way, I shall have to take the amateur business out of the hands of Miss Marbury (that is, I suppose, out of the hands of the American Play Company) if I do not receive my fees regularly as I used to. My American Income Tax returns were upset last time by a quite inexcusable delay. Perhaps they will wake up if you jog them.

# 6. Bernard Shaw Talks about Actors and Acting, 1929. [*Shaw on Theatre*, pp. 186–97]

[*Shaw gave this talk, originally titled "How it Strikes Me," for The Royal Academy of Dramatic Art at the Academy Theatre in London on December 7, 1928. It was broadcast live on the BBC, which always made the management nervous, as Shaw had a history of improvising to insert his own often-controversial opinions. This excerpt from the talk was printed in the* New York Times *in January 1929.*]

Ladies and Gentlemen: The greatest number of listeners to this address of mine have just been informed that what is happening is "London calling the British Isles." What is actually happening is Bernard Shaw calling the universe. I want to emphasize that, because some of my audience consists of our young students here, and I want to remind them at the outset that their parents might probably hear them, no matter how remote may be the part of the globe in which they happen to be at this moment. So, if they feel tempted at any moment to interrupt me with use of epithets or anything of that kind, I want to remind them that their voices may be recognized. ...

Being in the school, perhaps I had better talk about it, because this Royal Academy of Dramatic Art is a very peculiar place. The subject is difficult for me, because the government is always very nervous, for some reason or other, whenever I speak in public. I do not know why, because, after the performance of some of their own members in that way, I should imagine that they would not be afraid of anything. But they are a little afraid of me, and they always appeal to me not to deal with any controversial subject. But, unfortunately, I am driven here to speak on one of the most controversial subjects in the world, and that is whether a member of a family shall go on the stage or not. We are a school for training the member of the family who wants to go on the stage, and the differences between ourselves and other schools will at once occur to you. In the case of the other schools, the parents want the child to go to the school to get rid of it; the child does not want to go and would rather stay at home. In our case, the child wants to go very desperately and determinedly, and the parents usually object very strongly indeed. They used to object still more strongly than they do today, but, nevertheless, there is the objection.

Before I come to the grounds of that objection, which are reasonable enough, I want to remind you how very strong it has been and still to a great extent is in this country.

*[Shaw's examples include Charles Dickens, who was as "a born actor" and in the process of going on the stage when his literary career took off, but who nonetheless refused to let his own daughter pursue a legitimate opportunity to become a professional actress; also French playwright Alexandre Dumas fils and theatre critic Clement Scott who cautioned against letting respectable women go on stage. He then explains how this caution is being overcome by the enormous salaries associated with film acting.]*

The bearing of this on this school is this: that we have the parents who really think that the child's salvation has been imperilled by coming here. In that case the child usually has some strong artistic bent in opposition to its parents. But you are now getting the other sort of parent, who comes here with an entirely hopeless daughter without any artistic qualifications whatever, and insists on our turning a film star into a great actress, earning heaven knows what sums of money, on which her family will be enabled to retire from business for the rest of their lives.

That being our position, I want to come to the question whether the old prejudice has anything in it. What is it that we teach here? To begin with, perhaps I had better ask you,

What does a parent desire its child to learn? Take the case of a daughter. Do respectable families in this country desire their daughter to spend a great deal of time in making herself attractive to men? I quite grant you that they all want her to make herself attractive to one man, with a pretty solid income and a good position; but when you come to the question of her absolutely and promiscuously making herself attractive to every man who sees her, no matter what his class may be, whether he is sitting in a stall which has cost 12s 6d or 13s 6d whether he is in the gallery, admission to which is perhaps obtained for 2d, that is another story. That she is to paint herself, so as to make herself irresistibly fascinating to all these people—does any respectable family contemplate that lot for its daughter without recoiling in horror? But that is what we teach young ladies to do here. Even in the painting part of it we give them elaborate lessons. We teach them to wear wigs; we teach them every single art that can fascinate and attract large bodies of men. So that there really is some reason in this prejudice, after all, on the surface of it.

Take the case of the young man. His parents desire a big career for him. The very last thing that they desire is that he should go out into the world and be laughed at by everybody. We teach young men here to be laughed at. We take the greatest care, we spend incalculable pains in training them to be ridiculous, in training them to such a pitch that we consider we have done our very best when we have turned out a young man who the moment he appears on the stage provokes a roar of laughter, even before he opens his mouth.

Well, that is certainly a very questionable sort of school, I think you will admit. And yet we have a royal charter [a formal document issued by a monarch to certify the rights, powers, and significance of an institution]. You will say: "What on earth was the King thinking of?" When I tell you that this theatre of ours was inaugurated by the Prince of Wales, you will say: "What! has the royal family gone mad to counte-

nance these proceedings, this sort of training of children?"
Well, it is so; they do this kind of thing. We have got our
charter, and I am speaking here without the slightest fear of it
being revoked, although I am within hearing not only of this
audience but of the government, who are probably anxiously
listening.

Why do people want to go on the stage in spite of all these
scandalous difficulties at the outset of the career? Well, partly
because it is an eligible profession to some people, and partly
because it is the satisfaction of a human instinct. Those two
things operate, and I shall have, I think, to deal with them
separately.

In the theatrical profession we have what are called theatrical families. They are old families, all the members of which
have been actors or actresses; and they are usually most des-
olatingly respectable. Usually they are extremely skilled in
their profession, and very satisfactory to work with, because
they know their business, which is not quite so common as it
ought to be on the stage. But they are there for some reason.
Whether it is that they are brought up with much greater
strictness than any other sort of families, the fact is that I
have never been in a Quaker family which was anything like
so strict as an ordinary theatrical family. But they produce the
actor who is on the stage, and who very often has a distinguished career there; and yet, so far from being stage-struck
is he or she that they positively do not enjoy acting; but they
are driven into it by the fact that they can get a living more
easily, they know how to go about getting a living more easily,
in the theatre than anywhere else.

I could give you some quite noted examples.... The actor
of my time who was most unquestionably our leading classic
actor in the special sense is Sir Johnston Forbes-Robertson.
He was an artist by temperament; he was a painter; but he
found matters so difficult as a painter that he went on the
stage, solely because he could live as an actor more easily

than he could in the other way. In his very interesting autobiography he makes a very curious statement: that he can only remember one period, one performance in his life which he enjoyed in which he was acting himself. There you see this curious thing, that it is not always the satisfaction of the instinct that settles a career; sometimes it is the economic pressure of the career. I want to say a very interesting thing about that. Those people who are driven by this outside pressure onto the stage are very often the best actors, and the people who are most hopelessly stage-struck are sometimes impossibly bad actors. I simply state that as a general proposition, because there may be in this audience some person who has never dreamed of becoming an actor, who has been brought up perhaps to be a clergyman, and is contemplating that career with some doubt as to whether it is a quite eligible one—it is difficult to get people to go into the Church now. But I just want to say this to encourage such a person: Even if he has not the slightest desire to be an actor he has just as good a chance to be a celebrated actor as people who devote all their lives to the theatre. I say that as a general encouragement.

But I am most interested when I come to that side of the matter which is the satisfaction of an instinct, because then it becomes psychologically very curious. Humanity produces two types occasionally. In their extreme form they are not very common; but these two types created the theatre originally. There must have been some man, probably in archaic Greece or anywhere you like, who, instead of earning an honest living as a carpenter or a mason or something of that kind, or even as a politician, although that might have satisfied his instincts—You find that this man—and the same thing applies to women, although it began with men—this man does not want to be himself. He wants to magnify himself, he wants to be a hero. You don't get opportunities every day of being what is called a real hero. You don't find battles ready for you in which to win Victoria Crosses. You may have no opportunity at all: and the result is that, not having an actual opportunity of being a real soldier, you have to pretend to be a soldier; so you develop your personality, you give yourself the air of a soldier. You wear your hair, or sometimes do, of a length at which heroes were supposed to have worn it at whatever particular period it happens to be; and you pose before your fellow-creatures, you utter heroic sentiments. If you are in a difficulty as to improvising the heroic sentiments, you may possibly get another person to do it for you, and learn them off by heart: in which case you invent the dramatic author—you invent me, in fact. But still there is this type of man, and he has to entertain. He begins by reciting, by playing all the different characters himself, and that is a propensity which still lingers among actors.

There are many actors nowadays who, although they do not play all the characters themselves, regret that they cannot do so. I ought in fairness to say that sometimes the author regrets that he cannot play all the parts as well. But at last the man who has spouted, if one may put it that way, to a crowd gets up on a soapbox, if there is such a thing, or stands on a barrel; and then finally he gets something more permanent. He wants a sort of stage or tribune to speak from; he gets beautiful costumes; he exaggerates his height with buskins. He still plays all the parts himself, but although he begins in that way he finds it is necessary to present a sort of something like what we now call a drama. Yet at first the necessity for playing all the parts himself brings him to this curious point. He says to the author, "I want to play both Romeo and Juliet, or Tristan and Isolde, whatever the case may be; but you must understand that Romeo and Juliet must never be on the stage at the same time; Romeo must come on and make love, and then he must go away; then Juliet must come on and express her sentiments." The author naturally says, "This is very awkward." I suppose that after a time the authors made a little struggle and said, "Well, would it not be nice to have somebody else to play the lady? I will not make her part very prominent, but still it would help you a great deal; and really it would make it more interesting to the public." And so you get your drama in that way.

But over against this particular actor who is the tragedian, and who dreads above everything else on earth being laughed at—the one terrible and fatal thing for him is ridicule of any kind—there, side by side, strangely enough, in order to restore that balance which Nature always appears to have in view, there arises the other sort of man, who is born with a tremendous desire to be laughed at and who will undergo the most extraordinary ignominy, who will paint his nose red, who will allow people to kick him about, who will have the most disastrous falls, if only he can make people laugh.

This is a curious psychological thing. It has prevented me from being a really great author. I have unfortunately this desperate temptation that suddenly comes on me, just when I am really rising to the height of my power, that I may become really tragic and great: some absurd joke occurs, and the anti-climax is irresistible. I am reminded that there is a very distinguished actress, who is among you today [Mrs. Patrick Campbell], who, instead of speaking of me respectfully as Mr Bernard Shaw, in the manner that is befitting to my age and years, always addresses me as Joey, the name of the clown in the pantomime. I cannot deny that I have got the tragedian and I have got the clown in me; and the clown trips me up in the most dreadful way. The English public have said for a long time that I am not serious, because you never know when the red-hot poker will suddenly make its appearance or I shall trip over something or other.

There is another thing. There is the desire that we all have to escape from reality. Now a very great actress, Ellen Terry, once told me of this, when speaking of a play which I had written for her. In writing the play I did the sort of usual thing that an author does. The author, in writing for a particular genius, a particular personality, instead of thinking of gratifying that personality and enabling her or him to escape for a moment from himself or herself, seizes on the personality and dramatizes it. I did this with Ellen Terry in a play which she played with great success. But she said to me on one occasion: "I wish somebody would write a part for me to act. In this play of yours I have nothing to do but go on the stage and be myself, and the thing is done." There, you see, there came in this curious desire, that she wanted to escape from herself; she wanted to be somebody else for a time.

You get that on the stage, and you also get very interestingly precisely the opposite. You get other sort of artists whose desire is not to escape from themselves. Their desire is self-intensification. They want to develop and intensify their own personality to a tremendously magnetic and overwhelming extent, and in doing so, pursuing this entirely egotistical aim, they sometimes attain a degree of fascination which is quite extraordinary, and then you see the influence that an actor or an actress may have....

The relations which arise between authors and actors owing to this difference, of course, are very interesting, although they ought to be preserved exclusively for behind the scenes, because what the author would like to do is to combine the intensity of the one kind of actor with the curious dramatic imagination of the other kind of actor who wants to be somebody else, wants to change his personality. The extreme, for instance, is well represented by certain actors who are called character actors. I believe that the reason that they go on the stage is an unconquerable shyness. You may think that shyness is about the very last thing that would drive a person on to the stage. You imagine that if a person wants to obscure himself, to be in the background, not to be called forward to say anything, the very last thing he would want to do would be to walk on the stage and face the footlights and all the other lights. And yet it is the most complete refuge that you can possibly imagine. If only you are a character actor, you can go and be somebody else, you never need betray your own personality....

From all this you will see how extraordinarily interesting the theatrical profession is to anybody who is behind the scenes, and perhaps the best way to get behind the scenes is to come to this school and get trained, to take up the profession of an actor. But it requires a great deal of character to hold your own on the stage. The impression which some people have that you require less character to be an actor than to be anything else is a most terrible mistake. You must get that out of your heads at all possible costs. The way in which the stage will find out every single weakness that you have got, every vanity that you have got, every folly that you have got, every little slip in self-control that you are subject to, is really very terrible. Therefore, to come back to the children whom parents may want to send to this school, they had better send us the pretty strong characters, even if those strong characters, by the way, have revealed themselves by kicking over the traces in every possible direction in ordinary domestic life. ...

But I want to say again, Why, after all, is it that this curious mad art of ours, this elaborate pretending to be somebody else, this satisfaction of instincts which are entirely irrational and many of them absurd—why is it, after all, that it does enjoy a royal charter and royal patronage and all the rest of it? and why is it that the public will forgive almost anything to this profession of ours except being bored, and that they are quite right not to be? Well, it is because we really render—the art of the theatre, like many other arts, renders—very conspicuous public service.

In the old days Aristotle said that tragedy purged the soul with pity and terror; and the old definition of comedy was that it chastened morals, chastened manners—because the word expressed both—by ridicule. I have never regarded that as a permanent definition. Ridicule may be rather unkind. I think the worst kind of play is the comedy in which the author sets you laughing at one another. The old-fashioned comedy, to take a simple example, always made fun of old women, simply because they were old. Well, that was abominable and detestable. And so on all through.

As to pity and terror, if people's souls could only be set going right by pity and terror, then the sooner the human race comes to an end the better. You cannot pity unless you have misfortunes to pity. That is the reason, by the way, why I am not a philanthropist, why I do not like philanthropists—because they love suffering of all kinds. They are never happy unless some one else is unhappy, so that they can exercise their philanthropy. I do not want there to be any more pity in the world, because I do not want there to be anything to pity; and I want there to be no more terror because I do not want people to have anything to fear.

But there are other things. You may throw pity and terror on one side, and you can reveal life, and you can stimulate thought about it, and you can educate people's senses. If you look on that life as it presents itself to you, it is an extraordinarily unmeaning thing. It is just as if you took a movie camera and went out into the Strand or Piccadilly and began to turn the handle, and afterward developed your film and then said, "Well, that is life—all those people moving about." Lots of them have tragic histories, some of them have comic histories; some of them are abounding with joy because they are in love, others are going to commit suicide because they have been disappointed in love. It is all very wonderful! But when you look at the film you say, "Well, I don't see anything there but a lot of people running about in a perfectly meaningless way." Now what the drama can do, and what it actually does, is to take this unmeaning, haphazard show of life, that means nothing to you, and arrange it in an intelligible order, and arrange it in such a way as to make you think very much more deeply about it than you ever dreamed of thinking about actual incidents that come to your knowledge. That is drama, and that is a very important public service to render....

## 7. Why Too True to be Good Failed: A Moral in Favour of a National Theatre, 1932. [*The Bodley Head Bernard Shaw: Collected Plays with their Prefaces*, vol. 6, pp. 532–4]

[*Shaw was a staunch advocate of establishing a subsidized National Theatre, recognizing that the plays he considered most important were often unlikely to recoup their production costs solely from box office receipts.*]

The opportunity is rather a good one to draw a moral in favour of a National Theatre. You may remember that after the old experiment made by Vedrenne and Barker at the Court Theatre in 1904, which was finally pushed as far as it would go, and ended a bit further, Granville-Barker came to the conclusion that he could make a west end London theatre, playing Shakespear and highbrow repertory, pay its way if it were rent free and rate free. An endowment to that extent would solve the money problem.

In those days, remember, rents and salaries and production expenses were so much lower than at present that George Alexander, running the most expensive theatre of its size in London, complained to me that he could not carry on unless his receipts were £1,000 a week.

Now it happens that this is the exact figure at which *Too True* was withdrawn last Saturday. Alexander would have run the play for six months at such business; but Barry Jackson has to throw in his hand unless the receipts are £1,600.

When Cochran gallantly produced [Sean] O'Casey's [1880–1964, Irish playwright] *Silver Tassie* he had to take it off, because his expenses were £1,700 a week.

*Too True* filled the cheaper seats and moved people as no play of mine has moved them before; the houses in Birmingham were crowded out for three weeks; and the tour is all right. But because the people who can afford to pay thirteen shillings for a stall do not care for that sort of play in sufficient quantities, and left the box office £50 short of "Stalls full" every night at the end, the play is described as a failure and has to give place to musical comedy. And meanwhile at the Old Vic and Sadler's Wells, *Caesar and Cleopatra* fills these big houses with their reasonable prices.

Thus the case for a National Theatre grows stronger as the commercial theatres and cinemas flourish more and more and raise the standard of expenditure to a pitch undreamt of at the beginning of the century. Here am I, expected to force intellectual drama to the utmost limits of human endurance—"as far as thought can reach," [a quote from Shaw's epic play cycle *Back to Methuselah*] in fact—rebuked austerely by every sap-head in the critics' circle if I humanely venture to give my audiences the least scrap of fun; and the reward I get is that when I have increased the takings more than sevenfold in thirty years, and had a success which in point of money would have ranked before the war as a silver mine, the play has to be withdrawn, leaving me hammered like an insolvent broker on the Stock Exchange. I must have a public pension of at least £10,000 a year if I am to carry on. *Too True* failed, as they call it, in America also. That means that after twelve weeks' roaring business, the receipts dropped in the last week to $6,500. Well, if the vanguard of the drama cannot live on the drama when the plunder amounts to $6,500 a week, it must perish unless governments and municipalities come to the rescue with endowed theatres. If this National Government will only pay the rent of the New Theatre; Sir Barry Jackson will run *Too True* for another year cheerfully. Neither he nor I can say any fairer than that, can we?

# 8. Playwrights and Amateurs, 1933. [*Shaw on Theatre*, pp. 228–36]

[*Shaw delivered this speech in the process of presenting a motion on behalf of the Welwyn Garden City (a town near Shaw's home in Ayot St Lawrence) Theatre Society to the British Drama League conference in Edinburgh. The motion called on playwrights to maintain their own right to negotiate licenses for non-professional productions on terms that were more reasonable and affordable for non-commercial theatre societies than the standard amateur fees. Shaw was personally and professionally invested in creating a more financially viable model for theatrical production, but also opposed in principle to the idea of unpaid "amateur" performances. See page 261 for letters on Shaw's own negotiations over non-professional productions of his plays.*]

...You see, I write plays. And when I was a young man, which is now an unreasonably long time ago, the man who wrote plays got paid by the manager of the theatre—usually in the first instance a London theatre. Then his play went a certain tour through the provincial towns which had theatres, where he got paid by the managers of the touring companies. That was how he got his living. But he had one other string to his bow. In all the big provincial towns, and the suburbs of London especially, bodies of infatuated ladies and gentlemen, when they went to a theatre and when they saw, say, my friend Sir Gerald du Maurier [1873–1934] and Miss Gladys Cooper [1888–1971] enacting a play in a very finished manner [*The Admirable Crichton* by J.M. Barrie], all the ladies thought they could do Miss Gladys Cooper's part, and all the gentlemen thought they could do Sir Gerald du Maurier's part. Accordingly, they used to get together, calling themselves amateurs because it was a very disreputable thing to act for money, and also by many excellent people was considered a very serious sin. They gave the best sort of performance they could; and if there were any profits—which there very seldom were—they were very careful to give them to a charity in order to expiate the sin....

You see in this the shady side of what you call the "amateur." The amateur was a person who was trying to give the best imitation of something that he had seen in the theatre; but he had to keep himself absolutely clear of any suspicion of doing anything so disgraceful as making money, and he had to expiate his sin by giving the money to charity. Every playwright who was a genuine artist and respected his profession and his craft naturally loathed such amateurs. They were a standing insult to our art; but nevertheless they were worth five guineas a time. In those days the amateur became a byword for incompetence and vanity; so all the playwrights, myself included, put down "Amateurs, five guineas." That was in the old time. My difficulty today is that this practice, which was quite proper at that time, now remains, in entirely changed circumstances, as a superstition, and a very mischievous one....

[Shaw explains that these early amateurs had no legitimate tradition in which they developed a genuine appreciation for dramatic art.]

All that is completely changed, though the five-guineas amateur still pays his five guineas. Allow me here to say with the greatest possible emphasis that the British Drama League is not the British amateur movement, as it has been called. I hope that the main business of the British Drama League will be to get rid of that sort of amateurism altogether. But all through the country in the villages and towns you find people who are genuinely enthusiastic for the drama, many of them really desirous to do the highest and most interesting type of play. This it is that brings them into personal contact with me. And now comes the question. Very often these little devoted bands, before they can give their performance—I do not say they actually have to pawn their shirts, but it often comes to something very near that. Anyway, they manage to get up a performance; and for an audience they may in a village have a few rows of seats, and perhaps a few of the gentry may be induced to come and pay half-a-crown to sit in the front row—not very many. The rest pay something like twopence. Sometimes performances of my plays take place under those conditions. Well the receipts are, say, fifteen shillings. Now what is the author to get? What can he expect under those circumstances? The authors who have never thought about their position, those playwriting ladies and gentlemen (we are not really ladies and gentlemen, though we are politely called so)—what do they do, many of them? They go to these unfortunate people who have beggared themselves to give a dramatic performance out of pure love of art and have managed to get back fifteen shillings; and they say, "Five guineas, please!" Well, are there any words of mine that can sufficiently contemn such outrageous and unreasonable rapacity? In that happy land Switzerland, plays can be performed by anybody on paying a specified percentage—I think it is only 2 per cent.

I am very fond of money; and the older I get the more fond I get of it; but if I were to charge five guineas, what would be the result? Well, I should not get it, because they could not afford to perform my play.... What do I do? I don't let them off, because if I let them off with nothing, that would be black-legging, that would be unfair competition with my fellow-playwrights. I charge them exactly what I charge the professionals—that is, a percentage of the gross receipts....

I come back to that five guineas with loathing and disgust. I ask whether there is any playwright—(I have a B.B.C. microphone here and I hope a lot of them are listening. I am supposed to be talking to you, but I am talking at them.) I say that they do not deserve to have their plays performed at all unless they are prepared to adapt them to the means of the very poorest people.... But if I treat all genuine drama lovers as I do, as professionals, if I give them professional terms, they must not call themselves amateurs. My difficulty is that unless we of the Drama League make it thoroughly understood that we do not hold a special brief for amateurs—that we do not want to encourage amateurs of the old type—we will have all those little societies innocently calling themselves "The So-and-So Amateur Players." Then if they come to me, I say, "Amateurs, did you say? Five guineas!" They must drop that term.

We had a meeting here this morning at which a member of our League moved, with the best intentions, a resolution to the effect that in certain performances nobody should be paid; that the producer should not be paid; and that nobody should make a living out of dramatic art. I did not say anything on that occasion, because I was speechless with rage. The rule I want the British Drama League to make is that *everybody* at all these performances should be paid.

What does constitute a professional performance? If all the profits of the performance are kept in the concern for future performances, if the people call themselves the Portobello or What-You-May-Call-Them Players, and if they keep a standing organization and keep on giving play after play, which is what they want to do, and if all the money that comes in is put to a reserve for future performances to build up a permanent arrangement, then unquestionably they are professional. What else is any professional supposed to do?

I have said that some professionals get drunk with the profits. Well, our people can do that also (see page 267). If they prefer to go and have a jollification with the profits, nobody can question the complete professionalism of that. But when we try to make distinctions between people who are paid and people who are not paid, we find it impossible to distinguish between one class of performance and another.

Take the most unquestionable professionals people who are at the top of their profession. Do you suppose that the old actor-managers—for instance, Sir Henry Irving, Sir Herbert Beerbohm Tree, or Sir George Alexander—do you suppose that *they* were always paid? There were many weeks in their lives in which, when they had paid everybody else, not only had they nothing left for themselves, but they were considerably out of pocket over the transaction....

I think that the only question is not whether these people should get professional terms, but whether they ought not to have less than professional terms. It sometimes happens that these people honestly write up to me in certain very difficult circumstances and say what they want to do, and my secretary writes back to them and says she does not think I have taken any notice of the letter and perhaps they had better go ahead and say nothing about it. But I don't want that altogether. I do like to get my ninepence or one and sixpence.... I have to live in my modest way of writing plays. It is a very difficult thing to do. Therefore I want to impress upon the minds of all the players in the country, whether they are British Drama League players or Repertory players or regular professional players, that an author is a person who has to eat and drink and clothe himself and lodge himself, and that therefore they must not perform a play without paying a little at any rate to the man who wrote it. So, you see, I have my own little axe to grind in the matter, as well as others.

You see now what I mean by this resolution. I want the League of British Dramatists to get rid of this nonsense about amateurism and professionalism altogether. All who are working for love of the drama honestly to give the best dramatic performances to the public they can, are entitled to professional terms. You cannot draw a line and say, "On this side is professional work, and on the other is amateur." The only meaning that the words ever had is that on one side there is bad work and that on the other there is good work. That has ceased to be the case....

Remember that Richard Wagner, the composer, said, quite truly, "Music is kept alive not in our great opera houses and in our concert rooms, but on the cottage piano of the amateur." I tell you—and this is my last word—that the drama in this country and in every country is not kept alive by the great theatres, although they do something for the highest departments of the art of acting, but by the love of the people for the drama and the attempts that they make themselves, when they are starved by the professional circuits, to give performances in the places the professional circuits do not reach. The object of the resolution which I now formally move is to make that as easy and as cheap for them as possible.

# 9. Rules for Directors, 1949. [*Shaw on Theatre*, pp. 279–89]

*[Shaw was always heavily involved in the rehearsal process for his plays, essentially performing the function of a "director," and sometimes producer, before those roles were widely instituted. He would recommend casts, read the play and explain character motivations to the actors, sometimes even demonstrate actions and intonations, and give notes during rehearsals and after opening performances. He could be very specific about the vocal tones and actions that were appropriate to a character, but is also often remembered for his respect and generosity towards actors, and his keen understanding of the practical aspects of theatrical production, evident throughout this handbook for directors.]*

*Play directing, like orchestral conducting, became a separate and lucrative profession less than a century ago. The old stage manager who arranged the movements of the players, and called every actor Old Boy and every actress Darling, is extinct. The director has sup-*

*planted him. Yet there is no established method of directing and no handbook from which a novice can learn the technical side of the job. There is not even a tradition, because directors do not see one another at work as players do, and can learn only by experience at the expense of everyone else employed in the production.*

*These pages are an attempt to supply a beginners' guide. They are not concerned with direction as a fine art; but they cover the mechanical and teachable conditions which are common to all productions, without knowledge of which the novice will waste hours of rehearsal time that should be devoted to acting. All playwrights should study these.*

*The most desirable director of a play is the author.*

*Unfortunately, as playwriting is a solitary occupation which gives no social training, some playwrights are so lacking in the infinite patience, intense vigilance, consideration for others, and imperturbable good manners which directing requires, that their presence at rehearsals is a hindrance instead of a help. None the less, they should know how to write for the stage as playwrights, and not as poets and novelists indulging their imaginations beyond the physical limits of "four boards and a passion."*

The director, having considered the play, and decided to undertake the job of directing it, has no further concern with its literary merits or its doctrine (if any).

In selecting the cast no regard should be given to whether the actors understand the play or not (players are not walking encyclopedias); but their ages and personalities should be suitable, and their voices should not be alike. The four principals should be soprano, alto, tenor, and bass. Vocal contrast is of the greatest importance, and is indispensable for broadcasting.

The play should be read to the company, preferably by the author if he or she is a competent dramatic reader: if not, by the best available substitute. If none is available, no reading is better than a bad one. To the first rehearsals the director must come with the stage business thoroughly studied, and every entry, movement, rising and sitting, disposal of hat and umbrella, etc., is settled ready for instant dictation; so that each player will be in the most effective position to deliver his lines and not have to address an intimate speech to a player at the other side of the stage, nor to follow such a player without a line or movement to transfer the attention of the audience accordingly. The exits must be carefully arranged so that the players leave the stage immediately on their last word, and not hold up the play until they have walked to the door. If the director arrives at the first rehearsal without this blueprint, and proceeds to waste the players' time improvising it at their expense, he will never gain their confidence; and they will be perfectly justified in going home after telling him not to call them again until they can devote all the rehearsals to their proper function of acting.

To appreciate the necessity for this laborious planning one has only to imagine a trial-at-law in a room without bench, bar, or jury box, or a service in a cathedral without altar, choir, or pews: in short, without an appointed place for anybody. This is what the stage is until the director has made a complete plan, called a prompt copy. Properly such a plan is the business of the author; for stage directions are as integral to a play as spoken dialogue. But the author may be dead. Or in view of the fact that writing dialogue (of Hamlet, for instance) is a pleasurable act of creation, whereas deciding whether the Ghost shall enter from the right or the left is pure drudgery, the author may leave the drudgery to the director. He mostly does.

It is not necessary to use a model stage for this job. All that is necessary is a chessboard with its chessmen, and a boy's box of assorted bricks. With these all scenes and furniture can be indicated and all movements made. Unless this is done some movements, especially exits, are likely to be forgotten by even the most experienced director.

The players should be instructed not to study their parts at this stage, and to rehearse, book in hand, without any exercise of memory. When the movements are thoroughly rehearsed and mastered, the director should ask the players whether they are comfortable for them all, and if not, what is wrong.

All being satisfactorily arranged, books are discarded, and rehearsals called "perfect": that is, with the parts memorized. The director now leaves the stage and sits in the front of the house with an electric torch and a notebook; and from that moment he should watch the stage as a cat watches a mouse, but never utter a word nor interrupt a scene during its repetition no matter how completely the play goes to pieces, as it must at first when the players are trying to remember their parts and cues so desperately that they are incapable of acting. Nothing betrays the inexperienced director more than dismay at this collapse, with outbursts of reproach and attempts to get everything right at every rehearsal. The old hand knows that he must let the players memorize the words before they can act their parts.

At the end of each act, the director returns to the stage to explain or demonstrate such of his notes as may be judicious at the moment. But no fault should be mentioned or corrected unless and until its constant repetition shews that the player will not correct it in his or her own way as the play is gradually learnt. When all the players are letter-perfect their memorizing will be so mechanical that if one of them makes a slip by repeating an early cue later on, the rest will pick it up again and repeat what they have just been through, proving that the memorizing phase is over. The director can now return to the stage and interrupt as often as may be necessary.

The danger is that as the players can now utter their words without thinking they will catch one another's speed and tone, betraying to the audience that they are only gabbling off a prearranged list of words, each knowing what the other will say next and fielding their cues like cricketers. The director must accordingly take care that every speech contrasts as strongly as possible in speed, tone, manner, and pitch with the one which provokes it, as if coming unexpected as a shock, surprise, stimulant, offence, amusement, or what not. It is for the author to make this possible; for in it lies the difference between dramatic dialogue and epic narrative. A play by a great poet, in which every speech is a literary masterpiece, may fail hopelessly on the stage because the splendid speeches are merely strung together without provoking one another, whereas a trumpery farce may win an uproarious success by its retortive backchat.

The final phase of direction is that of "dress rehearsal" with costumes, scenery, and make-up all complete as for public performance, instead of everyday dress and a bare stage with the doors marked with a couple of chairs. It is now the director's turn to be more upset by the change than the actors. Everything seems to have become wrong and incredible. However, the director soon learns to be prepared for this, even if he never quite gets over the first shock of it. He is now back on the stage, going through the passages that need finishing, and generally doing what he likes. A bad last rehearsal need not alarm him: in fact he should connive at its failure lest the players should be too confident of success "on the night" and not do their utmost best.

The time needed for the direction of a full-length play on this method is roughly a week for the stage movements book in hand, with the director on the stage; a fortnight for the memorizing, with the director off the stage silent, watching, and taking notes; and a week for the dress, with the director on the stage again, directing and interrupting *ad lib.*

Rehearsals should be most strictly private. No journalist or lay visitor of any kind should be present. When for some reason it may be necessary to allow strangers to witness a rehearsal, no instruction nor correction should be addressed in their presence to a player; and the consent of every player should be obtained before the permission is granted. To emphasize the fact that what the visitors are witnessing is only a rehearsal, a prearranged instruction should be addressed to a stage carpenter, never to a player.

During the memorizing phase a muffled passage must never be repeated on the spot, even if the players desire it. The director's word must be "No; you will not be able to repeat it on the night; and you must not make a habit of a mistake. Go right on." A director who says "We must go over and over this again until we get it right is not directing; he is schoolmastering, which is the worst thing he can do. Repetitions on the spot do not improve: they deteriorate every time.

Never find fault until you know the remedy; and never discuss a passage with a player; shew how the passage should be done as a suggestion, not an order; and exaggerate your demonstration sufficiently to prevent the player giving a mere imitation of it. A performance in which the players are all mimicking the director, instead of following his suggestions in their own different ways, is a bad performance. Above all, do not, instead of demonstrating a passage, say "This scene is essentially pathetic" (or comic as the case may be). If you do, the player will come to the next rehearsal bathed in tears from the first word to the last, or clowning for all he is worth all the time.

The notes taken by the director as he silently watches the players are a test of his competence. If, for example, he writes "Shew influence of Kierkegaard on Ibsen in this scene," or "The Oedipus complex must be very apparent here. Discuss with the Queen," the sooner he is packed out of the theatre and replaced the better. If they run "Ears too red," "Further up to make room for X," "Pleecemin," "Reel and Ideel," "Mariar Ann," "He, not Ee," "Contrast," "Change speed: Andante," "Shoe sole arches not blacked," "Unladylike: keep knees together," "More dialogue to give them time to get off,"

"This comes too suddenly," "?Cut this???" and the like, the director knows his job and his place....

In arranging hours players with only a few lines to speak should not be kept hanging about all day whilst the principals are rehearsing. Late night rehearsals are most objectionable. Neither players nor directors should work when they ought to be in bed. If such rehearsals are unavoidable the players who are kept too late for their last trains or buses should be paid their taxi fares home.

A play may need to be cut, added to, or otherwise altered, sometimes to improve it as a play, sometimes to overcome some mechanical difficulty on the stage, sometimes by a passage proving too much for an otherwise indispensable player. These are highly skilled jobs, and should be done by the author if available, or if not, by a qualified playwright, not by a player, nor by the callboy. Copyright in all such changes passes to the author. A player who reveals the plot or words of an unperformed play to the Press can be sued for breach of confidence at common law or under the Copyright Act.

These rules are founded on experience. They are of no use to a director who regards players not as fellow-artists collaborating with him, but as employees on whom he can impose his own notions of acting and his own interpretation of the author's meaning. He must let the players learn the play, and does not expect them to know it all as well as he does at the first rehearsal. He must distinguish between born actors who should be let alone to find their own way, and spook actors who have to be coached sentence by sentence and are helpless without such coaching. There are so many degrees between these extremes that the tact and judgment of directors in their very delicate relations with players are sometimes strained to the utmost; and there is no effective check on the despotism of the director except his own conscience, because only the most ungovernable players dare risk being blacklisted by an authority so potent in the selection of casts as the director. This is why docile players are usually less often unemployed (which means running into debt) than better rebellious ones....

A director sometimes has an antiquarian job. He may be called on to direct a play by, say, Euripides or Aristophanes as it was produced in Athens 2356 years ago. Or one of the pious Mysteries as the Church produced them in the Middle Ages. Or an Elizabethan drama on an Elizabethan stage. Or a Restoration or early Victorian play on a stage with proscenium, wings, and flats.

He should know that the Athenian stage was an imposing tribune in the open air on which the actors, in mask, sock, and buskin, strutted in conventional hierarchic costumes, and that as scenery and curtains were undreamt of, and changes of place impossible, the action of the play had to pass in the same place on the same day. These conditions are called the Unities. On later stages and on the cinema screen they are negligible superstitions; but their observance still has great dramatic value. On the medieval stage unity of place was got rid of by a wide stage on which half a dozen different places were shown simultaneously. Heaven, the jaws of hell, the throne of the Blessed Virgin, the Garden of Gethsemane, the Mount of Olives, the Court of Pilate, the house of Caiaphas, were all in full view together, with the actors moving from one to the other as the story dictated. The Elizabethan stage, adaptable to innyards, had no scenery. The stage was surrounded on three sides by inn galleries, and had a balcony and an inner stage in the middle with curtains called traverses in which indoor scenes were played.

This inner stage, still in use at Oberammergau [Bavaria] and elsewhere for Passion Plays, is important because it enables actors entering from the back at opposite sides to be seen by the audience before they can see one another, thus making possible such scenes as the first in *Romeo and Juliet*, in which the Montagues and Capulets talk out of sight of one another, and set the spectators wondering what will happen when they meet.... It was for the sake of such effects that when the Elizabethan stage was succeeded by the Restoration stage, with painted scenery viewed through a proscenium acting as a picture frame, the scenes were pierced to provide avenues through which the actors could be seen before they could see one another. There were also doors in the proscenium through which the principal players could enter, with pages bearing the women's trains, not in historic costumes, but in the full court dress of the period. Old toy theatres preserve this type of stage. Every director should possess one; for effects are possible on it that are not possible in modern built-in sets. For instance, when there are three wide entrances between the wings on both sides of the stage a crowd can be cleared off it almost instantaneously....

Modern direction includes film direction, in which there is no limit to scenic possibilities; and directors may spend millions of pounds profitably instead of a few thousands. The results so far include megalomaniac demoralization, disorganization, and waste of time and money. These evils will cure themselves. Meanwhile the art of the playwright and director remains basically the same. The playwright has to tell a good story, and the director to "get it across." This is all that can be learnt by a director from anything but experience and natural vocation. Like all methods it depends for success on the taste and talent with which it is practised.

There is no sex disqualification for directing. Women directors are at no disadvantage in comparison with men. As in marriage and queenship, the grey mare is often the better horse.

## 10. Letter to Barry Jackson, 17 August 1950.
## [*Bernard Shaw and Barry Jackson*, p. 195]

[*British theatre director Barry Jackson (1879–1961) founded the
Birmingham Repertory Theatre (1913) and the Malvern Festival
(1929). Jackson included at least one Shaw play in each of the
Birmingham Repertory Theatre's first ten seasons, and originally intended Malvern to be a summer theatre festival dedicated entirely
to Shaw's works, although it grew to include a larger variety of work.
Nonetheless, Jackson's founding of the Malvern Festival provided
the inspiration for Shaw to write most of his late-career plays. This
letter, in which Shaw poignantly reflects on his professional career,
was written less than three months before his death.*]

I am dead as a playwright. On my birthday I managed to
send off to the printer a half length attempt at a little comedy
[*Why She Would Not*]; but it is a pitiful senile squeak. I shall
probably burn it. My big plays did not blaze a trail to greater
heights: they reaped the harvest and cut down the trees, leaving nothing but a desert with a silly old stag trying to browse
in it.

Still, I am content to have said my say and shot my bolt. I
have done a good day's work, and now I must put up the shut-
ters.

All this drivel you have provoked by expecting another
*Heartbreak House*....

I can't think of anything more to say. The pump is dry: I
can spout nothing but metaphors, well mixed.

# Sources and Further Reading

*[For comprehensive and up-to-date bibliographies and other important research aids for work on Bernard Shaw in electronic and print forms see the Research Aids section on the website of the International Shaw Society: www.shawsociety.org. The selection here focuses on Shaw's theatrical interests and activities.]*

## Autobiography

*An Autobiography*. Selected from His Writings by Stanley Weintraub. 2 vols. New York: Weybright and Talley, 1970.

*The Diaries 1885–1897*. Ed. Stanley Weintraub. 2 vols. University Park: Pennsylvania State University Press, 1986.

*Sixteen Self Sketches*. London: Constable, 1949.

## Biography

Gibbs, A.M. *Bernard Shaw: A Life*. Gainesville: University Press of Florida, 2005.

———. *A Bernard Shaw Chronology*. Basingstoke: Palgrave, 2001.

Holroyd, Michael. *Bernard Shaw*. 5 vols. London: Chatto & Windus, 1988–92.

Peters, Margot. *Bernard Shaw and the Actresses*. Garden City, NY: Doubleday & Co., 1980.

## Letters

*Advice to a Young Critic and Other Letters*. Ed. E.J. West. New York: Crown Publishers, Inc., 1955.

*Agitations. Letters to the Press 1875–1950*. Eds. Dan H. Laurence and James Rambeau. New York: Frederick Ungar, 1985.

*Bernard Shaw: Collected Letters.* Ed. Dan H. Laurence. 4 vols.
New York: Viking Penguin, 1965–88.
*Bernard Shaw and Mrs. Patrick Campbell: Their Correspondence.*
Ed. Alan Dent. London: Victor Gollancz Ltd., 1952.
*Bernard Shaw's Letters to Granville Barker.* Ed. C.B. Purdom.
London: Phoenix House, 1956.
*Ellen Terry and Bernard Shaw: A Correspondence.* Ed. Christopher St. John. New York: G.P. Putnam's Sons, 1932.
*Selected Correspondence of Bernard Shaw.* Series Editors J. Percy
Smith and L. W. Conolly. Toronto: University of Toronto
Press, 1995– [ongoing]. *Bernard Shaw Theatrics*, ed. Dan H.
Laurence, 1995; *Bernard Shaw and H.G. Wells*, ed. J. Percy
Smith, 1995; *Bernard Shaw and Gabriel Pascal*, ed. Bernard
F. Dukore, 1996; *Bernard Shaw and Barry Jackson*, ed. L.W.
Conolly, 2002; *Bernard Shaw and the Webbs*, eds. Alex C.
Michalos and Deborah C. Poff, 2002; *Bernard Shaw and
Nancy Astor*, ed. J.P. Wearing, 2005; *Bernard Shaw and His
Publishers*, ed. Michel W. Pharand, 2009; *Bernard Shaw and
Gilbert Murray*, ed. Charles A. Carpenter, 2014.
*To a Young Actress: The Letters of Bernard Shaw to Molly Tompkins.* Ed. Peter Tompkins. London: Constable, 1960.

## Plays And Prefaces
*The Bodley Head Bernard Shaw. Collected Plays with their Prefaces.* Under the editorial supervision of Dan H. Laurence.
7 vols. London: Max Reinhardt, the Bodley Head, 1970–74.

## Theatre Reviews, Essays, And Addresses
*Bernard Shaw: The Drama Observed.* Ed. Bernard F. Dukore.
4 vols. University Park, PA: Pennsylvania State University
Press, 1993.
"The Censorship of the Stage in England." *The North American Review*, vol. 169, no. 513 (August 1899): 251–62.
*Dramatic Opinions and Essays with an Apology by Bernard Shaw.*
Ed. James Huneker. New York: Brentano's, 1907.

*Our Theatre in the Nineties*. 3 vols. London: Constable and Company, 1954.

*Platform and Pulpit*. Ed. Dan H. Laurence. New York: Hill and Wang, 1961.

*Plays and Players: Essays on the Theatre*. Ed. A.C. Ward. London: Oxford University Press, 1958.

"Preface." *Three Plays by Brieux*. New York: Brentano's, 1913. vii-liv.

"The Quintessence of Ibsenism." *Major Critical Essays*, vol. 19. London: Constable, 1930.

*Shaw on Shakespeare*. Ed. Edwin Wilson. New York: Applause, 1961.

*Shaw on Theatre*. Ed. E.J. West. New York: Hill and Wang, 1958.

*Shaw's Dramatic Criticism (1895–98)*. Ed. John F. Matthews. New York: Hill and Wang, 1959.

## Criticism

Bentley, Eric. *Bernard Shaw*. New York: Limelight Editions, 1985.

Conolly, L.W. *Bernard Shaw and the BBC*. Toronto: University of Toronto Press, 2009.

———. *The Shaw Festival: The First Fifty Years*. Oxford: Oxford UP, 2011.

Crawford, MaryAnn Krajnik and Heidi Holder, eds. *New Readings: Shaw at the Sesquicentennial*. SHAW: The Annual of Bernard Shaw Studies 26. University Park: Pennsylvania State University Press, 2006.

Davis, Tracy C. *George Bernard Shaw and the Socialist Theatre*. Westport: Praeger, 1994.

Dukore, Bernard F. *Bernard Shaw: Director*. Seattle: University of Washington Press, 1971.

———. *Bernard Shaw, Playwright: Aspects of Shavian Drama*. Columbia: University of Missouri Press, 1973.

Fromm, Harold. *Bernard Shaw and the Theater in the Nineties: A Study of Shaw's Dramatic Criticism.* Lawrence: University of Kansas Press, 1967.

Gahan, Peter. *Shaw Shadows: Rereading the Texts of Bernard Shaw.* Gainesville: University Press of Florida, 2004.

Gainor, J. Ellen. *Shaw's Daughters: Dramatic and Narrative Constructions of Gender.* Ann Arbor: University of Michigan Press, 1991.

Gibbs, A.M., ed. *Shaw: Interviews and Recollections.* Iowa City: University of Iowa Press, 1990.

Gordon, David J. *Bernard Shaw and the Comic Sublime.* Basingstoke: Palgrave Macmillan, 1990.

Hadfield, D.A. and Jean Reynolds, eds. *Shaw and Feminisms: On Stage and Off.* Gainesville: University Press of Florida, 2013.

Hugo, Leon. *Bernard Shaw: Playwright and Preacher.* London: Methuen, 1971.

Innes, Christopher, ed. *The Cambridge Companion to George Bernard Shaw.* Cambridge: Cambridge University Press, 1998.

Kent, Brad, ed. *George Bernard Shaw in Context.* Cambridge: Cambridge University Press, 2015.

Meisel, Martin. *Shaw and the Nineteenth Century Theater.* New York: Limelight Editions, 1984.

Morgan, Margery M. *The Shavian Playground: An Exploration of the Art of George Bernard Shaw.* London: Methuen, 1972.

Pharand, Michel, ed. *Dionysian Shaw. SHAW: The Annual of Bernard Shaw Studies* 24. University Park: Pennsylvania State University Press, 2004.

Stafford, Tony J. *Shaw's Settings: Gardens and Libraries.* Gainesville: University Press of Florida, 2013.

Weintraub, Rodelle, ed. *Fabian Feminist: Bernard Shaw and Woman.* University Park: Pennsylvania State University Press, 1977.

Weintraub, Stanley. *Who's Afraid of Bernard Shaw? Some Personalities in Shaw's Plays*. Gainesville: University Press of Florida, 2011.

91720497R00183

Made in the USA
Columbia, SC
22 March 2018